Enhancing Understanding—
Advancing Dialogue

Rodney Fopp

Enhancing Understanding—Advancing Dialogue

Approaching Cross Cultural Understanding

Rodney Fopp

ATF Press
Adelaide

.

Cover design: Original art work by Eloise Ford, graphic design by Astrid Sengkey

ATF Press
An imprint of the Australasian Theological Forum Ltd
P O Box 504
Hindmarsh
SA 5007
ABN 90 116 359 963
www.atfpress.com

Contents

Contents

Acknowledgments

There are many people who have been involved in one way or another in writing this book even though the responsibility for its contents rests with me. I am indebted to them all and thank them heartily even if they are not mentioned below.

Special mention should be made of the Hawke Research Institute for Sustainable Societies at the University of South Australia which provided both a fellowship to begin to explore the issues, and the outstanding and welcome editorial assistance of Kate Leeson (particularly with what turned out to be a very early draft) and Paul Wallace more recently.

I would also like to thank my colleagues in the School of International Studies for their encourage and support of this project. With the Head of School, Professor Elisabeth Porter, they have created a very congenial environment in which to pursue this and other work.

Mention should also be made of the staff at ATF Press. In particular the ATF's General Editor, Rev Dr Alan Cadwallader who commented on drafts, and Hilary Regan, the Executive Officer, have been extremely helpful.

It seems to me that there are times in life when those essential people who honour and charm us with their presence inspire us to do things we might not otherwise embark upon. To all those in that category I express my gratitude, and particualrly to Joan who has shared the development of this book with keen interest, unflagging encouragement and confidence in the outcome, just as surely as I have been inspired by her exceptional playing of Bach preludes and fugues on the pipe organ. This book is dedicated to her.

Introduction

The following is my attempt to introduce readers to this book about approaching the understanding of other cultures. In it I cursorily explain why cross-cultural understanding is an imperative task. I follow this with an attempt to delimit the scope and focus of the book, to explain what it is—and is not—about, which proved to be rather difficult, particularly as the scope and focus of this book may be a little unexpected or unusual. It is necessary to clear the path gradually. My hope is that by the end of this chapter the scope and focus are a little clearer. To foreshadow, the book is not a historical or sociological analysis of racism or an analysis of how discrimination is perpetuated; it concerns the powerful ideas about what counts as knowledge which are smuggled into cross-cultural understanding and which influence it (often adversely) from the start.

Later in this introduction, I give a brief outline of each chapter, followed by a description of the argument, and conclude with several qualifications, which include a statement about to whom the book is directed and a working definition of cross-cultural understanding.

As in the remainder of the book, I try to introduce the rather complex ideas in an accessible way. In the desire for clarity I decided that erring on the side of being a little repetitive but clear was preferable to being brief but vague or ambiguous. If it is a little repetitious in parts, the intention is to clarify.

This is a book about how cross-cultural understanding is approached. Even prior to 11 September 2001, there were a number of reasons for writing a book such as this. First, many nations contain a diverse range of people representing different cultural and racial groups; increasingly cultures mix and inter-relate. A mix of cultures within or near national borders is very common, whether it is workers from other countries in Germany, the previous forced merging of cultural groups in the Balkans, the Indian and Chinese communities in Fiji and Malaysia, the indigenous peoples in colonised countries, or the cultural diversity forged by migration or members of cultures seeking recognition of their identity.[1] For this reason alone, cross-cultural understanding is important.

Second, modern technology has narrowed the distance between people of different cultures and nations.[2] It is a relatively simple task to communicate across the globe. In a sense, the world has shrunk;[3] it no longer necessitates the ignorance and exaggeration of differences. Thus, even when cultures are not in close proximity, technological advances enable the great media corporations to feed information to us, to display the variety of cultural reactions to various events on our television or computer screens. The attitudes and beliefs, the values and cultural practices of other cultures, are beamed into our lounge rooms. Of course, such footage is not pure or pristine; it is loaded or skewed in a certain direction that does not always match how those portrayed see their culture. Nonetheless, the fact that we experience other cultures via the perception of others (particularly, in the media) is another reason to reflect on how we approach cross-cultural understanding.

Third, with globalisation and internationalisation, and with the influence of the world economy and inter-national events, comes the imperative to understand what

---

1. For an analysis of identity see Richard Jenkins, *Social Identity*, Second edition (London: Routledge, 2004).
2. Zygmunt Bauman, *Globalization: The Human Consequences* (Cambridge: Polity Press, 1998), 1–5.
3. See Zygmunt Bauman, *Globalization: The Human Consequences.*

is happening and why.[4] As other cultures and nations are involved in events which concern us, the need for cross-cultural understanding is self-evident. As we trade with other countries, as we exchange tourists, there is an urgency to understand other cultures.

Fourth, there is an increasing need in a variety of educational settings for a book such as this. Increasingly, educational institutions are driven by external and internal forces to introduce courses and subjects tailored to the dictates of the economy, and the labour market in particular. Tourism, trade with other countries, forging links with the region, understanding the effect that off-shore decision makers have on our economy (such as Wall Street on our stock exchange or on the value of national currencies), and internal matters such as the living conditions of indigenous people, migration policy and multiculturalism, all support the need for a book which attempts to facilitate and enhance the understanding of different cultures.

The need for this book has, of course, been thrown into sharpest relief since 9/11. While the necessity for cross-cultural understanding existed previously, 9/11 and subsequent events have sucked the earth's citizens into a vortex in which 'them' and 'us', 'us' and 'the other', 'good' and 'evil', the 'believer' and the 'infidel', are symptomatic of deeply entrenched perceptions, constructions, representations and misrepresentations of other cultures and religions. Even when large proportions of populations are opposed to the continuation of wars (in

---

4.   For an intriguing account of the influence of globalisation on individualism and multiculturalism, see Anthony Elliott and Charles Lemert, *The New Individualism: The Emotional Costs of Globalization* (London: Routledge, 2006).

Iraq, for example), the controversies over religious dress, wearing religious symbols, permitting, respecting or tolerating the religious observance of minority groups (for example, prayers during the day), provoke fears in populations that are seemingly unabated.

It seems that religion is pivotal to the polarisation depicted in the opposites just mentioned. Religious beliefs are alleged to be the cause of conflict and terror. For example, the world, and nations and communities, are divided into representations of Muslim and non-Muslim which define culture in terms of religion. There are grave dangers in such an approach, including the fact that the distinction between cause and symptom is not explored and may be confused, that context and history are rarely examined, and the approach used systematically fails to appreciate national, cultural and religious differences between and within Muslim nations and communities. According to some current social attitudes, people of one religion are, by definition, all the same. In this approach, a religion is homogenous and uniform while the diversity and subtlety within a particular faith per se, and cultural and national differences, are discounted and ignored. Such re-presentations are a travesty. But they also demonstrate how cultures are characterised and constructed in such a way that culture and religion are inextricably intertwined. So, in this and following chapters, whenever culture is mentioned, religion can be read into the text.

At this point I should acknowledge that the way I have written the above paragraph on religion could be regarded as a western construction. I have suggested that culture and religion are linked and that culture could be regarded as a synonym for religion. In this formulation religion is acknowledged as at least a part of, and inextricably linked to, culture. But, this formulation does not even canvass the possibility that religion could be the defining factor of a culture, that the culture (or the social) could be in the service of religion, rather than one institution among others (such as the family or education or government) as acknowledged so far in this Introduction. If a western secular worldview is smuggled into an exploration of what this book is about it is important that we consider the assumptions which we bring to cross-cultural understanding.[5]

However, the link between culture and religion is further complicated because the West is overtly secular.[6] It should, however, be conceded that to many others in the world the West carries the legacy of a Christian heritage with imperialist and colonialist associations, and with extremely conservative, pro-Israeli, and anti-Islamic permutations. As this book is intended for my contemporaries in the West, a vexed question is: how can we in the secular West understand other cultures which are inherently religious or when religious sensibilities have implications for other cultural arenas such as security and foreign relations? Simply put, if other nations are religious and the West, by and large is not, how can we understand them? Religious differences and differences in religious belief involve worldviews, values, and alternative views of history. Moreover, different things are cherished and treasured, and such values extend even to what is regarded as socially valid knowledge (that is, in one nation state religious knowledge is highly valued, whereas in a secular state scientific theories of knowledge might prevail).

---

5. For an account of how a religious concept such as mysticism has been interpreted through western eyes, see Richard King, *Orientalism and Religion: Postcolonial theory, India and 'the mystic East'* (London: Routledge, 1999).
6. For an account on the rise of secularism see, Alistair McGrath, *The Twilight of Atheism; The Rise and fall of Disbelief in the Modern World* (London: Random House, 2004).

A good case can be made for examining all the above issues with a critical eye. It is imperative that they be analysed and the consequences and implications of each carefully unravelled and disclosed. Where possible I will do this in this book, but it is *not* the focus. The main aim of this book is more fundamental. It is to explore what we bring to cross-cultural understanding in order to become more fully aware of what it involves, the obstacles to it, how they can be overcome, and how cross-cultural understanding can be enhanced and fostered.

One of the obstacles to cross-cultural understanding is that the past still haunts us. The consequences of past imperialism, colonialism, and chauvinism of the most heinous varieties, including religious parochialism and proselytising, are characterised by anything and everything but cross-cultural understanding—or at least the mutual and more comprehensive understanding of another culture which is the concern of this book. The past invasions of nations in Africa, the Americas, the Indian subcontinent and parts of Asia and the Pacific, have had enormous consequences for the people of those nations and cultures. Since the end of the Second World War, the consequences of resultant independence movements have been felt by the invading and colonial powers themselves. Vietnam, the defeat of the French and the Vietnam War, is but one example.

Yet genocide and the decimation of cultures, including religious beliefs, are not only things of the past. The conditions of indigenous peoples in their native lands are deplorable (for example, in Australia, Canada, New Zealand and the United States). With few, if any, exceptions their standards of living are far lower than that of their non-indigenous compatriots. Furthermore, some of the gains for indigenous people which resulted from the movements in the 1960s and 1970s, such as positive discrimination, are currently being criticised by conservative, and even some middle-of-the road, social and political groups and their supporters.

The need for cross-cultural understanding is also demonstrated by the debates over migration that have arisen in many of those countries in which the indigenous nations and cultures have been invaded and decimated. In Australia and the United States restricted migration policy has been a feature of past public policy. The White Australia Policy in Australia effectively barred people from the Asian region in preference to migrants from the United Kingdom and Europe, including Italy and Greece. In the United States after the First World War, consideration was given to selective migration policies which were intended to exclude the citizens of some European countries on the basis of their alleged inferior intelligence. Debates about work permits, and the migration of indigenous people to the colonising power, have also highlighted the need to understand other cultures. This has happened in both France and the United Kingdom where the racial and cultural mix has increased dramatically with people from (for example) the West Indies and Nigeria migrating to the former colonists' shores.

In Australia, in the 1990s, three controversial issues dominated the media. They highlight the relevance of a book about cross-cultural understanding, relating to people of other cultures or studying other cultures, and finding ways of thinking which facilitate such activities. There are other issues, of course, but the three about which I am thinking arouse particular passions. The first is the High Court ruling known popularly as 'Mabo'.[7] In effect, the Mabo ruling held that Australia was populated prior to 1788 and that the country was therefore

---

7. High Court of Australia, Mabo v Queensland (No.2) (1992) 175 CLR1.

colonised. This meant that before 1788 the land was owned by the indigenous people, a position which overturned the previous legal understanding which legitimated white colonisation. As the country was 'settled' (itself a euphemism for 'invasion') in 1788, indigenous people had a right, according to the Mabo judgment, to make a claim on the land they once owned, negotiate about what activities occurred on it, and seek compensation for any loss of its original use. The legislation designed to implement the Mabo ruling provided the mechanisms and the alleged safeguards for this to happen.

A second issue which has emerged since the 1995 election of the Federal Government in Australia is the perennial one of migration, and particularly migration from Asia. Leading the discussion was Pauline Hanson who was disendorsed by the Liberal Party in Australia for her comments on racial issues, and later formed her own party. Hard times, particularly when the national economy is incapable of providing anything approximating full employment (as was the case then), are reflected in the extent of cultural amnesia, the production and reproduction of social myths, and the scapegoating of other cultures.

Thus, the Mabo decision and the immigration debate in Australia raise the thorny issue of relations between various cultures and the problems involved in cross-cultural understanding. The subsequent division and conflict make reaching agreement about such issues difficult, if not impossible. So there are disagreements about many of the implications or consequences of the Mabo judgment. There are also disagreements about the effect native title claims may have on land leased from the Commonwealth or the states and territories. Facts are contested just as energetically as interpretations of law. The immigration debate has been just as controversial. For some, the extent of the controversy aroused by the Mabo decision, and by Pauline Hanson's statements, is the sign of a mature democracy in which matters can be debated in a free and unfettered way. For others, it is cause for grave concern.

A third contentious issue in Australia has been mandatory sentencing in the Northern Territory and Queensland. Under this legislation, non-custodial options for offenders are not available to courts. Whereas, in the past, first or second offenders may have been fined or given suspended sentences or, in the case of young offenders, been put into diversionary programs which attempt to keep them out of custodial institutions, such options were no longer available. The burden of this legislation has fallen heavily on indigenous people, and particularly indigenous young people, who were already over-represented in custodial institutions compared to their white counterparts. In Australia this policy has been particularly controversial, and has been debated in federal parliament and referred to a United Nations sub-committee.

The book: what is it about, and not about?

In the light of the above, the need to understand other cultures would seem incontrovertible. However, as significant as they are, analysing such controversies and disagreements is not the focus of this book. It is also not about policy debates or why some people have certain attitudes to other cultures or races. It is not about why some people are ethnocentric (that is, judge and act on the basis that their culture is the centre and all others are on the periphery) nor why Australian history has been characterised as xenophobic (the fear of foreigners). It is not about structural racism in social institutions (such as the way the judicial system, for example, relates to indigenous Australians) nor the way that dominant views are popularised to highlight negative images of cultural groups to their detriment, while advantaging dominant groups. These issues are mentioned in part, but a detailed analysis of them will not be found in this book.

I acknowledge that all of the above are obstacles to cross-cultural understanding, that they involve the per-petuation of various dominant and popular ideas, and that the issues as described above are about power, how it is unequally distributed, the consequences of wielding such power, and the responses to being on the receiving end of it. Even the production and reproduction of myths about cultures and races is best explained by which group has power to effect their plans and which does not. Again, these issues are mentioned in part, but a comprehensive and detailed analysis is not the focus of the book.

This book examines the way cross-cultural knowledge is approached, the obstacles to it, and the manner in which they can be overcome. It is about some of the attitudes, beliefs and values we bring to cross-cultural un-derstanding. In particular, it is about the way in which some knowledge counts and other forms of knowledge are discounted, and the relevance of this to cross-cultural understanding. In fact, these views which are brought to cross-cultural understanding are often taken for granted. They include a set of assumptions which are culturally approved, and rarely examined, let alone questioned. It is argued that these plague the understanding of other cultures before we even begin the task itself, that is, before we even engage with members of other cultures.

For example, something as obvious as defining what is reliable and valid knowledge is a potential obstacle to cross-cultural understanding. Consider a university student studying another culture for a project of some sort. The student may accept without question dominant western views about what reliable and valid knowledge is and the methods used to acquire it. The culture or even sub-culture being studied may have an entirely different world view, leading to a different idea of what constitutes valid knowledge, perhaps one which relies much less on observation and scientific method as the source of information. If a culture explains a fire or a storm or illness by invoking what the western student may regard as unscientific, unverifiable explanations, then misunderstanding is almost inevitable.

One might argue that an analysis of cross-cultural understanding should examine not only the differences in world view, but also why one is more powerful than another. Overall, I agree. An analysis of the difficulties of cross-cultural understanding will inevitably examine the broad power relations in society which perpetrate and reproduce a particular view about, or representation of, the dominant culture and its relationship to different cultural, ethnic or racial groups. Such an analysis will ask why selective dominant and negative images of a culture are amplified, and why opposing but positive views are excluded or diminished. Such an analysis demands a probing investigation of power relations in our society. It requires questions such as: what social function is performed by the negative pictures of certain minority groups? in whose interests or to whose benefit?

However, here again in this book I do not examine such matters specifically. It is not about the practice and implications of past and present cross-cultural relations and understanding. The focus of this book is not about representations or even relations which lead to inequalities and oppression. It is about something that is powerful, but not about the power of those who make images. It is the power of certain forms of knowledge, and the value of that knowledge, which guides our attempts to understand other cultures. It is not about contesting information about cultures and sub-cultures and such issues as whether they are assisting the economy or not.

My focus is more fundamental (which does not necessarily mean more important).

I concentrate on exploring some taken-for-granted assumptions about cross-cultural understanding which seem to be operating before we engage or converse with members of other cultures. In this context our interest is to ask if it is possible to understand other cultures at all, whether our own cultural background and socialisation (the process whereby we learn about our own cultures) render us constitutionally incapable of understanding across cultural divides.

This book is not about claim and counter-claim over a specific culture, but about more fundamental assumptions of knowledge and its contribution to cross-cultural understanding. These are often regarded as being philosophical and epistemological (that is, philosophical questions about theories of knowledge and knowledge claims). In this book such issues are examined. For example, the criteria by which we conclude that we know something and the question of whether members of different cultures live in different worlds or live in the same world but experience it differently, are usually regarded as points of philosophy and epistemology. Yet they are clearly relevant to cross-cultural understanding (indeed, to any form of understanding). There are other matters which are pertinent, such as whether all cultures and values are equally valid, whether the fact that all cultures are equal is a reason for being tolerant, and whether claiming that values are unequally valid logically means that I want to impose my values on others.

The method used in this book originates largely in social theory, political philosophy and the sociology of knowledge (although the last with important qualifications).[8] The sociology of knowledge, among other

---

8.   The sociology of knowledge is often associated with Karl Mannheim's, 'Ideology and Utopia', in *Ideology and Utopia An*

things, is concerned about why certain forms of knowledge are more important than others, why know-ledge is
arranged socially in a hierarchy, why certain forms of
knowledge are included and others excluded, why some
forms of knowledge have social credentials and others
don't, why certain forms of knowledge count and others
are discounted, and why certain forms of knowledge are
admissible and others not. For example, the sociology of
knowledge which motivates the approach I adopt
analyses why scientific knowledge might be regarded as
more valid than say, religious knowledge, why reason
rather than emotion is considered to be the soundest basis
for knowledge, and why the voice of the most powerful is
heard and those on the margins disregarded? There are
issues of power here. But integral to the general matter of
power is what counts as privileged knowledge and why.[9]

The distinction used here is between knowledge and
factual claims, on the one hand, and claims about knowledge, on the other. Knowledge claims (the former)

Introduction to the Sociology of Knowledge (London: Routledge
and Kegan Paul, 1960). This enterprise was much criticised for
different reasons by Karl Popper, *Poverty of Historicism*
(London: Routledge and Kegan Paul, 1957) and Roger Trigg,
*Understanding Social Science: A Philosophical Introduction to
the Social Sciences,* Second edition (Oxford: Basil Blackwell,
2001), 23-43. For more recent attempts to formulate the
sociology of knowledge see Richinda Power, *A Question of
Knowledge* (London: Prentice Hall, 2000) and Tim May and
Malcolm Williams, editors. *Knowing the Social Word* (Bucking-
ham: Open University Press 1998).

9. By the sociology of knowledge in the following I am keen to
   analyse what forms of knowledge are valued and devalued in the
   West and what are the implications for cross-cultural
   understanding. It will become clear that I do not adhere to the
   epistemological relativism that is sometimes associated with the
   sociology of knowledge project.

concern things such as what percentage of a minority group are living in poverty compared to the whole community. Or, what proportion of indigenous people is in police custody compared with other non-indigenous groups. Another example is whether all people in a culture have certain beliefs, practices and values, or whether such beliefs, practices or values are held by only a small percentage of the culture. It may be that the public perception, or the view peddled in the media, is quite inaccurate. These are knowledge or factual claims. They can be tested. As important as they are, this book is not so much about them.

The focus of this book is socially accepted and prevailing claims about knowledge, about what beliefs about knowledge are used in cross-cultural understanding. It is about our approach to socially powerful forms of knowledge. As I suggested, it is about aspects of our culture which influence, if not determine, how we come to a cross-cultural understanding, what we think it is, whether we think it is possible, and the social standards of what counts as valid knowledge by which we judge the beliefs, practices and values of other cultures.

In a way, of course, there is a link between knowledge and power. But my concern is not about claims that are regarded as factual even if they can be disputed (such as levels of poverty). It is about popular and powerful taken-for-granted assumptions. For example, why is a version of scientific knowledge the standard for all knowledge claims in the West and how does this influence cross-cultural understanding? The following does not merely describe these hierarchies of knowledge linked to commensurate hierarchies of relative power. It challenges these claims about what is regarded as valid knowledge. In this way, it offers a different approach to some sociologies of knowledge. Yet this is not, strictly speaking, a philosophy book, although it does not recoil from using philosophical arguments to expose some of the popular, privileged and powerful thought forms.

Herein also lies one intended difference between this book and other excellent books on this and related issues by philosophers.[10] Most philosophers writing about similar issues to those in this book do not use their critical analysis to ask what to the sociologist of knowledge, or the social and political theorist, are the most obvious questions. Philosophers, rightly criticise claims about what knowledge is reliable and valid and, in this book, in so far as necessary, their arguments and approach are adopted. But they tend not to ask why that particular form of knowledge is socially credentialed. It is sociologists who are inclined to ask the following questions. If the dominant perspective about knowing is so inadequate (philosophically speaking), why is it so popular and powerful? What social function does this popular but inadequate perspective perform? If all scientific claims do not have the qualities of certainty and reliability that we have been taught are crucial, why does it remain popular? Why is the scientific method credited with providing the criteria for valid knowledge claims when, since the late 1920s at least, such a view has been seriously challenged? Why do we believe that we can arbitrate between facts when it can be argued that facts, like values, are a product of social convention? What is the social function of acting as if values are absolute but claiming merely that they are relative?

It is important to note that I am not criticising philosophers for not asking sociological questions any more

---

10. See Brian Fay (1996), *Contemporary Philosophy of Science A Multicultural Approach* (Oxford: Blackwell, 1996), and Roger Trigg (1985), *Understanding Social Science*.

than I am criticising sociologists for ignoring philosophical and epistemological questions. In fact, philosophers and sociologists have done both. For example,
philosophers as different as Karl Popper, Michael Polanyi,
Jean-Francois Lyotard and Richard Rorty, critical social
theorists such as Theodor Adorno, Herbert Marcuse, Jurgan
Habermas and Max Hork-heimer, and feminists such as
Sandra Harding, have done both.[11] In the following I
attempt to highlight the sociological significance of
popular and powerful perspectives which have been at
least challenged, if not debunked, by more philosophical
(and sociological) analyses, and their relevance in approaching the task of cross-cultural understanding.

Philosophers and sociologists both explore and
question appearances, that is, things as they seem. One of
the themes of this book is to use philosophical and sociological questioning to explore how cross cultural-under-
standing is approached. A pre-condition for this is that we
consider the issues both philosophically and socio-
logically, using a more philosophical analysis to challenge
the validity of the taken for granted assumptions by
which we approach other cultures, and using a sociological approach to examine the social reasons for popular
knowledge claims and beliefs about knowledge. The latter
is at the heart of what I mean by the sociology of knowledge.

Chapter outline

In Chapter 1 I begin the task by exploring what it means
to say we understand another culture. In this chapter
several obstacles to cross-cultural understanding are also
examined. In particular, the influence of our own culture
as a barrier is explored. After this three possible responses
to such barriers are analysed: the response of the ethnocentric, the cultural relativist and the cultural pluralist.
Chapter 1 concerns understanding in the cognitive sense,

---

11. Some of the theorists mentioned are discussed later in this book.

in the sense of knowledge from the head. It asks: how can we know cognitively?

In Chapter 2 I pose another question. This time it is not about how we can know about other cultures, but what it means to 'be understanding' in the sense of being sympathetic to other cultures, respecting them, and appreciating their diversity. This attempt is based on the distinction in everyday parlance between 'to understand' as knowing about something and being understanding as being sensitive to and respectful of others. I also argue that, in addition to cerebral knowledge, being understanding involves values and commitments which are difficult to defend in the West, where they are regarded as mere ideologies. Is there a way out of this stalemate? Is there a way to defend the values required of cross-cultural understanding?

In Chapter 3 I ask whether science can provide an agreed neutral ground which would facilitate the adjudication of ideologies and find a neutral place conducive to cross-cultural understanding. The chapter explores some of the influences of scientific knowledge which have adversely affected cross-cultural understanding. It discusses the criteria by which certain forms of knowledge are elevated and others are devalued and, particularly, whether there is any justification for the social construction and popularity of scientific knowledge.

Postmodernism, the topic of Chapter 4, offers a rather complicated, fluid and quirky critique of what is known as modernity (ending roughly after the Second World War), and the latter's faith in progress and absolute standards. Superficially at least, it would seem to offer important insights which might be thought to facilitate cross-cultural understanding. After all, postmodernists tend to emphasise difference and diversity, and they read texts and stories in a way that is said to emphasise the voice of the powerless. In addition, they tend to be relativists and advocate tolerance. I explore their contribution to cross-cultural understanding in this chapter.

In Chapter 5 I examine the implications of one of the themes in the following chapters, namely, the meanings of value absolutism and value relativism. These are like two sides of the one coin. On one side we have the argument that because we cannot arbitrate between values (value relativism) we should be tolerant. On the other side, some argue that it is possible to say that one value is preferable to another (value absolutism) which, according to their critics means that value absolutists want to impose their values on their antagonists. The seeming aid to cross-cultural understanding which comes from value relativism, and the impediment which allegedly comes from value absolutism, are examined in Chapter 5.

Tolerance as a political virtue, something worthy of advocacy, is implicit in calls for cross-cultural under-standing and seems to be a precondition for it. But what does tolerance mean? What social function does it serve? Is it commensurate with the task of cross-cultural under-standing, as tolerance is socially certified and propagated? Or does it constrain or limit understanding? Public documents often advocate tolerance, but is it sufficient? In Chapter 6 I explore these matters.

In Chapter 7 I examine some of the implications of the argument in the previous chapters. If, as I argue, value relativism cannot defend tolerance, and value absolutism (as I use the term) does not necessarily entail the tyranny of imposing our views on dissenters, why are these arguments or perspectives so popular? If, contrary to popular thought, they are not an aid to cross-cultural understanding, why are they so popular and powerful? What social function do they serve? In particular, in Chapter 7 I assess the alleged neutrality and impartiality of objectivity to determine its social function. If, as is argued, objectivity fulfils social functions which are inimical to cross-cultural understanding, from whose perspective should we begin?

Chapter 8 is about the possibility of defending a commitment to cross-cultural understanding. In many ways, it is most unlike a work of social science. Nonetheless, if there are values on which cross-cultural understanding depends it would be ideal, to say the least, to consider how they can be defended. The chapter engages with the some of the most influential ideas in recent social science, including anti-foundationalism, social constructionism, and notions of truth.

In Chapter 9 I attempt to overcome an acute dilemma that has emerged from the previous chapters. It concerns investigating another culture without falling into either of two traps. One trap is trying to avoid imposing western scientific thought on those with whom we wish to engage and understand. The other trap is rushing to the other extreme. In an endeavour to avoid imposing western scientific methods and theories about what counts as knowledge, this alternative adopts as its own and without question the accounts and self-descriptions of members of the other culture with whom they are engaging. The alternatives seem to be: see through the lens of western scientism or accept the way other cultures describe their own way of life. Both positions, and an alternative, are examined in Chapter 9. In Chapter 10 the arguments in the book are synthesised and applied to cross-cultural understanding. The Conclusion applies the findings to religion.

The argument

The argument I advance is that while understanding involves knowledge which is descriptive or factual, acquiring such knowledge is not as straightforward as is assumed (Chapter 1). Cross-cultural understanding also requires us to be committed to being understanding in the sense of being interested in other cultures, in respecting differences, in appreciating diversity, and in being tolerant (Chapter 2).

In this way, understanding involves values and commitments. We are motivated to understand because we have a sense, however tacit and for whatever reason, that other cultures are worthy of respect, that dialogue cannot only resolve misunderstanding and tensions but can also be illuminating. There are certainly pragmatic reasons for understanding other cultures, but they are not the only ones. Whatever the reason, however, a commitment to being understanding is difficult to defend in the West because it presupposes the value of under-standing, which in turn is undermined by the prevalence of the view that it is impossible to defend one value against a competitor, and that values are only reflections of our own subjective preferences. They have no other status. They are ideologies. If we cannot defend cultural values, including the value of understanding other cultures, cross-cultural understanding seems to be thwarted almost from the beginning.

Despite some potential for providing the preconditions for cross-cultural understanding, I argue that the methods and theories of knowledge in science are not optimal to the task. In fact, western science and social science have been a cause of much misunderstanding by arrogating to themselves the standard for all knowledge (Chapter 3). Postmodernism, which assists in some respects, still leaves us with some way to go largely because of its relativism (Chapter 4).

This notwithstanding, one popular justification for the values which support cross-cultural understanding, including tolerance, is relativism. This might come as a surprise. Relativism might seem to undermine the defence of values, but it is often argued that it is precisely because we cannot arbitrate between values that we should be tolerant. In Chapter 5 I argue that neither of the conclusions which purport to follow from value relativism and value absolutism necessarily follow; tolerance neither follows from value relativism nor does intolerance necessarily follow from value absolutism (as I use the term and as a contrast to value relativism).

In Chapter 6 I claim that liberal notions of tolerance that are popular and powerful in the West are more likely to seek changes in individuals rather than structures, that they defend the positions of large powerful majorities against repressed minorities and are largely oppressive. These criticisms notwithstanding, I argue that a tolerance which avoids these pitfalls is a necessary pre-condition of cross-cultural understanding. I base this conclusion on a bolstered or reinforced notion of tolerance. Such a maximised notion of tolerance also allows the possibility of intolerance, which is sometimes necessary for genuine cross-cultural understanding. This may seem contradictory or perverse. However, this intolerance is not necessarily directed at the people or groups with whom we are conversing, but against the structural obstacles and rival views which oppose tolerance and cross-cultural understanding.

In Chapter 7 I argue that relativism, neutrality and impartiality, although seemingly indispensable to cross-cultural understanding, fulfil a social function which is often hostile to them. In brief, although not too crudely, this occurs because, in the plethora of cultural and value positions, a power vacuum is created which the power brokers control. Even the ideal and practice of objectivity, when connected with neutrality, disguises the very power relationships which dictate it. It is argued that the notion of standpoints and a particular view of deference, best circumvents the problems associated with relativism and neutrality.

But beginning our cross-cultural understanding and research from the standpoints of the marginalised, and deference, is yet to be defended. In arguing that it is possible to arbitrate between values by rational means I take issue with many of the fancied views of our times, such as anti-foundationalism, a strong or a full-blown social constructionism, the impossibility of approximating truth, the coyness about values and the presumed virtue of value relativism. While exploring how some of these ideas may assist cross-cultural understanding, I highlight their inadequacies.

I argue that approaching cross-cultural understanding requires alternative methods, and different theories of knowledge, and how it is obtained—at least compared to those currently feted. If the approaches of the past, including those of science and social science, limit cross-cultural understanding and skew it in repressive ways, then different methods are essential. I make a modest, inchoate and introductory attempt at deriving such methods in Chapter 8. I am inclined to the view that our methods and theories of knowledge are more likely to be conducive to cross-cultural understanding if they are pluralistic rather than relativistic, if they are multicultural rather than monocultural. The reason for this is not because there are no valid values but because there are, and not because we should be eclectic and choose a little from here and there, but because the very pluralism and diversity of cultures warrants discovering the values and the tools to engage in, and defend, cross-cultural understanding.

Having attempted to defend the values which underpin cross-cultural understanding, in Chapter 9 I explore the possibility of overcoming both an imperious social science and taking the perspectives of other cultures for granted, taking their self-descriptions as our own, or accepting their own culture in their own terms. I argue that both are ethnocentric in their own way, and that an alternative approach is contrasting cultures so that we discover terms from our language that can be used to describe another culture. This has the advantage of alerting us to inadequacies in our own culture which, in turn, minimises the prospects of ethnocentrism.

Several more qualifications

There are other aspects to the argument, but the above will suffice for now. What should be clear is that this is not a recipe book for cross-cultural understanding or a policy which might be called multiculturalism. It does not provide a step-by-step account of the ingredients and what to do with them. It offers no instructions for cross-cultural understanding that could be used either in the field, in encounters with people of other cultures, or when studying other cultures for a research project or reading their literature (either past or present).

The book is about some (but by no means all) of those things we bring to cross-cultural encounters which are usually assumed or taken for granted when we engage with other cultures (often unconsciously). Of necessity, in daily practice we use certain concepts, devices, methods, tools and understandings about how we should proceed without really thinking about them critically. In daily life there is no time for dillydallying. And mention of every-day life points to how ubiquitous cross-cultural under-standing really is. It does not only refer to engaging in long-term conversation with a person from another culture or studying another culture or living overseas. The tertiary assignment which requires us to read an ancient text is set and we have to do it. We see someone in the street from another culture purchasing unfamiliar food. We see people moving toward a mosque or a temple, or hear of colleagues fasting during the day. The media reports show conflict in which the antagonists seem to be members of different cultures. A cultural festival is advertised on television and we are involved in understanding other cultures.

In such activities there is an immediacy and urgency about cross-cultural understanding which precludes prevarication. As cross-cultural encounters are often un-predictable, it is impossible to delay the encounter to consider the things we bring to it. We simply engage, whether by conversing with another person, reading, observing the street or office or education situation, watching television or in discussion. That is why it is important to take stock, to reflect upon those things we find it difficult to reflect upon in our daily encounters.

So this book is about those things which predispose cross-cultural understanding in certain directions, those preliminary aspects which influence communicating and understanding in the cross-cultural context, even if we are unaware of them. Once analysed, many of these in-fluences are obstacles, rather than facilitators of cross-cultural understanding. For example, the adverse influence of cultural filters, ethnocentrism and western science may be more readily identifiable than the negative influences in cultural and value relativism, and post-modernism. Nonetheless, the latter are influential.

A basic premise of the following is that whatever we bring to a task by way of beliefs, concepts and objectives, influences if not determines the outcomes, the results. It is important to know what we bring, even if hitherto we were unaware of them. Thus, an imperative for cross-cultural understanding is disclosing such influences even if the emphasis appears to be more about obstacles to it rather than the prerequisites of it and, certainly, how to do it. Moving forward often necessitates clearing the path. It is not different in cross-cultural understanding.

Values are also emphasised. As you will discover, my concern about values is not that some conservatives oppose value relativism because they perceive a decline in traditional values. My concern is that despite appearances, some varieties of popular relativism are conducive to repression rather than freedom. My concern is that the advocates of some movements which advocate greater freedom in the West, including some multi-culturalists and postmodernists, have associated value relativism with political values such as freedom, tolerance and pluralism while, simultaneously, linking the oppon-ents of value relativism with intolerance and autho-ritarianism.

They, the advocates, have found what they believe to be a problem with their opposition (who they allege want to foist their views on others), while being unable to see the political and social function of the relativism they espouse or that their position is inherently incapable of defending or justifying the very political values they advocate. It is this shyness about declaring value positions, recoiling from those values which underpin cross-cultural understanding and multiculturalism (max-imally understood), which is one of the prime targets and main concerns of this book.

Several further clarifications by way of caveats, disclaimers and qualifications are also in order. Firstly, this book engages with my western colleagues and coun-terparts. It makes no claim to understand what indig-enous peoples and nations, or cultural minorities in the West, or anywhere else, feel or think about cross-cultural understanding. I do hear indigenous groups say they want to enter into dialogue, to understand us and to be understood. I could be wrong about this, but media reports, protests outside parliament and the work of advocacy groups would suggest this. But I am not presuming how they might approach the task. If, for whatever reason, non-western readers find my argument helpful, or a sympathetic account, I would be heartened and would be committed to exploring the conversation.

However, the argument in this book is primarily directed at powerful ideas and practices in the West which are inimical to genuine cross-cultural understanding.

Secondly, cross-cultural understanding is not confined to the attempt to understand individuals from other cultures. It undoubtedly includes person-to-person understanding. However, as Chapter 9 attests, this book is also an attempt to ascertain the best approach that the social sciences could adopt. If social scientists wanted to understand another culture, what form would the social sciences take? What would be their motivation? What would be their objectives? This is an important task, particularly in the light of my conclusion in Chapter 3 that much of the science which has influenced the social sciences has been, and remains, constitutionally incapable of maximising cross-cultural understanding.

Thirdly, overall the style is intended to be accessible. While (hopefully) not chatty or conversational in style, examples, including imaginary stories, are used to clarify or make points. While most chapters have some footnotes I have tried to keep them to a minimum. Only when it is necessary to defend an interpretation of another author do I follow the work of others closely. On some occasions critical comments are made, on other occasions they are not. For example, it might seem that I am uncritical of Marcuse's view of 'repressive tolerance' (Chapter 6) and Charles Taylor's approach to understanding and social science. However, it should not be assumed that I agree with everything they argue or that I feel it necessary to anticipate every argument against them. That might make my argument a little vulnerable in places but why should I give critics ammunition?

Finally, it is necessary to say something about what I mean by cross-cultural understanding. Optimally, cross-cultural understanding has at least three features. Firstly, it is usually a process which is recognised as one which maximises mutually beneficial and respectful interaction.[12] Secondly, its objective is an enhanced, but not necessarily acritical, appreciation of another cultural perspective and world view, which includes beliefs, practices and values. Thirdly, it produces an increasingly critical picture of our own culture and its relations with other cultures. Cross-cultural understanding does not absolve another cultural world view of its adverse implications and consequences. Yet, cross-cultural under-standing is less likely to be ethnocentric, chauvinistic, jaundiced and prejudicial if it challenges one's own cultural beliefs, practices and values. It also challenges our relations with our cultural interlocutors in order to ascertain how they might view our attempts to understand them, and they us.

---

12. A further qualification is required here. I might consider that I have come to understand, yet those with whom I engage may feel no benefit of any newly acquired awareness of their culture on my part, even if they agree that I have understood.

1

Approaching cross-cultural understanding: questions and reactions

Introduction

At first glance it might seem that cross-cultural under-standing is a relatively simple affair. Even when we disagree with other cultures and their values or outlook, we take it for granted that we can understand them. Even if we disapprove of some of their beliefs and practices, our very disapproval is based on, and presumes, some sort of prior understanding. So what does it mean to say we understand another culture or its members?

In the first part of this chapter I ask a number of questions which are intended to demonstrate the complexity of cross-cultural understanding, something often taken for granted. Several examples are used to illustrate the points which, to some extent at least, are summarised in the idea that our own cultural beliefs and values are the filter through which we make sense of the world, including other cultures. Indeed, this filter has the potential to be an obstacle to cross-cultural under-standing, because it limits our outlook. I examine three responses to this cultural filtering.

The first is ethnocentrism which sees a particular culture and ethos as the centre of the world and (usually) judges all others as inferior. A second response is cultural relativism which is an extreme version of cultural filtering. Cultural pluralism is a third response. This position recognises that there are cultural filters which influence the prospects of cross-cultural understanding but which do not limit it altogether. For the moment, though, let us consider some pertinent, if not basic, questions.

What does cross-cultural understanding mean and involve? An example and questions

Consider first what it might mean to understand another culture. At first blush it may seem quite uncomplicated to say, 'I understand something of another culture'. In everyday life the ability to understand, and to acquire understanding, may be assumed and taken for granted. But a moment's reflection reveals a series of questions which suggest that understanding is not quite as straightforward as it might seem.

For example, some people (let us say in the dominant economic, social and political group) might be quite satisfied with their understanding of other cultures. They might claim to know all about 'them', 'those others'.[1] They might insist that they know all they need to know to make the necessary judgments and decisions about them. But how much do they really know? Further, the subordinate cultural group may object strongly to the traits attributed to them; they may contest what others purport to know and claim. This too, is common. The powerful group may claim they understand the other culture and its members (the other), but such a claim is vehemently denied by the subordinate group.

So who really understands? Whose view is privileged in the sense of being given the most social honour or

---

1. In this chapter, 'understand' is used in the sense of knowing about. It is cognitive rather than affective knowledge about which we are concerned in this chapter. The latter is the focus in Chapter 2.

standing, the most clout or power? In other words, whose view is given the most social credit? Whose view counts for those who organise society, defend it and agree with it? If you were to arbitrate between the perspectives, whose would you prefer? I'll try to clarify the relevance of these questions with a concrete example.

Suppose a small group of indigenous people object to a structure being built (say a bridge) on the grounds that it would be sacrilegious.[2] By that they seem to mean that the building of the bridge would see the destruction of a place which for them has great cultural and religious significance. Upon completion of the bridge, the topography would be permanently changed so that the cultural (and I might say the religious) significance of the place would be lost. Let's also suppose that a group of powerful developers and their supporters claim to understand the cultural and religious significance of the building of the bridge for indigenous people.

However, according to the indigenous people, the developers do not understand at all. The developer's claim to understand is belied by their plan to build the bridge in the first place. According to the indigenous people, if the developers came anywhere near to understanding, they would realise that to build the bridge would not only alter the landscape forever, but it would also destroy the cultural meaning of the site. They feel the way the developer might feel if a mosque or church was

---

2. This is based on an actual example, although the details are not the same. For one example from the academic literature see the exchange between James Weiner, 'Anthropology, Historians and the Secret of Social Knowledge', in *Anthropology Today*, 11/5 (1995): 3–7 and Ron Brunton, 'The Hindmarsh Island Bridge: and the Credibility of Australian Anthropology', *Anthropology Today*, 12/4 (1996): 2–7.

destroyed.[3] The indigenous people claim that their position has not been properly understood or appreciated or respected.

Now, I concede that I may have neither understood, appreciated nor respected the positions of the indigenous group or the developers. In fact, as I wrote I was really struggling to express the little I know about the way indigenous people are generally integrated with the land. However, thankfully the illustration hinges neither on the limitations of my understanding, nor on the details of an actual story. The issue is: one side (the developers) claim to understand, and those on the other side—the indigenous people whose customs are adversely affected—repudiate the developer's claims.

In this illustration, the indigenous people are claiming to be misunderstood, and grievously so. So do the developers understand? Is their understanding disingenuous or tendentious? In what sense is the word understanding being used? Is it a matter of degree? Further, how would we judge? What criteria would we invoke to judge whether the group claiming to understand really did? And on what grounds were these criteria chosen?

---

3.   This argument is sometimes used as though destroying a church corresponds to building a bridge across land that is regarded as sacred. Clearly the correspondence does not appear to represent the indigenous claim on three grounds. Firstly, the land claims are significantly different. To destroy a church does not necessarily mean that the land title on which it is built is lost. Secondly, the area of land involved is vastly different. If lost, indigenous peoples stand to lose much more than a block of land. Thirdly, the parallel is inadequate because the building and the land are regarded differently. Churches are often built and extended or rebuilt; the sacred quality of the land for the indigenous people in the example is not so transitory or mutable. I concede that in some ways the very illustration disadvantages the indigenous position—but then so does most of the dominant language and argument!

And why use these criteria to decide what it means to understand and not others? Is it a matter of searching for the facts? If so, which facts, or what sort of facts, would decide the matter? Is understanding the only issue here? Or is it a matter of the relationship between knowledge and power? Is it possible to be objective?

More questions

These are very important questions, some of which I will address as we proceed. In addition, there are even more questions which are usually answered in everyday life by default, that is, they are assumed. An example will help to tease them out. Let's say I claim to understand a particular cultural group. What does this mean? Does it mean I understand all aspects of their culture, the majority of it, some of it, or just a little? And how did I come to understand the part that I claim to understand? What contact (if any) did I have with the cultural group which led me to draw that conclusion? And is that conclusion justified? What are my sources? For example, if I had only met one member of the other culture could I claim to understand? Would that be sufficient to warrant my claim?

Furthermore, is it justifiable to extrapolate from claiming to know people of another culture to maintaining that I understand the culture sufficiently to generalise about it and its members? Put differently, is it permissible to jump from private, anecdotal evidence about a member or members of a cultural group to generalising about the entire group? My source may only partially understand. Worse, their misunderstanding might be infectious!

Even if I read in the media something about the other culture that confirmed my view, it would not necessarily validate my claim to understand. The source of the material may be inaccurate. Even if someone else confirmed a claim about the other culture, would that justify my claim to understand? Would my claim to understand be validated if I knew everyone in the culture or had spent my life studying the culture or living in it? Is it possible to understand a culture without being a member of it? Is it possible to understand a culture if not born into it?[4]

This business of understanding can be explored even further. If I claim to understand another culture, do I understand it by my standards of understanding or by their standards? Is there consensus about the criteria for what constitutes understanding? Does there have to be? Is there agreement about indicators of understanding and whether I meet them or not?

Consider the situation in which I claim to understand culture C and I am describing and explaining culture C to you in the presence of members of that culture. If on hearing, the members of C correct me, if they insist that I misunderstand, who would you believe? Would you accept their description of their culture, or my version which members of the culture say is a misunderstanding? Of course we could all be wrong, in part or altogether. Would you agree that I understood even if the members of culture C agreed that I did, or would you suspect that we were all misguided? So, when we say we understand do we insist that our understanding is correct or do we defer to the diagnosis of members of culture C?

---

4.   On this point see Brian Fay, *Contemporary Philosophy of Science: A Multicultural Approach* (Oxford: Blackwell, 1996), 9–29.

More obstacles: different accounts of what counts as knowledge

There are many cultures and cultural attitudes and values and, importantly, perceptions about them. Such perceptions can be influenced by things which are regarded as obvious, taken for granted, unquestioned. For example, what is considered socially as the normal ways of obtaining reliable and valid knowledge is a potential obstacle to perceptions that facilitate optimal understanding. Consider a student studying an ancient book for a project of some sort.[5] The student may accept without question the dominant western views on what reliable and valid knowledge is, and the methods used to acquire it. However, the author of the book under study may have taken a different view of valid knowledge, perhaps one which relied much less on observation as the source of information (empiricism) and the scientific method as a means of obtaining it (positivism).

For example, ancient authors, cultures and religions, did not depend on the western view of science to explain the world in which they lived. Instead other world views were used to explain their beginnings, the origins of their physical and social worlds, the reasons for their existence, the relationships between the physical and human realms, and so on. Some of these practices and the explanations are now judged as non-sense by the rationalist and largely scientific western world. For example, beliefs about non-physical forces are considered to be irrational. Consequently, realities for members of another culture, which are revealed in ways that are not amenable to verification

---

5.　This example bears a striking resemblance to an illustration outlined in the Introduction. But I've used a different scenario (studying an ancient book) to illustrate the point that cross-cultural understanding is not restricted to contemporary political situations.

by the scientific method or the theory of knowledge on which it is based, are relegated to the status of myths, legends or mere stories. So beliefs about the spirit world, or ascribing divine-like qualities to physical objects such as trees or stones, or explaining natural forces by attributing creative energy to animals and the like, do not measure up to the standard of rationality used in the West and so are found wanting.

Similar examples are not only found when studying ancient texts. Alasdair MacIntyre gave a more recent example of the ease of smuggling parochial issues into comparative investigations.[6] He cited the example of an argument used by political scientists Almond and Verba in their book *The Civic Culture*.[7] Almond and Verba evidently argued that:

> Italians are less committed to and identified with the actions of their government than are Germans or Englishmen, offering as evidence the fact that the Italian respondents, as compared with the English and German respondents to their survey, placed such actions very low on a list of items to which they had been asked to give a rank order in terms of the amount of pride they took in them.[8]

As MacIntyre pointed out: 'At no point did Almond and Verba pause to ask whether the concept of pride is the same in the three different national cultures, that is, to ask, whether the different respondents had after all been

---

6.   This is example is used by Alasdair MacIntyre, 'Is a Science of Comparative Politics Possible?', in *The Philosophy of Social Explanation*, edited by Alan Ryan (Oxford: Oxford University Press, 1986), 170–88.

7.   Gabriel Almond and Sidney Verba, *The Civic Culture*, (Princeton: Princeton University Press, Princeton1963), 173.

8.   MacIntyre, 'Is a Science of Comparative Politics Possible?', 173.

asked the same question'.[9] Yet, as MacIntyre pointed out, in Mediterranean and Middle Eastern cultures to have pride is associated with maintaining and preserving one's honour and that of one's family.[10] Pride as honour is entirely different from saying 'I am proud of the Australian institutions of parliamentary democracy'. It is about ensuring that one's honour is protected, that one's good name and reputation are maintained and recognised by the community. To exclude such possibilities from analysis renders misunderstanding almost inevitable.

Misunderstanding may also occur when one or either party believes they understand each other when conversing. Subsequently, one party discovers that the other did not really understand at all—their so-called understanding amounted to inserting what they heard into their own cultural perspective. In other words, they appeared to be communicating, that is, there was dialogue in the sense the words were heard as the speaker intended. However, as the words were internalised and interpreted by the listener, they were given different meanings reflecting a different world view. The speaker and listener were at cross purposes. One party may believe their understanding is accurate but the other party comes to realise that they are really cultural worlds apart.

The influence of our own culture

A common view amongst people who consider these and similar matters is that we do import aspects of other cultures into our own; we tend to see other cultures from our own culture's perspective. It is as if we see other cultures and their members through our own cultural windows or filters. Inevitably, understanding another

9. *Ibid.*
10. *Ibid.*

culture is filtered by our own experiences and background. But does the filter prevent us from gaining an accurate view? Is the filter so coloured that it is impossible to see and understand anything except from my perspective? There are at least three responses to the effects of our cultural filters which translate into three positions or reactions to other cultures.

Ethnocentrism

One response is to ignore the possibility that our own cultural background influences how we see other cultural beliefs and practices, and to assume (presume is a less neutral but probably more accurate word) that our culture is the benchmark by which we should judge all others. In this sense our cultural world is the centre around which others exist and from which they are judged.[11] This is usually known as *ethnocentrism*. Ethnocentrism in this sense usually entails a person or group insisting that their culture is superior to other cultures which are, by definition, inferior. It is an explicitly and overtly malignant view because it is usually racist (for example, the Ku Klux Klan, Nazism and other policies which have led to ethnic cleansing).

This chauvinistic outlook also characterised the imperialist colonising of 16th–19th century Europe which destroyed cultures and pillaged indigenous nations on the grounds that it was 'the white man's burden' to bring the benefits of technology and European culture to 'primitive' people. Such domination was at least justified, if not in a

---

11. Here the metaphor of a circle is used. Ethnocentrism adopts the centre of the circle and interprets (or reads) everything beyond it from the perspective of that nucleus. In the version used here (which will be known as E_1) the ethnocentric position deliberately and purposively arrogates to itself the centre point around which all others revolve. E_1 regards its position as superior to all others.

sense motivated, by the superior world view, or the Eurocentric outlook, of the imperialist colonisers who invaded, conquered, raped, and exterminated nations of indigenous peoples—the adverse consequences of which continue unabated in many places today.

The economic, colonial, political and military motivations for this imperialistic aggrandisement are not denied, but the invaders also considered their world to be the centre of civilisation and, by definition, all others to be eccentric (at best).[12] According to this view, the land being colonised was inhabited by people who were inferior, whose world views, technology, language and religion were primitive compared to European cultures. This was ethnocentrism, in this case Eurocentrism, which in many, if not most instances, thoroughly disparaged and belittled indigenous cultures.

Yet colonisers believed they understood the peoples and cultures they were invading, so that they felt they were justified in calling them barbaric, indigent and primitive. In other words, to assert that a nation and culture is primitive presupposes a superior technological society, and that something about the inferior culture is known to the extent that it is believed to be understood (however dismissively). Undoubtedly, some cultural practices led to the colonists' conclusion. Perhaps it was the use of spears or bow and arrow which prompted this view. It may have been that they did not wear European-type clothes, or live in European houses. With more contact came more knowledge, and the claim to under-stand meant that the colonists could say that, 'these

---

12. In the case of economic colonial and military motives, being the centre was the objective to be realised. The point is that ethnocentrism was a part of, and essential to, imperialistic designs and action.

people roam around', 'they are transient', 'they don't wear clothes', 'they are illiterate', and so on.

In one sense, of course, where the indigenous nation was overrun and largely destroyed, claiming the invaded culture is inferior may have diverted attention from the reality of the conquest. So, in one sense, ethnocentrism is not the only factor in the decimation of indigenous cultures and genocide of nations. Nonetheless, the colonists' perception of the indigenous culture and nation supported their colonising, economic and imperialist objectives. In other words, ethnocentrism may not have been the only factor motivating invasion but, as a system of beliefs, it justified and supported imperialistic aims.

Thus, the invaders did have a view about the indigenous nation and culture. They did claim to see and experience. They did draw conclusions about what indigenous people did and believed. In this sense they knew something about the culture. Now it might be argued that knowing something about a culture is different from understanding it. That is true and we will examine it further in the next chapter. However, the point at this juncture is that the invaders claimed to know certain things from their encounters and justified their actions on the basis of their knowledge.

In summary, one response to the cultural influences that modify our understanding of other cultures is ethnocentrism. This involves, at least, an attitude of cultural superiority by which the ethnocentrist's culture becomes the standard, the centre, from which to judge all others as inferior. This usually presupposes some claim to know or understand something about the allegedly inferior culture.

Now, it is conceivable that someone could be so chauvinistic that they might even claim to be ignorant of all cultures and yet still retain their claim to cultural superiority on the grounds that their culture is the standard by which all others are measured. Such a position is fraught with difficulties, but it can be imagined. However, ethnocentrists usually claim to know something of other cultures.

An example is the dominating influence of the Dutch Reformed Church in South Africa, which for decades insisted that apartheid was justified by their belief in the validity, and their interpretation, of their Bible.[13] This church has since renounced its previous position, but nonetheless, its legitimisation of apartheid depended on knowing something about the indigenous people. They compared what they understood to be the characteristics of the majority black cultures with the teachings of their religion which, in turn, justified their position as superior and denounced the black population as inferior. It helped them to justify and defend apartheid.

Another example is the enforced removal of Aboriginal children from their parents in Australia. This policy involved removing children from their parents and taking them to homes or institutions which were operated almost exclusively by white people. The reason for the policy was a belief about the inferior child-rearing practices of indigenous people, and the racist and ethnocentric view that Aboriginal children would be better off in white custodianship than with their parents.

Whatever the rhetoric, the official and stated reasons for this policy were based on information about Aboriginal people. Many, if not most Australians would now agree that the information was inaccurate and the policy anathema. Nonetheless, certain knowledge claims were made; claims about understanding were presupposed. In a nutshell, powerful white people and their

---

13. It should be acknowledged that there were elements of resistance in the South African Christian churches. Desmond Tutu was one very active figure.

supporters believed they knew something about, and understood, Aboriginal culture.

It is hard to determine which came first, the ethnocentrism and the white culture of superiority (more accurately, the ideology of supremacy), or the information on which it was claimed to be based. Ultimately, in the hands of the dominant groups, ethnocentrism and claims to knowledge were mutually reinforcing. But the powerful who implemented the policy claimed to under-stand, a claim which was seriously flawed. They may have known something, but clearly they did not understand.

It is now time to recollect some important issues from the above discussion. You will recall that the discussion of ethnocentrism was the first response to a series of questions about the influence of our own background on the determination of our views. The position was that, inevitably, our understanding of another culture is filtered by our own experiences and background. I also asked if cultural filters prevent us from developing an accurate view, and if it is possible for the filter to be so strongly coloured that it is impossible to see and under-stand anything clearly through it.

So, what is the response to cross-cultural under-standing from those who uphold the ethnocentric position? Firstly, they seem to act as if the cultural filter does not exist. They believe their knowledge claims about other cultures are correct. What they see and hear about other cultures confirms their view, and they do not factor in the possibility that their experience and knowledge, and therefore, their understanding are influenced by their own cultural background. Moreover, they are often sufficiently powerful to position themselves in the centre.

Secondly, their perspectives are held stridently. That is, in addition to ignoring the possibility that their conclusions are influenced by their own cultural background and that their perspectives could be biased, their views are held with a certainty which verges on dogmatism. Ethnocentric positions are almost, by definition, as narrow as they are excluding.

In other words, again almost by definition, ethnocentric groups are intolerant. In fact, their very position depends on their being intolerant. They decide much earlier than other more tolerant groups that certain behaviours, cultural practices or beliefs cross the threshold of what they regard as acceptable. Such unacceptable behaviour, practices and beliefs are advertised as abhorrent, along with the associated cultural group. The cultural group is undermined to varying degrees and by methods which range from disparagement of its integrity to overt hostility and aggression. This intolerance may enter the political arena or be acted out in non-political, extra-legal and violent means.

Thirdly, the stridency of ethnocentrists is the result of them believing that some of their values are jeopardised by the culture at which their ethnocentrism is directed. Values are things which are treasured or cherished. This explains their intolerance, their entrance into the political foray and the violence that may result.

At this point some readers may be wondering if I am being fair here. After all, I am arguing that the ethnocentric person pretends that cultural filters do not exist and that they regard their conclusions as absolutely correct. Surely, some might aver, that is a reasonable response? I disagree, but you might respond by pointing the finger at me. The retort might be as follows: if it is impossible to observe and communicate with members of another culture without being influenced in some way, shape or form by our native culture, then surely seeing other cultures from within the framework of my own is unavoidable? In so far as our own culture influences our perceptions, they become the centre from which we operate. If they become the centre, how does this differ from ethnocentrism? So the argument is not so much that

I am wrong about ethnocentrism, but that inevitably I am ethnocentric too.

In this sense, ethnocentrism may be inevitable, even if there are other versions of it which are not as malignant and sinister as the one described above (call it E_1). The critical issue is our response. Do we recognise our ethnocentrism? If it is, what is our reaction? My response to this argument is that it makes good sense to differentiate between two versions of ethnocentrism. One version (call it E_1) fantasises that our native cultural filters have little or no influence on our perception, that it is possible to understand other cultures. The other version (call it E_2) argues that some form of ethnocentrism is inevitable, but it does not necessarily lead to us becoming members of the Ku Klux Klan. In fact, the E_2 form of ethnocentrism may advance liberal or tolerant values. In E_2, cultural filters mean that we see and judge the world as if our own values were at the centre with all others on the margins, but the intention is not to trigger bigotry or intolerance.

Nonetheless, there looms a seemingly insurmountable obstacle to cross-cultural understanding. We might denounce E_1, but if we are inevitably saddled with E_2, how will it ever be possible to communicate effectively with and understand another culture? The next response to the dilemma of cultural influence being an obstacle to cross-cultural understanding is largely a response to this issue.

Cultural relativism

This second response to the difficulties associated with cultural filtering accepts that it is largely impossible to understand another culture except via our cultural filters. The problem is that we are usually a product of our own culture and our cultural filters effectively restrict our understanding. We can only see from our cultural viewpoint, which so skews the image that it effectively prevents us attaining an accurate insight. Importantly, this does not only apply to our own culture. According to this response, all members of all cultures are in the same position. We are locked into our own cultural frameworks which we have internalised to such an extent that we are all incapable of understanding each other's cultures - or that's the position.

This position is sometimes known as relativism.[14] There are several forms of relativism. One form is a description of the diversity or plurality of human cultures. Sometimes this is called sociological relativism. However, I call it descriptive relativism because it describes the myriad of cultures. There is also another popular form of relativism from which are derived certain attitudes and beliefs which encourage tolerance and cross-cultural understanding. This will be addressed in Chapter 5. For now though, I will consider relativism as a response to the pervasive influence of our cultural background. To facilitate this, I use another metaphor, namely, a frame within which we work (a framework).

The form of relativism described here asserts that cultural influences are like a frame within which our cultural concepts have developed, and that from this frame we see the world. For example, imagine an empty picture or window frame within which our cultural values are framed. The frame includes our norms of behaviour, laws, the expectations we have of each other, the things we take for granted about our religious and legal traditions, and the institutions of education, government and family. If we perceived everything through this frame then, as axiomatic as it sounds, we see with and through one frame of reference and members of another

---

14. While I did not rely on the following, readers may find some of the chapters in Paul K Moser and Thomas L Carson, *Moral Relativism: A Reader* (New York: Oxford University Press, 2001) relevant and helpful.

culture see through another. This position could be called *cultural relativism*. Unlike ethnocentrism (E_1) which ignores the cultural framework (or filters), cultural relativism takes them very seriously indeed.

The difference between descriptive relativism, which points to the sheer diversity of cultural forms and practices, and cultural relativism is that the latter does more than describe. Cultural relativism claims that we see the cultural and social world from the perspective of our cultural frame of reference and that, as there are different cultural frameworks, there are different perspectives. Some cultural relativists take this to an extreme, arguing that the cultural worlds seen from the various perspectives are altogether different. According to the extreme cultural relativist, if I have one frame of reference I am not going to understand another; likewise another culture will never understand mine. The problem is that the very building blocks or concepts of different cultures are at such variance that they cannot be compared with, or measured against, one another. In this sense the respective cultural frames of reference are incomparable, or incommensurable.

Although sometimes used as almost synonyms, it is helpful to distinguish between *cultural* relativism and *conceptual* relativism.[15] Both refer to the existence of frameworks or frames of reference which are incommensurable, with no external reference point to assist in discovering anything common between them. However, whereas cultural relativism refers to the frameworks which arise from cultural divergence, such as the plurality of values or norms, conceptual relativism refers to the more elementary but essential building blocks usually associated with meaning. These include the names for things (for example, mat or cat, or what constitutes a

---

15. Roger Trigg, *Reason and Commitment* (Cambridge: Cambridge University Press, 1973), 14–26.

cause or an explanation). In one sense, conceptual relativism refers to more fundamental things than values and laws; in fact without such concepts, discussing values and laws would be meaningless and difficult, if not impossible. For example, without names it would be impossible to say what a value was and how it was different from a law or norm.

Thus, conceptual relativism refers to the plurality of fundamental building blocks through which we perceive and think about things, while cultural relativism refers to the conventions of particular cultures, such as beliefs, expectations, practices and values, by which the social worlds are conceived and explained. These conventions are internally coherent in the sense that they are justified by their own criteria.[16] So, one culture's norms and laws may be explained and defended from the culture's overall value position. Likewise, another culture with different, perhaps even inimical norms, will justify their laws from their very different value positions. The conceptual relativist agrees about the incomparability and incommensurability of different frames of reference, but usually in relation to the meaning of concepts and words.

So far I have emphasised the differences between cultural and conceptual relativism. Nonetheless, they are related by the fact that they outline the same issues for cultures and concepts and their implications are similar: different concepts and cultures have frameworks from which the world is seen differently.

One very intriguing question which arises from the discussion of relativism concerns the nature of the social world seen by the respective adherents of a frame of reference. If the framework determines the view, do they

16. Roger Trigg, *Understanding Social Science: A Philosophical Introduction to the Social Sciences*, second edition (Oxford: Basil Blackwell, 2001), 76–7.

live in the same world but see it differently, or do they live in different worlds? Do they live in the same reality which they see differently, or do they live in different realities? Is there one reality seen variously or are there multiple cultural realities?

If there is more than one conceptual and cultural world, and these are incomparable and incommensurable, the implications for cross-cultural understanding are serious. For example, if as a result of living in different cultures we effectively live in different worlds, how is it possible to communicate with another culture? An answer: it would seem impossible because there is no external world to which both cultures could point; there simply are no common cultural values (cultural relativism) and there are no common concepts to which both could refer and which could be translated from one cultural language into another (conceptual relativism). There is no external reference point; there is no independent reality which transcends the concepts, values and norms of the respective cultures which would seem necessary for cross-cultural communication. A common reality independent of the conceptual and cultural frameworks is the very thing that is denied by conceptual and cultural relativism which, in turn, has significant adverse implications for the possibility of cross-cultural communication.

Cross-cultural communication, which is a prerequisite for understanding, presupposes a common reference point from which an appeal for meaning can be made. Consider what in English is called a cat. Assume that in other languages, L_1 and L_2, (in cultures C_1 and C_2) there is a word for cat but they are, not surprisingly, different words (tac and gom, respectively). In order to identify and communicate about cats, two people from different cultural backgrounds may point to a cat and say their respective words. As they do, they will surmise that they have heard the word for cat in the other language. The

English speaker will say 'cat' and hear 'tac' or 'gom' as the non-English speakers say their words and hear 'cat'. They will be able to confirm that their meaning is correct when they repeat the experience. The word for cat may be different in L_1 and L_2, but, because there is something to which they can point, the members of C_1 and C_2 and the English speaker will be able to understand one another.

Whatever word is used in the respective cultures, the three words for a small, four-legged furry animal with slit eyes which purrs and hisses, mean the same thing. Whatever the language, the meaning of the word cat refers to something that is a real part of common experience. In this sense, the cat they perceive is not limited by their conceptual framework; it goes beyond, or transcends, cultural and language differences. This is what usually happens in translation; translators provide a short-cut because they know the word for cat in both L_1 and L_2. Nonetheless, there is something to which they can refer which is common to the worlds they share—a cat. This is precisely what extreme cultural and conceptual relativists would seem to deny (because they are locked into their cultural frameworks).

There are several points to be made about relativism, both cultural and conceptual. The first point underscores the difference between the ethnocentrist and the cultural relativist. Unlike the ethnocentrist, the extreme cultural relativist takes the cultural filter so seriously that it becomes an effective barrier to any understanding. Unlike ethnocentrists, who are confident about their understanding of another culture, cultural relativists claim that their respective world views are totally different and incomparable (at least to varying degrees), that the different cultures are locked into their frames of reference and that it is impossible to understand or communicate with another culture. Where the ethnocentrist is confident, if not cocksure, about matters of fact regarding other cultures, the relativist maintains that such certainty is impossible. The cultural relativists, eschewing any claim to understanding, are resigned to understanding only within the confines of their own culture and concepts, as are members of all other cultures. There is really only one cultural world: our own.

A second point concerns an alleged implication of relativism. Whereas ethnocentrists insist that they are correct in their understanding of another culture to the extent of being dogmatic and intolerant, cultural relativism is often used to support less dogmatic and more tolerant attitudes to other cultures. In other words, certain political implications follow on from relativism. This position is sometimes stated in the following form (although often not as blatantly for reasons that will be suggested later): it is precisely because there are different incommensurable worlds and world views that we cannot say that one culture's world view is better than another's, and therefore, we should be respectful of them all.

This is a very seductive argument which justifies and defends the political values of tolerance (by which I mean more than a begrudging acceptance) and perhaps certain policies, such as multiculturalism. Whether it is up to the task is another matter and one which I examine in Chapter 5. However, the point here is to highlight the link or connection between relativism and some political values which are deemed to follow. Accordingly, cultural relativism is sometimes used to lend support to the political values associated with respecting and appreciating other cultures, cultural diversity, and policies which are intended to guarantee the rights of cultural groups to retain and learn their languages, cultural values and cultural practices.

The third comment is that it is conceivable that some cultural relativists could adopt a seemingly modest position on the possibility or otherwise of being able to understand another culture. They concede that, as members of one culture, they are locked into their own cultural framework, and therefore, live in an entirely different world to the members of another with whom they cannot communicate, and therefore cannot understand in any sense of the word.

Again, this modesty seems commendable, but it would be inaccurate to conclude that such cultural relativists draw no conclusions at all. In fact, they seem to make two claims: (1) it is impossible to understand another culture, and therefore it is impossible to communicate with members of it because we live in different conceptual and value worlds, and (2) we do know there are other cultures and we have concluded that they are different from our culture. It might sound as if this is a very modest claim, but the question which immediately comes to mind is: if they are totally locked into their own world, how do they know that other cultures even exist and are different? How can they recognise them at all if they have tunnel vision as a result of being locked into their own conceptual and cultural world? If the cultural relativists can see a difference, does this mean that they can see beyond their own cultural world?

Further, if they can see beyond their own cultural world and locate cultures different from their own, does this mean there is something they share, or something to which they can appeal, which highlights the concept of difference, what it means to be different? If there is a comparison it would seem to presuppose a standard or criterion by which to compare two cultures in order to recognise their differences. So the third point can be summarised in the following question: what is the standard or criterion by which cultural relativists can understand that there are cultures different from their own?

This, of course, is precisely what the extreme conceptual and cultural relativist denies, namely, the existence of criteria by which we can compare, translate, understand and communicate with other cultures. An illustration may clarify the argument here. Imagine that members of a culture, C_1, come across a member of another culture, C_2. Imagine also that members of C_1 come to realise that members of C_2 believe that the sea is a happy eternal place to which the soul passes on death, whereas members of C_1 believe the sea is the home of demons and would be a diabolical place in which to die and spend the afterlife.

Leave aside for the sake of the argument the fact that to come to this understanding necessitated C_1 to transcend their cultural prison to become aware of other perspectives, and that they were willing to communicate with members of C_2 which, of course presupposes a willingness to listen and learn and to take on the translation required. If we retrace the steps of C_1's acquired understanding (that is, we come to realise C_2's beliefs about an afterlife) we note that C_1 was able to communicate sufficiently to realise that they were different, yet shared certain concepts. They shared the tangible concept of sea and death and more abstract ideas such as an afterlife, the abode of the dead. They even shared the idea of a belief in the sense that members of both C_1 and C_2 assented to the idea that there was a place to which the dead pass. They not only believed in such a place but they shared the concept of belief. The net result is that members of C_1 and C_2 were able to include in their world certain concepts, ideas and values which would have been excluded by cultural and conceptual relativism. C_1 and C_2 were not totally locked into their frameworks; they could transcend their own world and engage with another culture.

The point of this example is to demonstrate that cultural relativism may not be as modest as it claims. There may seem to be humility in the cultural relativist's approach; after all, they are not making bigoted, dogmatic, peremptory claims like the ethnocentrist. They simply claim they cannot know or understand. Accordingly, they do not arrogate to themselves an understanding of another culture because they believe that we are locked into our own cultural framework which makes understanding impossible. But this ability to describe is at the heart of the point being made here. If they can identify another culture as being different from their own, then they would not seem to be locked into their own culture —at least to some extent. Furthermore, despite their claims to the contrary, the other culture and its concepts seem to be accessible from their cultural world.

The cultural relativist might respond by attempting to suspend their own cultural filters and understanding the culture on its own terms, to take the other's understanding as their own. On the face of it, this seems a very accepting thing to do. After all, in so doing, their own cultural beliefs, concepts, practices and values are put to one side. They suspend their own view of another culture and express cultural traditions and understandings as the other culture does. I do not want to completely rule out the possibility of hearing and understanding another culture on its own terms (discussed in Chapter 8 and 9). However, the very project remains in tension with what the conceptual and cultural relativist proposes. If it is possible to understand another culture on its own terms or, more accurately, use the culture's own expressions, then cultural filters do not entirely act as a block.

Moreover, a further implication of this response is that a partial perspective from our cultural vantage point is impossible, but complete acceptance of another's world from their perspective, on their terms, is possible. How and why the cultural filters act when initiated from our perspective, yet are inactive when viewed from the other perspective, is difficult to fathom. In any case, such a move contradicts the very relativism which they espouse (because it shows that it is possible to escape our cultural frameworks). It is to an examination of this option that the discussion now turns.

Cultural pluralism

Another response to the influence of cultural background is to acknowledge cultural influences but to recognise that there are differences in the degrees to which this argument is taken. This position I will call *cultural pluralism* because its proponents claim that (1) cross-cultural understanding is possible and (2) it should be encouraged as a political virtue and a goal in any civilised society. This alternative accepts some of the points made in the preceding examination of cultural relativism. Advocates of cultural pluralism are under no illusion about how difficult it is to understand and communicate across cultures. Nonetheless, they would claim that, as difficult as it is, there are real things to which it is possible to point and to which it is possible to attribute names because they share some common attributes, qualities and traits. Once members of C_1 and C_2 agree that it is the same thing to which they are referring, they can learn the different names for it. In this way, it is possible to engage with other cultures to enhance cross-cultural under-standing.

The cultural pluralist claims that translation is possible because we do not live in entirely different worlds of concept and culture. We live in the same world although we experience it differently because of geographical and cultural differences. Hence, we see it through the concep-tual and cultural lenses which we use. Unlike the extreme cultural relativist, this alternative suggests that it is one thing to say that C_1 and C_2 have a different angle or pers-pective on the world, and quite another to say they live in entirely different, incommensurable and incomparable worlds.

There are several points worth making about the cultural pluralist's position. The first concerns an implication about how we should treat those who are different. It will be recalled that the cultural relativist argues that it is precisely because there are so many cultures and resultant worlds and world views that we should be tolerant. In other words, the political value of tolerance is derived or deduced from cultural relativism. The cultural pluralist agrees with the cultural relativist that tolerance is an important political value. For the cultural pluralist, the appreciation of diversity and the political freedom of other cultures to hold and uphold their traditions is an important political virtue.

But what is significant is that the cultural pluralist defends or justifies tolerance on different grounds. For the cultural pluralist, tolerance does not necessary follow as a political value merely because there are so many competing cultural values (which is what the cultural relativist argues). For cultural pluralists, tolerance is to be advocated, defended and justified on the basis of values such as respect, an appreciation of diversity and the rights of others, which are essential if cultures are to exist co-operatively and peacefully.

Thus, like the cultural relativist, the cultural pluralist insists that there is an enormous difference between the anti-Semitic organisation on the one hand, and on the other, the organisation which assists migrants, or the groups which give haven and assistance to political refugees. Cultural pluralists agree that their cultural background influences their understanding of the people they are assisting. But they would also claim that their cultural background does not override core values which motivate and are consistent with their actions. In fact, they would argue that their cultural values include the values on which their tolerance and political resistance to repression is based.

The cultural pluralist claims that the values which oppose repression and oppression, which fight for justice, which resist all forms of sinister, bigoted, racist ethnocentrism (E_1), which are open and tolerant, which encourage and appreciate diversity of cultural expression, and which encourage difference, can be defended on the grounds that some values are preferable to others. Now, it is true that the cultural relativist may also advocate similar political values, but the point I am emphasising here is the difference between cultural relativism and pluralism on the important point of the origin or defence of their similar political values.

The cultural relativist insists that it is impossible to arbitrate between values and so, precisely because there are so many cultures and cultural values, we should appreciate them all. As it is impossible to say that any one cultural value is superior, they therefore conclude that we ought to be tolerant. Again, the cultural pluralist agrees that tolerance is an important political value but does not derive it from relativism and the diversity of cultures. Against the value relativism of the cultural relativist, they claim that some values are more important than others, that there is a hierarchy of values which can be defended and which defends tolerance over intolerance, freedom over oppression, and equality over inequality.

You may now have a sense a déjà vu, or worse, of going round in circles. Perhaps you may be thinking that some of the above paragraph, particularly the appeal on moral grounds for tolerance, sounds very similar to the ethnocentric position. Those who hold this position believed that their values were correct; they arrogated to themselves the right to assert that their values were superior. They still do in many parts of the world. In a sense, there is one similarity between ethnocentrism and cultural pluralism. Both positions oppose value relativism, the view that it is impossible to arbitrate between competing values.

However, this should not blur the enormous difference between ethnocentrism and cultural pluralism. They have fundamentally different views about the appreciation of diversity, the celebration of difference, freedom, respect, rights and tolerance. While it may seem to be stating the obvious, the significance of this point should be emphasised: people who are ethnocentric and cultural pluralists are *not* value relativists but there the difference ends. They may both oppose value relativism but they are poles apart when it comes to tolerance. The ethnocentrists are intolerant; the cultural pluralist advocates tolerance of the difference and diversity the ethnocentric loathes.

An interesting comparison between the cultural relativist and pluralist can also be made. When discussing cultural relativism I made the point that it seemed to be very modest in its claims. Extreme cultural relativists claim that it is impossible to enter another cultural world. They argue that because there are different cultures there are different worlds which we cannot understand, but of which we should be open and tolerant. For many that seems to be a simple statement of fact. However, we noted that any suggestion of modesty is not necessarily benign if one uses such arguments to propagate the misguided or the inaccurate.

Superficially, it would also seem that cultural pluralism is far from modest. After all, it maintains that cross-cultural understanding *is* possible—and defensible —despite our different perceptions of the world. There is only one world which, by difference of geography and culture, is seen and experienced differently by different people. There is something to which all cultures refer despite their differences. It is this that, according to the cultural pluralist, renders cross-cultural communication possible. The obvious point to be made is that this need not be an immodest, sinister or repressive view of the world; it may not be such a grand claim. Further, if the arguments advanced are more convincing than those of cultural relativism, then we have the potential for cross-cultural understanding (rendered difficult, if not impossible, by the extreme cultural relativist). Moreover, cultural pluralism offers us the chance to justify the values which cultural relativism shares with the cultural pluralist, but which the former is constitutionally incapable of rationally defending (because values cannot be defended other than from within a cultural framework). This issue is an important theme of this book, albeit with some rather long, but hopefully pertinent, digressions (to be discussed in Chapters 5 and 8).

Concluding comments

The issues raised in this chapter are important in themselves, but they are particularly significant if we are keen to understand other cultures. We have discussed a plethora of issues. Superficially, it seems a simple task to understand other cultures. However, the questions about it, and the preconditions for it, suggest that it is much more complex than is sometimes thought. In fact, a probing question I did not ask in the first section of the chapter, but consistent with the task of this book, concerns the social function of the seemingly socially popular, taken-for-granted simplicity of cross-cultural understanding. In a world where cultures cross each other's paths continually, why is there a view that understanding other cultures is so easy, particularly when a little reflection reveals how complex it is? What social function is served by the view that it is relatively uncomplicated, that we can just do it?

Some readers may disagree that the taken-for-granted nature of cross-cultural understanding is powerful and popular but, even if by default, it seems to be the presumption. In other words, the powerful and popular view is that cross-cultural understanding is relatively straightforward. Not only can individuals and groups understand other cultures in ordinary interactions, but it is appropriate to draw conclusions, make judgments and evince what are in effect policy decisions about what should be done.

What funding should be made available for indigenous health and housing services, whether other cultures should be accorded so-called equal or preferential rights, which cultures are regarded as suitable sources of migrants for our country and what expectations we have of them when they arrive, are to a large extent influenced by how we understand them. Yet, if the above analysis is sound, there is little emphasis or attention paid to how we come to that understanding, and the influence of our own cultural filters. So a good question is: What is the social function of this perspective? What social function is served by ignoring the issues discussed in this chapter?

One answer is that it defends and legitimates current policy and practice. If understanding is taken for granted, then the acritical approach does not even explore or challenge the dominant and powerful ideas. If understanding is assumed, current ideas about what it means to understand, how we can best do it, remain unchallenged. Yet to accept the taken for granted is to accept the given; to accept the given is to think and behave in ways that further entrench the very conditions which determine existing social arrangements and power imbalances. The pursuit of cross-cultural understanding can no more ignore such factors than the more theoretical issues discussed in this chapter.

Another issue arising from adopting the taken-for-granted meaning of understanding is the question of whether this is a form of ethnocentrism, of perceiving and judging the world from the presumed vantage of our own culture. In other words, is our notion of what is meant and involved by cross-cultural understanding—exacerbated by taking it for granted—an example of perceiving and judging the world from our cultural values and standards? Is the attempt, is the claim, to understand indigenous people, an example of ethnocentrism, even if we regard ourselves as cultural relativists or cultural pluralists? Is the way we understand other cultures an indicator of our ethnocentrism (E_2) even if we advocate tolerance, affirmative action and other policies which attempt to redress existing imbalances of power and wealth?

You may be surprised at this response. Surely, it could be argued, cultural relativism is most unlike ethnocentrism (E_1). However, if there is only one cultural world we can know and understand, then one conclusion is that our culture is not only the centre but it is the only one. The retort may be that something must be added to this claim, namely, it is the only one we can know! But being locked into our own cultural worlds is tantamount to acknowledging only one culture: ours.

Raising such issues is an example of reflexivity, of not exempting ourselves from the same questions we ask of others. Thus, diagnosing ethnocentrism in others also involves challenging ourselves. For example, it is essential that cultural relativists and pluralists expose as ethnocentric the excluding, chauvinistic and narrow-minded groups in a culture (E_1). It is important to identify the beliefs, the alignments and networks, and the power exerted by neo-Nazi and racist groups, including political parties.

However, the issue of reflexivity reminds us that on the international scene there are some countries which consider concern from outsiders over their human rights record and other abuses to be meddling in their affairs. In the Asia-Pacific area this criticism has been levelled at Australia by various governments, including those of

Indonesia and Malaysia.[17] They argue that they have different values and ways of dealing with breaches of their laws. In the West we often find these to be particularly harsh and undemocratic, and abuses of human rights. However, this prompts the question: are both sides being ethnocentric? Are both sides judging the others as if their own ethos and culture were the only ones? Maybe the cultural relativist is correct. Perhaps we are locked into our own cultural worlds. Yet, as I've already noted, to appeal to a descriptive reality, which applies across cultures and by which they are discerned as different, is contrary to what the cultural relativist espouses, at least in its extreme version.

This raises a further point about the possibility that cultural relativism is ethnocentric in another sense, namely that the very knowledge claim that we are locked into our culture is a western idea. It would seem that various forms of relativism are found in very early literature which influenced the origins of western thought. Moreover, relativism has been a rampant twentieth-century view in the West. It is, hence, a possibility that cultural relativism is a form of ethnocentrism (E_2) about even our most basic claims about knowledge, about whether it is possible to understand another culture. In reality, though, even the cultural relativist defends such values as tolerance and cross-cultural understanding. A critical issue is why, particularly when they argue that it is impossible to arbitrate between conflicting values. Why does the cultural relativist advocate tolerance and cross-cultural understanding?

---

17. See, for example, Anthony J Langlois, *The Politics of Justice and Human Rights: Southeast Asia and Universalist Theory* (Cambridge: Cambridge University Press, 2001).

Perhaps one more point about cultural relativism is in order. It should be obvious that I regard cultural relativism as defined to be unsustainable. The conclusions drawn from the influence of cultural filters are unnecessary, and ultimately rebound to undermine the integrity of the position. However, this does not mean that I either ignore or underestimate the issue of the extent to which our cultural background influences our ability to understand other cultures. They do influence our understanding but not only in the way cultural relativists insist. The critical issue is how we deal with or manage them. Further it is possible to agree with the cultural relativist's conclusions about the virtue of acceptance, the celebration of diversity and tolerance, and yet note that such values presuppose the very reality that cultural relativism denies, namely, the existence of 'the other', 'those who are different', and values which we can defend. If we are locked into our cultural worlds this recognition is impossible; if the cultural relativist is correct we cannot defend the very values—indeed any values—required for the appreciation of diversity and tolerance.

2

Should we 'be understanding' when approaching cross-cultural understanding and how can we defend such a stand?

Introduction

In the previous chapter I began by exploring the meaning of cross-cultural understanding. After examining several impediments to understanding, I outlined three responses to a frequently experienced obstacle, namely the cultural filter. In this chapter I begin with a similar issue, namely, the meaning of understanding, but understanding in a very different sense. In the previous chapter I used understanding cognitively, that is, to express the idea that understanding presupposes the exchange of information. This use of the word denoted head knowledge, or reports that triggered the brain into action. In this chapter, I explore the meaning of understanding in an affective sense, in the sense of being understanding, as we might say in everyday English.

The affective side of our personalities—our emotional and feeling side—is discounted in our society. This is in part a result of the privileging of male over female gender stereotypes and a particular view of knowledge due to the powerful influence of science.[1] Nevertheless, this more-than-cognitive aspect comes to the fore when we ask:

---

1. The nature and implications of science for cross-cultural understanding are examined in Chapter 3.

What does it mean to be understanding? That is, what does it mean to claim that we are sympathetic or empathic towards other people whom we see as different, and who might want to be seen as different, at least in some respect?

It is an important question because how we feel about other cultures and their people makes all the difference to cross-cultural understanding. If we feel that their culture is inferior and ours superior, then this may (and probably will) compromise our attempt at cross-cultural understanding. Such feelings and thoughts are pre-judgments and affect our final judgment; they are prejudices that distort our attempts at cross-cultural understanding. We might also concede that they will influence the way we learn about other cultures.

Thus, the value we assign to other cultures influences how we learn about them. This is not only because how we value other cultures will influence how we interpret what we see and hear, and how much effort we will put into understanding them, but also because it will influence how we weigh up knowledge, whose perspective we would adopt in a dispute between another culture and the dominant culture, whose stories we will believe, what evidence we will regard as admissible and inadmissible, and so on.

Even here, whether we use words that indicate a predisposition can be telling. For example, most people would claim to be tolerant, just as very few people would admit to being racist. But what do we mean by tolerance?[2] Do we mean that we 'will put up with them'? If this niggardly, parsimonious and stingy view of tolerance is adopted, can we claim to be understanding? Is a self-congratulatory, begrudging tolerance simply a guise for an extremely censorious approach masquerading as acceptance and understanding? Even when

---

2.   Tolerance is the topic of Chapter 6.

we make seemingly neutral or benign prejudgments, our understandings, and whether we are being understanding, influence our exploration of other cultures. For example, we might say that the voice of a culture is inaudible; we don't often hear from them. But central to our judgment is the way we explain their silence. Is our judgment that they are silent, or is it that they have been silenced? It makes all the difference!

I concede that this is not necessarily a one-way street, that it is not only our feelings towards another culture that may influence our information gathering and our overall attitude. Our understanding, as in our knowledge about another culture, may influence our feelings and emotions; what we discover intellectually about another culture may be more or less conducive to being understanding. However, the general point I am making here is that it is inevitable that we come to our encounter with other cultures with (pre)existing knowledge, sympathies and values. Thus, cultural pluralists will approach the gaining of information about other cultures differently from those who are inclined toward ethnocentrism. The very origins of our engagement with another culture are not as neutral as we may purport—if they are neutral at all. The question then is: how can I identify and deal with my prior attitudes to other cultures before I begin my fact-finding?

Put differently, when finding out about other cultures, neutrality is out of the question because one has already taken a stance.[3] The stance might be tacit, or perhaps unrecognised or smuggled in, but a prior stance there is and it is inevitable. The stance may involve varying degrees of valuing. Some may value the presence of other cultures as

3.   In this I agree with the cultural relativist about the influence of our culture. But my analysis differs and I do not draw the same conclusions.

something to celebrate and value; some may take opposing views. We will now examine this cluster of issues more systematically, starting with what it means 'to be understanding' (as distinct from 'to understand').

The meaning of understanding

So far the meaning of understanding has been largely assumed. Understanding as used in Chapter 1 was about gathering information. So, to the question, 'what does it mean to understand another person or culture?' we might answer that we need to know something about the other culture, about their institutions, language, folklore, stories, and so on. So to understand can mean that I know something about the other culture because I learnt about it at school or university, or experienced it first-hand when I travelled, or because I have read about it. In some senses, this is a minimalist view of understanding. I will use the designation U_1 to refer to this kind of understanding that emphasises head knowledge and fact finding.

There is another sense in which understand is used in everyday English. The phrase, 'do I understand?' can mean 'am I understanding?' or 'do I sympathise with?' In the sense of the word used here, understanding refers to a number of related (and presupposed) attitudes and actions including an inclination towards, and an acceptance and tolerance of (say) another culture.

As used here, for example, this to 'be understanding' does not refer to a begrudging acceptance or a perfunctory toleration as in 'I tolerate them'. To be committed to tolerance, to understand in the sense of being understanding, means that 'I respect cultural difference even though I may not or don't know all about another's culture or values'. It means that 'I enjoy the differences they bring'. It means that 'whatever I think of another culture, except for some major violations of human rights, they have the right to practise their culture as I do mine, and just as biodiversity is crucial so is cultural diversity'.

A play on the word identify can be used to clarify the meaning of understanding in this second sense, which hereafter I will designate as U_2. If we say, 'I want to identify the hallmarks of a particular culture' we are referring to U_1. If we say, 'I want to identify *with* the people from that culture or nation', or 'when I approach cross-cultural understanding I want to come as one who identifies with the people from that culture', then I am referring to U_2.

It is the argument in this chapter that the sympathy involved in being understanding (U_2) is an essential prerequisite of, and is integral to, any full and serious approach to cross-cultural understanding. In this sense 'to understand' (U_1) necessitates 'to be understanding'; U_2 is a precondition of U_1.

An implication of U_1 and U_2

It is important to tease out an implication of the two meanings of understanding. The first meaning (U_1) is concerned with my factual knowledge of a culture or members of it; the other meaning (U_2) is of my allegiances and sympathies that, in turn, are based on certain values. The first meaning (U_1) can be thrown into sharp relief by the questions: 'on what knowledge does my claim to understanding depend?', 'does my claim to understand depend on my knowledge, the accumulation of cognitive information which is processed in my brain?' and 'if I didn't know anything about a culture could I claim to understand it?'

Of course, understanding depends on knowing something about the culture. How can I say I understand if I don't know anything? And in the sense that understanding is based on knowledge then it seems obvious that knowing is an important ingredient of understanding in this first sense (U_1). If I say that we understand that cultures in polar environments have many words for what in a warmer climate is simply called snow, we are making a claim to understand on the basis of some knowledge. If we say that the indigenous people of Australia who live in the desert can find water where I cannot see it, then that is understanding based on knowledge I have gleaned.

But what about understanding in the other sense outlined above (U_2). What about understanding as 'being understanding', or respecting or even appreciating or celebrating the diversity of other cultures? In this sense, understanding does not depend on what I know because I may know nothing or very little about other cultures. For example, imagine a person of culture C comes to Australia to live. Suppose we know nothing about this person's culture. We don't know anything about their language, their beliefs, their food or values. For many Australians, this ignorance would have very little to do with their view about the migrant's right to live in Australia, or express their culture when they are here, or to become active and equal participants in social and political life. Yet our determination to understand still represents and involves our sympathies, our commitments, our allegiances. In fact, it would seem to be a precondition of U_1. For if we approach U_1 with antagonism to the culture, or a lack of sympathy (U_2), how will we ever really understand them?[4]

---

4.   A related point was made by Charles Taylor, 'The Politics of Recognition', in *Multiculturalism: Examining the Politics of Recognition*, edited by Amy Gutman (Princeton, New Jersey: Princeton University Press, 1994), 66–7, and Charles Taylor, *Varieties of Religion Today: William James Revisited* (Cambridge, Mass: Harvard University Press, 2002), 50.

A comparison of ethnocentrism and cultural pluralism

At this point it may be helpful to compare the positions of ethnocentrists and cultural pluralists. Ethnocentrists claim to have an understanding (U_1) of another culture that they believe is inferior to theirs. They would claim that they know things about the cultural beliefs and practices that give them grounds for their conclusion. The cultural pluralist, on the other hand, may or may not know the same things as the ethnocentrist, but irrespective, is committed to respecting the other culture. The reason for this is that the cultural pluralist acknowledges that cross-cultural understanding involves U_1 and U_2. Thus, unlike ethnocentrism, cultural pluralism is committed to approaching cross-cultural understanding with acceptance, tolerance and the appreciation of diversity (U_2), some of which may be invoked before any understanding (U_1) is gained.

Cultural pluralists do not depend entirely on information about other cultures, but on a prior commitment to, or decisions about, an ethical or moral stance, namely that the diversity of cultures is a cause for celebration, that cultural diversity is enriching, that cultures deserve to be respected and cherished in the same way I would like my own culture to be respected and treasured. That is, to cultural pluralists, the appreciation of cultures—being understanding—is of great, if not the greatest importance. Among the many differences between the ethnocentrist, and the cultural relativist and pluralist are radically opposed value positions that affect how they regard and approach other cultures.

However, this poses a problem, because making decisions on values and ethics is always regarded as difficult in western culture. The rhetoric is that making decisions about values is up to the individual. There is a pervasive view that it is impossible to arbitrate between value positions. So, you have your values and I have mine. If we disagree, we agree to differ. Apart from a value that is presupposed in such a view—I want to respect your values even if I disagree with them—there is, nonetheless, a powerful and popular view that it is impossible to adjudicate between competing values. This position is called value relativism.[5] It says that it is impossible to justify the values associated with understanding as 'being understanding' (U_2).

This causes a dilemma, namely, how can we defend our value positions so as to show that cultural pluralism is preferable to ethnocentrism? How can we defend the position that acceptance, tolerance and respect for the rights of members of other cultures is preferable (I would say superior) to rejection, intolerance and disrespect? Despite what is at stake, in one sense there is a vacuum created by the popularity of value relativism. In Chapter 5 we will explore the implications of this vacuum, but for now the issue is the great difficulty, if not impossibility, of defending and justifying our value positions in western culture, including the values involved in approaching cross-cultural understanding.

In summary, we began our discussion of cross-cultural understanding in this chapter wishing to explore what it might mean to understand another culture. I argued that while knowledge of the culture was a prerequisite for one meaning of understanding (U_1), more than information was required if we were attempting to be understanding in the sense of appreciating diversity and valuing cultures in their own right (U_2), irrespective of what information we have about them (U_1). In fact, I argued that U_2 was a precondition of optimal U_1. Yet this valuing of other cultures introduced the idea that, in our society, it is difficult to justify and defend our values, because

---

5.   In Chapter 5 I call this 'epistemological value relativism' or 'e-value relativism'.

disputes about such matters seem unresolvable and, ultimately 'it's up to the individual'. Needless to say, if we want our society and its institutions to be understanding (U_2) and to adopt the values I've associated with it, then it requires more than being 'up to the individual'.

Several qualifications: on the relationship between knowing and being understanding

Before pursuing the theme of this chapter (U_2), it is worth emphasising several points on the relationship between the two meanings of understanding. Taking our stand in favour of understanding (U_2) does not mean that we cannot modify or change our position if we discover new information (U_1). If on the basis of better knowledge we discover that there are aspects of certain cultural practices that we deplore, if we discover that there are aspects that we find unconscionable and totally unacceptable, the additional information has assisted us to make our decision.

But here several points are noteworthy. Firstly, while this new information (U_1) has led us to deplore a particular cultural practice, we do not necessarily know that all members of the culture concerned hold the same position, or even if there is an expectation that they should. In other words, we do not know if the cultural practice that we find objectionable is a cultural norm. In any event, it may be that the cultural norms are shifting. If we were to assume that all members of a culture hold a particular view we may be essentialising or homogenising that culture, that is, denying or ignoring the brindled, motley and variegated character, the nuances and subtleties, which cultures possess.

Secondly, the new information (U_1) concerns one aspect of a cultural practice, but we may not know how significant it is. It might be that we are exaggerating its significance by taking it out of context. Further, as repugnant as it might be to us, we may reconsider our position if members of that culture explain to us the reasons for the practice. We may continue to repudiate it but try to overlook it, given the overall contribution the culture's members make to our society.

Thirdly, even if we are outraged, our reactions are not merely based on our additional information. In fact, by itself, the new information may be a rather small proportion of all we know about the culture concerned. However, when it is coupled with our own values, it takes on new dimensions. The reason for this is significant, for it would seem that our reaction is due to this new piece of information being considered in the light of our values. It is our values that are the criteria we use to judge the practice that we have only just discovered; it is our values that render certain factual information (U_1) significant. That is, our values are important not only in how we come to cross-cultural understanding (U_2) but in how we evaluate (in U_1).

To be understanding

We thus return to the point made previously, namely that understanding (U_2) is critically important to our attempt at cultural understanding; increasing our knowledge is not the only thing involved. Further, in both (U_1 and U_2) our values are central. To want to be understanding is a value. That is, we value understanding rather than being misunderstanding, and we want that understanding to be sympathetic rather than unsympathetic—even before we begin. This component, which defends the value of understanding and the values associated with being understanding (sympathy and tolerance), I will call U_3.

Yet a dead end we noted previously, reappears: if values are so important but it is impossible to say that one set of values is preferable to another, how can we justify any value conclusions we make? How can we defend the values that are involved in, central to, and justify being understanding (U_3)? If all values are equal—at least in the sense that it is impossible to say rationally that one is preferable to another—on what basis are we drawn to conclusions about the values we espouse? These would seem to be extremely important questions. It would seem to be important to be able to justify our value positions, to defend them and to attempt to persuade those who hold different views. However, as we have seen, value relativism would seem to render this difficult if not impossible.

We have come to a critical intersection in our discussion. It seems that value relativism disallows the defence of being understanding (U_2) which is a precondition of cross-cultural understanding. That is, value relativism prohibits us from defending the position that being understanding (U_2) is preferable to mis-understanding; value relativism prohibits the view that understanding is preferable to a patronising or condescending understanding (which is not what is intended by U_2). That is why defending understanding, and the value of being understanding (U_3), is so important.

Further, if value relativism is correct in its diagnosis of claims about knowledge, then the ethnocentrist, the cultural relativist and the cultural pluralist have no common point on which they agree and on which they could begin to engage. All views are ideological; they merely represent our background or culture or emotions or preferences but whatever their content and origins, there is absolutely no common ground. Value relativism results in all views being ideologies. If we cannot overcome this impasse somehow we will not only be bogged-down when it comes to cross-cultural understanding, but sinking in the quicksand over just about everything else!

Is it possible then to overcome this problem of values being ideological?

Helpful distinctions about ideology

The well-known sociologist, Karl Mannheim, provided an insightful analysis of the dilemma being discussed here. Mannheim defined ideology in a somewhat different way to that above which nevertheless does not detract from its relevance to this discussion. Unlike the above use of 'ideology', which insists that ideas, preferences and commitments are merely personal, and between which it is impossible to arbitrate, Mannheim used the term to describe the thinking of 'ruling groups' which becomes 'so intensively interest-bound to a situation that they are simply *no longer able to see certain facts* which would undermine their sense of domination'.[6] This distortion, however, is not restricted to the ruling groups. Utopian thinking occurs when 'certain oppressed groups are intellectually so strongly interested in the destruction and transformation of a given condition of society that they *unwittingly see only* those elements in the situation *which tend to negate it'*.[7]

For the moment the salient issue here is the similarity between ideological and utopian thinking. Although expressed differently and directed in opposite political directions, in both positions there is a distortion of sight. People who think ideologically are 'no longer able to see certain facts' and those who think in a utopian fashion

6. Karl Mannheim, 'Ideology and Utopia', in Karl Mannheim, *Ideology and Utopia: An Introduction to the Sociology of Knowledge* (London: Routledge and Kegan Paul, 1960 [1936]), 36 (emphasis added). Central to the following are Mannheim's distinctions. It is not necessary to concur with his entire sociology of knowledge project in order to find them helpful in this context.
7. Mannheim, 'Ideology and Utopia', 36 (emphasis added).

'unwittingly see only those elements in the situation which tend to negate it'.[8] Both are hoodwinked by their political positions; the ideologue cannot see the facts that undermine their domination, while the utopian can only see those things that negate it. That is, utopians cannot see the things that support the social; they can only see the forces of destruction and transformation, and not the counter forces that support the society.

However, Mannheim then distinguished between the particular and total conceptions of ideology, and it is here that his distinctions become particularly instructive for our purposes.[9] In the particular conception of ideology, adversaries are dubious about some of the ideas and positions advanced by those who uphold them. In the total conception of ideology antagonists are suspicious of the entire world view of their opponents. The names or labels are good indicators of Mannheim's intention: the particular conception of ideology judges that only a part of an opponent's world view is false and, therefore, ideological; the total conception charges that all of the opponent's world view is ideological. For example, some-one who reads this book might be sceptical about some aspects of the cultural relativist or the cultural pluralist position (the particular conception) yet suspicious of the entire world view of someone who espouses ethno-centrism (the total conception).

Another difference between the particular and total conceptions of ideology is in the agreed criteria for evaluating a position, the criteria for validity. In the particular conception, even if it is thought that an adversary is 'concealing or distorting a given factual situation, it is still nevertheless assumed that both parties

---

8.   Mannheim, 'Ideology and Utopia', 36.
9.   Mannheim, 'Ideology and Utopia', 36, 49–50.

share common criteria of validity'.[10] Put differently, in the particular conception, 'it is still assumed that it is possible to refute lies and eradicate sources of error by referring to *accepted criteria of objective validity common to both parties'*.[11] Unlike the total conception, in which agreement about criteria is not shared, in the particular position the protagonists share common criteria by which, at least theoretically, it will be possible to discuss their position and attempt to persuade their antagonists.

Mannheim also made another distinction within the total conception of ideology. The key point here is whether at least one of the protagonists regards their own view as exempt from ideological bias or not. In the special formulation (of the total conception of ideology) one of the protagonists believes that all their opponent's views are wracked by ideological distortion while their own are undistorted.[12] For example, some versions of ethnocentrism may claim that all the cultural pluralist's views of their opponents are ideologically distorted but their own position is not. In the general formulation (of the total conception) those who diagnose another position as ideological are also prepared to acknowledge the possibility that their perspective is skewed as well.[13] In this formulation those who claim their opponent's views are distorted recognise theirs may be too. For example, in the general formulation, cultural pluralists not only recognise the ideological bias in their opponent's position, but they would also acknowledge the possibility that their own position may be biased. In fact, this is what the extreme cultural relativist may also do; they may accuse their opponents of being locked into their own culture, but they are also prepared to say that of their own

---

10. Mannheim, 'Ideology and Utopia', 50 (emphasis added).
11. Mannheim, 'Ideology and Utopia', 50–1 (emphasis added).
12. Mannheim, 'Ideology and Utopia', 68–9.
13. *Ibid.*

position.[14] It is timely to consider Mannheim's distinctions and their implications in a little more detail.

Applying Mannheim's distinctions

In the following the political aspects of Mannheim's distinctions between ideology and utopia are not the main focus. However, Mannheim's other distinctions enable us to explore the issue of the ideological nature of being understanding (U_2), the value of defending sympathetic understanding (U_3) and our own cultural values from which we assess other cultures (hereafter V_1). If, as Mannheim claimed,[15] we live in times characterised by the general formulation of the total conception (when I call all my opponents views ideological and mine are not exempt from the same judgment) then all views are potentially ideological.

According to Mannheim's diagnosis, ideologies, including those required for cross-cultural understanding, are the distortions of partisans. We will call this use of ideology I_1. According to this view, U_2 (the sympathy with

---

14. This, of course, says nothing about the consistency of the cultural relativist's position per se. In fact, that they can even recognise another culture suggests that they are not entirely locked into their own cultural world view. Nonetheless, according to Mannheim they may subject themselves to the same judgment they make of their opponents which, of course, is what the general formulation of the total conception of ideology is addressing. A fuller discussion of this issue can be found later in this chapter.

15. At this point I am using Mannheim's distinctions because, in my view, they reflect a powerful view in the West. While it is the case that Mannheim claimed that the total formulation describes a powerful western perspective, he did not draw the completely relativist conclusions others have. See Mannheim, 'Ideology and Utopia', 68–9.

which we approach the task), the values (sympathy, tolerance) which underlie and by which we defend U_2 (U_3), and our own cultural values which we use to judge other cultural beliefs and practices (V_1), are all ideological (I_1).

Several issues are noteworthy. The first is that the implication of Mannheim's definitions of ideology for understanding (U_2) includes allegations of another person's or group's distortions of knowledge claims of the facts (U_1). This distortion of facts is certainly a hindrance to cross-cultural understanding (U_1). If knowledge of such things as what a cultural group may value, how many of the group may speak a language or a dialect, or what they expect about the behaviour of their adolescent children, is inaccurate then, at the most elementary level, cross-cultural understanding is difficult if not impossible.

The second point is that in the particular conception of ideology (in which only part of a world view is regarded as distorted) it is theoretically possible to resolve some differences because they possess common criteria for validity. There is room for discussion and persuasion because both sides, the protagonist and the antagonist, agree on the same criteria for validity. For example, they may agree about what constitutes a fact. As they engage, both sides can appeal to the same criteria because they both assent to them. They agree on what evidence is admissible, about how to demonstrate what is factual and what is not. To summarise the point, Mannheim claimed that in the particular conception of ideology, one side is alleged to see things askew, to perceive amiss. Nevertheless, both sides at least agree about the criteria to which they can appeal. For example, they may disagree about the facts but agree on what a fact is and how it is derived.

This raises a number of questions when applied to cross-cultural understanding. For example, consider a disagreement over facts between one group committed to ethnocentrism and one committed to cultural pluralism. The debate is then about the distortion of facts in relation to their perspectives. The ethnocentric group may claim that unemployment is increased by immigration, while the cultural pluralist contends that unemployment may decrease with more demand in the economy. Both would appeal to the same set of data, the same policies and, while they disagree, they at least refer their opponent to the same independent data or criteria. This exemplifies ideological disagreement in the particular conception.

If the allegations of distortion of the facts are between a minority cultural group and an ethnocentric organisation, then they may or may not agree on common validity criteria. Imagine that there is no agreement about what valid evidence is. For example, the groups may not agree on an appeal to scientific methods or procedures, or statistical devices (such as correlation coefficients or analysis of variance). The members of the ethnocentric organisation may appeal to such evidence but the members of a minority culture may not.

If there is no agreement on criteria for validity between the two groups, this would indicate the total conception of ideology is operating. Both sides disagree; there is no common, external point to which both groups might refer. Or, to mix metaphors, there is no point at which they intersect on the criteria they use to establish the validity of their respective positions. There is simply no common ground of any sort to which they can refer.

Thirdly, imagine two opposing cultural groups. If one group were to say that your, but not their, view of the world is totally ideological, that your perceptions are totally warped by the ideological position you take, by your social position, and theirs is not, then that would exemplify the special form of total conception (at least for the group making the judgment). If the group making the judgment is also prepared to subject their own position to ideological analysis, to exploring the social origins of their positions, then that is indicative of the general form (of the total conception of ideology).

Of interest here is that in the special form one group is allegedly exposing the ideological nature of their opponent's perspective or world view without subjecting their own position to the same analysis. Somehow they are exempt. Mannheim was convinced that at the time he was writing *Ideology and Utopia* (1929) that the general formulation of the total conception prevailed. He argued that 'At the present stage of our understanding it is hardly possible to avoid this general formulation of the total conception of ideology, according to which the thought of all parties in all epochs is of an ideological character'.[16] Mannheim believed that the social origins of thought were so pervasive that they applied to all social groups, that the total conception was generally applicable.

It is now timely to apply the distinction between the special and general forms (of the total conception of ideology) to the engagement between the members of the ethnocentric organisation, and the members of a minority culture. In such an engagement we might anticipate that the ethnocentric group is most likely to assert the ideological nature of the minority group's position while exempting their own from similar analysis. Whether Mannheim was correct to insist that all thought is ideological is not as relevant to our discussion as the obvious fact that, whatever the ideological basis of world views, most groups do not submit their own view to the analysis they make of their opponent's. Certainly, members of ethnocentric organisation are unlikely to concede that their views are skewed in any way, shape or form by their ideology, yet simultaneously they charge their opponents with being riddled with ideological bias. The opponent could be a minority cultural group or a cultural pluralist.

16. Mannheim, 'Ideology and Utopia', 69.

A paradox seems to emerge here. On the one hand, few, if any, advocacy groups would concede that their position is ideological. They refuse to be reflexive, that is, to subject their own position to the possibility that it may be ideologically biased, to apply to themselves the same standards about the origins of their world views as they apply to others. On the other hand, as I argued in the previous chapter, the dominant view in the western world is that world views are relative, either to culture, social position, or to socially acceptable ways of determining what counts as knowledge, values or ways of thinking. Thus, when it is of others that this judgment is made, there is general agreement with Mannheim's diagnosis (the views of others are ideological); when the perspectives of those who make the judgment are also charged with ideological distortion they dissent (their own perspectives are not ideological).

Mannheim drew attention to the possibility that the world views of all groups are ideologically skewed. If so, the cultural relativist mentioned in the first chapter may be correct; there may be no other way to see the world but through our own cultural lenses and filters, our own ideologies. If so, then it is possible that we can only see the world from our own cultural perspective. It may be true that not all world views are ethnocentric in the sense of seeing and judging other cultures from the perspective of one's own culture in a malignant and racist way (E_1). But if some form of distortion is inevitable, does this mean that all judgments about other cultures are likely to be ethnocentric in the sense of E_2, of seeing another culture only through our own conceptual and cultural filters?

As cultural relativism is not necessarily ethnocentrism (E_1), seeing other perspectives as ideological does not necessitate the blatant chauvinism and racism of ethnocentrism (E_1). Indeed, as the cultural relativist usually espouses understanding (at least U_1 and U_2), it is likely that other cultures will be perceived from the vantage of liberal versions of tolerance, or the respect and dignity of all human beings. This is not parochial or purposively ethnocentric (as is E_1). Nonetheless, the question remains: is it inevitable that we will perceive others from the vantage of our own culture to such an extent that, even if issues of racial superiority are not part of our perspective, other cultures are still perceived and judged by our criteria, expectations, standards and values?

For example, western cultures tend to be secular, although (perhaps begrudgingly) tolerant of religion generally. If we can only see and judge with secular cultural assumptions, how can we see and judge without distortion (what westerners might label) more religious cultures? If we judge from a secular perspective, the influence of which is difficult to detect because we are so immersed in it, can we avoid seeing another culture except from our irreligious cultural centre, except in our own cultural image? A similar question can be asked of extremist religious groups in the United States: is it possible from their parochial and fundamentalist Christian position to see Islam through any other than their religious position?

As I hinted in the previous chapter, there seems to be another meaning of ethnocentrism (this time E_2). This ethnocentrism (E_2) may reject a narrow, rabid ethnocentrism that is based on, and reinforces, racism (E_1). It may even be committed to liberal traditions of freedom of the individual and tolerance, and respect for the dignity of other people and cultures. But, given the ubiquitous cultural influences we have been examining, the question remains: how is it possible to avoid our cultural influences that make up this form of ethnocentrism (E_2)? As an example of E_2, consider those western countries that accuse other (usually non-western) countries of human rights abuses, which are in turn sometimes accused of chauvinism because they are seen as imposing their western perspectives.[17]

Imagine a group of western students undertaking a research project in which they are expected to draw conclusions about another culture. Suppose that beliefs about previous existences, life after death, the value of flora as remedies, or the existence of transcendent powers that explain daily events (such as rain) are part of the culture under investigation. Ethnocentrism (E_2) says it is possible, even if the student were an implacable defender of cross-cultural understanding, multiculturalism and tolerance, that their own cultural assumptions would be so deeply entrenched that it would be difficult to see and judge other cultures except from the perspective of the secular and scientific culture in which they live. In fact, E_2 suggests that even if some of the students adhered to similar beliefs, or were members of the Natural Medicine Society or the Alternative Explanations Group, they would still be worlds away from understanding the other culture.

Even if they adhered to beliefs which were compatible with (although not identical to) the beliefs of the other culture, those students would remain outside the cultural world they are investigating and would, therefore, be unable to understand it. Adherents of E_1 may only see the world from their racist vantage point. But, while not necessarily racist at all, it would seem that we are all limited by E_2. If this position prevails, our assumptions, the knowledge which becomes tacit and within which all cultures immerse their members, our descriptions, what

17. As suggested in a previous chapter, on this issue see Anthony J Langlois, *The Politics of Justice and Human Rights: Southeast Asia and Universalist Theory* (Cambridge: Cambridge University Press, 2001).

counts in the taken-for-granted explanations and understandings on which our everyday lives rely, what counts
as knowledge and many other things, are part and parcel
of E_2.

Another example (which also summarises some of the issues in this chapter)

Consider another example. Imagine person D sees a huge
tree on the perimeter of a national park become a ball of
fire. D's theory or explanation for the fire is that it has
been a very hot, windy day on which there was an
electrical storm. In brief, lightning caused the fire, which
the wind blew into a bushfire.

Imagine there are two other people (B and C) whom D
meets as they escape the bushfire. They are all alarmed by
their experience but B and C tell D that the gods were
fighting in the heavens. The roar of their voices caused the
gale-force winds, and when the gods met in combat the
force of their contact caused sparks to fly over the entire
sky. This caused the lightning that struck the tree and
caused it to burn.

There are several pertinent questions that we might
ask. Did the threesome escaping from (what I call) a
bushfire experience the same things? In one sense they
did. They all referred to the gale-force wind, the lightning
and the fire. But for D the hot wind was explained by
winds coming from inland and represented on a weather
map by isobars which were very close together, the
lightning was the result of an electrical storm, and the fire
was caused by the lightning arcing to a tree.

For B and C, the gale-force winds were explained by
the gods huffing and puffing at each other, and the
lightning was explained as a by-product of the deflected
energy as the gods were locked in hand-to-hand combat.
The fire was caused by the winning god whose lightning
was the strongest and hit the ground, which in turn was

the winning god's way of telling the inhabitants that all was purified and cleansed.

Note that this threesome agrees that they have all experienced the same things (wind, lightning, fire) but they account for them very differently. But if their account or explanation is different, are they referring to the same thing? After all, D experienced wind, lightning, fire. B and C experienced the same phenomena but the wind was the gods huffing and puffing angrily at each other, the lightning resulted from the gods fighting and the bushfire contained a message. We might be inclined to say that the threesome saw similar things (wind, lightning, fire) but explained them in different ways; the facts were put together differently so that the explanations or theories were also different.

But were the descriptions, or even the experiences, really the same. If someone sees wind, lightning and fire, and someone else tells you that the wind is the gods huffing and puffing, the lightning is the gods in combat and the fire is a divine message, are they actually describing the same things? They have different explanations or theories but do their theories mean that when they feel the wind, and see the fire and lightning, that they are describing the same things? Or, are the descriptions the same (wind, lightning, fire) but their meaning or significance is different? But then the question arises: if the meaning or significance of the same phenomena differ from person to person, are they really the same things? Are they living in the same world?

Imagine that the threesome meet and discuss their different theories. B and C are most reluctant to accept D's theory of what caused the bushfire. So D expounds all the scientific theories he has learnt in Meteorology 1 at university. B and C listen attentively but then ask: why do you put so much faith in what you call science? Why do you trust the instruments that measure? Why should we adopt your explanation? So D then informs them about scientific knowledge and how reliable and certain it is. B and C are informed about the importance of the senses, of not allowing our personal beliefs and values to cloud our descriptions and theories, about how only those things that can be sensed make sense, are sensible, and really count as knowledge.

D explains the difference between scientific knowledge and non-scientific opinions (because for D the opposite of science should not be elevated to knowledge). D tells them about what counts as knowledge and what is discounted, what is credited and what is discredited, and that what he was talking about is called epistemology, our theories about what makes knowledge true or false. D was confident that the perspective he was proffering was persuasive and they would be convinced. Can you imagine D's surprise when B and C responded by saying that they had other ways of deriving knowledge?

In fact, they argued, the senses can be quite misleading. Moreover, they said, the knowledge that counts is the knowledge we bring to understand our experiences. The knowledge that counts is that which helps us not merely understand our experiences, but also what they mean, their significance. B and C said, 'It's not so much that we accumulate evidence and then believe something to be true; we believe certain things and then witness them all around us. In fact, if we didn't believe them first we would not see them at all'. And, they added, 'Whether you like it or not, you do that too. You believe your scientific knowledge will lead you to knowledge which you say "counts". Then, when you find this knowledge, your views about scientific knowledge and what knowledge counts are confirmed. Well, we do the same thing but we start from a different place'.

'So', B and C continued, 'we are not too sure if we live in different worlds or explain the same world differently. Sometimes our differences are so great that it appears we are worlds apart'. After some discussion B and C concluded that they share the same world with D because they all experienced the wind, lightning and fire. But because they explained these things so differently from D, they concluded that they perceive it or understand it differently. It was not a matter of being worlds apart; they live in the same world. It was not just a matter of being words apart either; more than mere words were at stake. B and C also concluded that there is a relationship between the culture we live in and what counts and does not count as knowledge; there is a connection between our cultural milieu and what counts as knowledge and what does not.

D was not too sure where he stood on all this but he remembered a discussion among his student friends about whether culture influences our theory of knowledge, or our theory of knowledge influences our cultural understanding. D was rather bamboozled by all this, but he remembered someone asking the question: which comes first, the chicken or the egg? Which comes first, our views about what counts as knowledge that influence the world we discover, or does the world we live in shape our theories of knowledge? D recalled that someone had said this raised the issue of the relationship between ontology and epistemology. Ontology considers the real world around us, and epistemology how we come to know it and what counts as knowledge. So the question becomes: does ontology shape epistemology, or does our epistemology shape our ontology?

D had an answer to this chicken and egg problem. D claimed that our cultural worlds should not influence our way of thinking and that our culture, our values, our personal preferences are merely subjective and distorting influences. D claimed that we should eliminate these contaminating subjective influences so that we can see the world as it really is. B and C were not so sure. They responded by noting that it was obvious that D was mightily influenced by a certain powerful socially accredited theory of knowledge (epistemology) that prevailed in D's western culture.

More particularly, they pointed out that it seemed that D's epistemology was influenced by the surrounding cultural environment or milieu (in this case, the belief and confidence in the scientific method), and that D's position was not as objective as the position advanced made out. In fact, they claimed that, while socially popular in the West, D's epistemology was rather restrictive because it could not investigate meaning, which is what they felt was absolutely essential. It was the meaning of life, exploring the significance of our place in the universe, and the like, which really mattered. An epistemology that did not, and could not do that, was very restrictive and limiting. Does this mean that D's position exemplified E_2? It would seem so—and C's and D's! For the moment, however, we leave our examination of E_2. It is continued in the concluding comments of this chapter and in Chapters 3 and 9.

Conclusion

In this chapter we have explored many salient issues. Some may have been a little unexpected. However, it is becoming evident as we explore cross-cultural understanding that many things are presupposed in our attempts to understand other cultures, and which influence, if not determine, its direction and success. Some of these are taken for granted—they are in the background—although hidden in cultural beliefs, expectations, practices and values. Nonetheless, they are there, influencing our communications considerably. Without identifying them, it is difficult to determine their influence and desirability.

At first glance, the matters covered in this chapter may seem rather theoretical. However, we have seen just how important theory is to practice. It reveals that even the most practical of actions, such as understanding another culture or a member of another culture, is grounded in theory on which we may rarely reflect and which is largely assumed. Yet, even here, to say assumed might be misleading, since it may denote a previous awareness which is settled in the deep recesses of our mind and which now controls our thinking. The previous understanding is there and, even if we do not have much contact with it, we can retrieve it if necessary. However, most of the time we do not reflect on it, we take it for granted.

Yet, this taken-for-granted reality—and beliefs about it—has enormous influence in cross-cultural understanding. This reality that is taken for granted is like a theory which influences, if not determines, practice. It may be theory but it guides cross-cultural understanding. One way to imagine the practical use of the theory that drives cross-cultural understanding is to think of a highway along which we drive our car. This highway has no exits and, as long as where it leads to is where we want to go, it is ideal. But what would happen if we realised we didn't really want to go to where it led? Perhaps we had heard that the place at the end of the road did not live up to the advertising? What would happen if we decided that we wanted to go somewhere else?

Applying this analogy to cross-cultural understanding, the question becomes: what if we thought we were on the right road to understanding another culture but realised that we were travelling on the wrong road? Or, what if we thought we had successfully negotiated the road to cross-cultural understanding when we discovered that we did not really understand (U_1)? Perhaps we sensed that our understanding was inadequate. Perhaps a member of the other culture told us. Perhaps we had a hunch that we were on the wrong road. In that case, something as practical as our limited understanding or misunderstanding, or additional information, is informing our theory. That is what normally happens when something does not work in practice: we come to realise there is something amiss with our theory. Then our practice, inadequate though it is, begins to inform, question and challenge our theory. It has been exploring our theory that has been my focus in this chapter, in particular our theory of understanding.

In this chapter I began by distinguishing between understanding as cerebral, cognitive, as factual knowledge (U_1), on the one hand, and as being understanding, or sympathetic (U_2), on the other. I argued that both were integral to cross-cultural understanding. I also argued that to be understanding was an approach we valued and which was, in turn, problematic because in our western society it is considered impossible to say whether one value is preferable to another. If it is impossible to defend one value against another, how is it possible to defend the goal of being understanding rather than being misunderstanding? It might be crystal clear that being understanding is preferable to its opposite, but is it possible to defend such a view when it is generally regarded as impossible to say that one value is preferable to another on rational or reasonable grounds?

The subjectivity of value positions raises the possibility described by Mannheim that value positions are ideological. I argued that Mannheim's distinctions are particularly useful when applied to the cross-cultural setting. The particular and total conceptions are relevant because they throw into sharpest relief whether the sides accept similar criteria for validity. If they do (as in the particular conception) they, at least, have a common ground on which disagreements and misunderstandings might be resolved.

As we have seen, however, this is not always the situation in cross-cultural understanding. In addition to the fact that there may not be common criteria of validity between cultures, it is also possible that the members of different cultures may recognise the values of other cultural groups as being related to their culture, but not acknowledge the same relationship in their own culture. This insight was gained from Mannheim's distinction between the specific and general in the total conception of ideology. What is germane to our interests is whether we are prepared to see a similar relationship between culture and values in another culture and, in particular, whether or not we are prepared to submit our cultural values to the same possibility.

This led us to a discussion that may also have surprised some readers who, in good faith and with good reason, denounce the bigoted and racist form of ethnocentrism (E_1). It may have jarred when I tentatively suggested that ethnocentrism (E_2) may be inevitable and the cultural relativist may have been correct all along. You may not want to be tarred with the ethnocentric brush even if E_2 totally repudiates the narrow and racist policies. That was how I felt when I first reflected on E_2, being locked into our cultural frameworks.

However, the encounter between B and C, and D, illustrates the difficulties nicely. They did seem to be worlds apart. They did seem to have totally different understandings of the common things they experienced. Does this mean that the cultural relativist is correct? Do we live in our conceptual and cultural worlds to such an extent that we can only see through them? If so, the cultural pluralist position would seem to be ethnocentric even if in the more benign sense of E_2. Furthermore, I keep on insisting that E_1 is malignant and E_2 is potentially benign, but is it that certain? How can I be sure? Is it possible that E_2 could slide into the bigotry and racism of E_1?

My conclusion in this chapter seems to be that the cultural relativist may be correct and cross-cultural understanding is difficult if not impossible. If so, cultural pluralism is unsustainable because it is impossible to defend the values of respect and tolerance on which it rests. It seems that the choice is between ethnocentrism or cultural relativism, between judging all other cultures as if ours is the centre (E_1), or accepting that we cannot escape the clutches of our own concepts and values (conceptual and cultural relativism; E_2). In either case, cross-cultural understanding would appear doomed.

However, before we accept that rather gloomy conclusion, it is necessary to ask if there is a form of knowledge that transcends ethnocentrism and cultural relativism. Is there a form of knowledge that is neutral, independent, absolute and objective, and universally acceptable which may help us out of the impasse we appear to be in? In the next chapter I explore that possibility.

3

Can science contribute to cross-cultural understanding?

Introduction

In the previous chapter I argued that being understanding is a precondition for cross-cultural understanding. However, being understanding involves engaging with other cultures in a manner which is not hostile or antagonistic; it requires values such as empathy, tolerance and an appreciation of cultural diversity. This is a problem in western society because values are not regarded as amenable to validation (as are facts) and may be considered merely ideological (I_1). If we allow the possibility that our views could be ideological, then it would only be possible to see the world from our own point of view which, in turn, raises the spectre of ethnocentrism of the E_2 variety.

Is there a way of dealing with our own deeply ingrained cultural concepts (such as what counts as knowledge) so as to be able to extricate ourselves from them? Is there some way to rid ourselves of our own cultural and conceptual filters? Is there a neutral and universal vantage point from which cultures can communicate with each other free from their own cultural perspectives?

In most spheres of human activity and learning in the West, science allegedly does this. We learn very early that science is purportedly free of the distorting influences of culture, and the subjective and emotional factors which supposedly clutter other forms of human activity and learning (for example, in philosophy or religion). This raises the question: can science in its search for objectivity free us from the filters that seem to make ethnocentrism such as E_2 inevitable? If we used the scientific method to understand other cultures would that improve cross-cultural understanding? If the answers to these questions are yes, we will have a foot in the doorway to cross-cultural understanding.

In this chapter I begin by discussing the theory of knowledge, or epistemology, which supports popular notions of science. This is germane because the underlying theories of knowledge on which science is based will assist us to appraise whether science can provide that independent, neutral and universal vantage. If science can do this, it will contribute to cross-cultural understanding. In fact, it will render it possible.

The socially popular view of the scientific theory of knowledge

The popular and powerful view of the scientific theory of knowledge can be concisely stated. But before this I want to emphasise that the perspective of science described in the next few pages is what I take to be the popular view of science in the West. This view claims that reliable knowledge is derived from sensory experience—if it can't be sensed, it's nonsense. This is usually known as empiricism. Linked with this empiricism is the view that the most valid knowledge is acquired via the scientific method. This is commonly called positivism. The knowledge derived from empiricism and positivism is claimed to be certain, reliable and valid.

Knowledge so derived is objective in the sense of being an accurate representation of the object under scrutiny, an object which exists independently of the human mind and senses (a position usually known as realism). In addition, scientific facts are derived by accumulating evidence (usually called induction) so that scientific theories are only determined by the facts which are known to be true by induction; scientific theories are factual. As scientific observations are repeated and theories confirmed, areas or disciplines of science develop and grow into a body of knowledge.

Another key point about this popular version of science is that it has become the benchmark of what constitutes knowledge; all claims are tested by the standards of science. If the area of study follows these standards then that discipline is regarded as being scientific, or as providing reliable knowledge. Such knowledge is at the top of the pecking order of knowledge claims. Knowledge claims not derived in this way, or not acquired in this way, are considered unreliable, invalid, subjective (as opposed to objective) and relative (as opposed to absolute). Further, it is alleged that scientifically derived knowledge neutralises bias and so does not come from a particular vantage point or perspective; it is thus value-free.

You may recall from the discussion at the end of the previous chapter that knowledge of this kind is precisely the sort we hoped could overcome the ideological distortion that I highlighted there. Knowledge based on this theory of knowledge (epistemology) and the resulting empirical and positivist method would seem to be precisely the sort of knowledge we need to provide a neutral meeting ground, a mutually agreed, external reference point which could enable us to extricate ourselves from our own distorting frameworks and world views. This form of knowledge seems to meet all the criteria for the sort of knowledge that might assist cross-cultural understanding, and to which we have only found obstacles as we have proceeded.

Arguably, the Vienna Circle of Logical Positivists in the late 1920s and early 1930s held a similar view of science (even if they didn't always hold the views attributed to them).[1] They were concerned about what they regarded as the role that certain universal and metaphysical and political beliefs played in Europe before, during, and particularly after, the First World War. They advocated 'the elimination of metaphysics from science'[2] and believed that a form of knowledge which was neutral with respect to these political dogmas, and which could neutralise them as mere ideologies, was the new form of knowledge that would create a more politically stable and just Europe.

According to the Vienna Circle, which included mathematicians, philosophers, physicists and sociologists, scientific knowledge would challenge the old political absolutes; it was their epistemology which would provide the solid foundation for the knowledge which deserved the name. The epistemology which they believed was qualified for the role was derived from scientific method and empirical observation. Their verification principle stated that the validity of a statement was determined by how it was verified.[3] If a statement could be verified by empirical and scientific means it was knowledge; if it could not be demonstrated by scientific means it was not.

This approach was relevant to all forms of knowledge as far as the Vienna Circle were concerned. The important distinction was not between the natural and physical sciences, and the humanities and the social sciences; all inquiry would be scientific if it followed the same

---

1.   For an accessible introduction see Oswald Hanfling, *Logical Positivism* (Oxford: Blackwell, 1981). The following rendering of the Vienna Circle is one which became influential in the social sciences in the post-Second World War period.

2.   See Hanfling, *Logical Positivism*, 123–48

3.   See Hanfling, *Logical Positivism*, 1–13

principles. In a nutshell, if any discipline used the scientific epistemology and method they recommended, it was science, and its results merited the epithet scientific knowledge. Put bluntly, the converse was: if it could not be sensed, it was nonsense.[4]

At first glance, the Vienna Circle's solution may seem effective for establishing a universal knowledge to which all could appeal. There was a universal theory of knowledge and a method for obtaining 'true' knowledge, namely, their theory of knowledge and their interpretation of the scientific method. According to the Circle, if the respective disciplines of human inquiry adopted their theory of knowledge and followed the methods of science as they conceived them, then the resulting knowledge was worthy of acceptance by all human beings.

Of course, this view of scientific epistemology and scientifically verified results was not new. The Vienna Circle, who devised their manifesto in the mid-to-late 1920s, were not the first to advance an empiricist and positivist view of science under which all other disciplines could be subsumed. Even in the social sciences, August Comte and Emile Durkheim seem to have advocated similar approaches. Durkheim, in particular, advocated that the social sciences should emulate the natural and physical sciences. However, few if any had previously so systematically proposed a theory of knowledge which was to be so influential in the humanities and social sciences. When Hitler usurped power in Germany, the members of the Vienna Circle who were of Jewish descent (and that was most of them) were dismissed from their academic positions and migrated to the United States

---

4.   See R Carnap, H Hahn and O Neurath, 'The Vienna Circle of the Scientific Conception of the World' [1929], in *Empiricism and Sociology*, edited by O Neurath (Boston: D Reidel, 1973), 301–18.

where their post-Second World War influence was to be considerable.

Their work meshed with another view which was the canon in the burgeoning social sciences. This was the fact-value dichotomy. Briefly, this distinction upheld the validity of facts but denied any equivalent validity to ethical, moral, political or religious beliefs. Again, if such topics could be made the object of genuinely scientific research, such as by ascertaining how many people held a religious position, they could be studied scientifically and, therefore, could be considered to be real knowledge. But beliefs about justice, tolerance or abortion, for example, could not make the scientific grade. Such ultimate values could not be defended by science. Accordingly, as they are based on emotion, the validity of religious beliefs, or beliefs about justice or equality, for example, were not amenable to scientific scrutiny and were thus subjective.

Before we attempt to assess whether logical positivism contributes neutral, universal, absolute and objective knowledge, there is one more point, particularly relevant to the social sciences, about the fact-value dichotomy which is worth noting. It is this: in order to emulate the natural and physical sciences, be objective and gain knowledge which meets the standards of the scientific canon, the social sciences must be free of commitments and values. This means social scientists must shun their own values when investigating the object of their research; it means they must eschew personal commitments so that the results of their research are unbiased and thus scientific.

At this point there are several points worth making. The first may not be very controversial, but is germane to our consideration of cross-cultural understanding. A view of knowledge which, as interpreted in the social sciences, bears some resemblance to the one originally adopted by the Vienna Circle, remains the standard, popular and powerful view of what constitutes valid knowledge—at least in the West. There are some exceptions, of course, and there is suspicion about the use and abuse of technologies which have emerged from science. Likewise, there is concern about the uneven distribution of the burdens and benefits of technology, namely, that the poor receive more of the burdens and fewer of the benefits. Nonetheless, science does set the recognised cultural standards of what constitutes valid knowledge.

There are, of course, religious and other beliefs of various persuasions which resist scientific epistemology. But even the main religion of the West, Christianity, has some adherents who are inclined to assert the reliability and the validity of their sacred texts on the basis of scientific standards. Thus, in order to demonstrate that their sacred stories are literally true, they invoke the scientific theory of knowledge. When their scientific research allegedly confirms the truth of their sacred stories, they denounce opposing views as wrong.

The debate about creation versus evolution is a case in point. In this sense, the empiricist and positivist view of science does become a standard to which they both refer, and the evolutionists and creationists use it as such.[5] Whether this confidence is justified is another thing, but both sides accept scientific criteria as such. In effect, the creationists argue that there is a neutral standard by which absolute, objective truth can be demonstrated, and the truth of the Bible is confirmed by archaeological and other findings which adhere to the same standard that their adversaries use to adjudicate disputed facts and theories. By this neutral standard, by their opponents' standards, this religious story is scientifically proven. So they argue! The point is that even some religious groups,

---

5.   This is similar to Mannheim's particular conception of ideology. The opponents see part of each other's view as flawed yet agree on the criteria for validity.

who have been criticised for their subjective knowledge claims, have used a scientific theory of what valid knowledge is as the key criterion when attempting to establish the validity of their claims. That exemplifies how powerful the dominant form of scientific knowledge is in the West.

The second point relates to two questions: firstly, can this popular view of science deliver the neutral, external, independent standard to which we can appeal in order to approach cross-cultural understanding sympathetically (U_2), the values by which we defend such understanding (U_3) and those values we use to assess other cultural values (V_1)? Secondly, can science give us a neutral ground from which we can derive knowledge of other cultures (U_1)? Regarding the first question, I am pessimistic about science being able to provide a reference point to which we can appeal to settle disputes about the values associated with being understanding. The reason for this should be clear: the view of science we are discussing insists that values cannot be held with the same conviction or certitude as facts. According to this view, justifying values, by their very nature, is not a task which is amenable to sensory perception and the scientific method.

This conclusion should not surprise, as it is consistent with the fact-value distinction. According to this position, facts can be ascertained by empiricism and positivism (and if they were established by anything less they would not be facts). But as we have seen, according to the fact-value dichotomy, values cannot be so ascertained. Thus, science cannot help resolve the problem of justifying why we should be sympathetic (U_3) rather than unsympathetic in cross-cultural understanding. If such a resolution is possible, it will not be found in the view of science popular in the West today.

The second question is whether science could afford that independent and neutral standard by which the accuracy of understanding (U_1) can be judged. On that question, judgment must be postponed until we examine other aspects of the Vienna Circle position. Such an examination would include an analysis of the scientific enterprise, including the adequacy of key concepts such as empiricism, positivism, induction (the idea that scientific facts and theories are established by confirming examples), and the eschewing of metaphysics and values.

However, even at this stage the prognosis is not good. What happens, for example, if we can be led astray by sensory perception? What would happen if the scientific method was more about agreements between scientists rather than an independent, neutral method of testing theories and probing things physical and social? What would happen if we could not prove by scientific means that empiricism yielded reliable knowledge? Would our confidence in this neutral knowledge be compromised if it was argued that it is impossible to approximate or get closer to the real world of physical things, except through the lens of a particular framework, world view or paradigm?

As the Vienna Circle came to realise,[6] some fundamental questions arose from the empiricism and positivism of their original position. There are several criticisms of both positions, but there is one strategy that is as straightforward as it is effective in identifying the deficiencies of empiricism. It is the problem highlighted by an argument from reflexivity.[7] In a reflexive statement a claim is directed at itself (not only at antagonists) and is shown to be self-refuting, as in the statement 'there are no

6. See R Carnap, 'Intellectual Autobiography', in *The Philosophy of Rudolph Carnap*, edited by Paul Arthur Schilpp (Illinois: Open Court 1963), 50–7.
7. See Hilary Lawson, *Reflexivity* (Illinois: Open Court, 1985), 9–31.

facts'. Consider that sentence. The claim is that there are no facts when the statement requires at least one—that there are none! Likewise with: 'don't believe a word I say!'

If we apply reflexivity to empirical claims which are alleged to be the only source of valid knowledge, we discover that this claim cannot be validated empirically. We cannot see this statement or its veracity (it has no physical existence, as does a tree for example), and even if we could, we could not claim it to be true before we had proven it by physical means. Yet support for the claim at that stage would be too late because it would show that we had already presumed it rather than knowing it to be true. It was empiricism that was supposed to reassure us that seeing could justify believing that something was absolutely true. But we can't demonstrate the validity of that statement empirically.[8]

Other criticisms of the Vienna Circle came from Karl Popper, the noted philosopher of science. There are several ways in which Popper's views undermined the scientific theory of knowledge proposed by the original Vienna Circle. Firstly, Popper argued that the Vienna Circle's distinction between meaningfulness and meaninglessness was an inappropriate and unhelpful distinction.[9] For Popper, the salient issue in science was not about meaning, but about the demarcation between science and pseudo-science, between scientific knowledge

---

8.   It might be argued that we can defend it after the event. But that is not what is usually argued. It might also be said that we deduce the efficacy of empiricism because we have seen it in the laboratory. It happens over and over again. But there is a problem with confirming examples or induction as well. We know something is true because it can be confirmed. But such a claim cannot be tested beforehand by induction!

9.   This arose from the verification statement principle which is about meaning. See Footnote 2 in this chapter and the next paragraph.

on the one hand, and knowledge which purported to be scientific but which was not, on the other. According to Popper, many a theory which claimed to be scientific, including Marxism, was pseudo-science.[10] Thus, Popper emphasised that science was not about meaning (as it seemed to be for the Vienna Circle) but about rigorously testing theories.

Secondly, Popper also challenged a consequence of the original Vienna Circle's position, namely, the distinction between science and metaphysics. Unlike the Vienna Circle, Popper did not consign metaphysical statements to the epistemological rubbish bin. Popper wrote that the Vienna Circle were 'trying to find a criterion which made metaphysics meaningless nonsense, sheer gibberish, and any such criterion was bound to lead to trouble, since metaphysical ideas are often the forerunners of scientific ones'.[11] Likewise, he also claimed that the demarcation between meaningful scientific statements, which 'must be logically completely reducible to (or deducible from) single observation statements', and meaningless metaphysics, undercut the validity of scientific statements:

> It might appear as if the positivists, by drawing this line of demarcation, had succeeded in annihilating metaphysics more completely than the older anti-metaphysicists. However, it is not only metaphysics which is annihilated by these methods, but natural science as well. For the laws of nature are no

---

10. See Karl Popper, *The Poverty of Historicism*, second edition (London: Routledge and Kegan Paul, 1961).
11. Karl Popper, *Unended Quest: An Intellectual Autobiography*, revised edition (Great Britain: Fontana/Collins, 1976), 80.

more reducible to observation statements than metaphysical utterances.[12]

According to Popper, the scientific laws of nature (for example, the law of gravity) are not totally reducible to observation statements, and theories about them comprise far more than the accumulation, or the sum total, of observation statements. Yet, such non-empirical claims are an essential feature of science. Eliminate the metaphysical issues about which Popper was concerned and the consequence is that scientific laws collapse.

Thirdly, Popper disagreed with the Vienna Circle in three other areas: (1) whereas the Vienna Circle emphasised verification in the growth of scientific knowledge, Popper emphasised falsification; (2) whereas the Vienna Circle emphasised induction in the growth of scientific knowledge, Popper emphasised deduction; (3) whereas the Vienna Circle emphasised that the laws of nature must be reducible to observation statements, Popper argued that observations were influenced by theories.

Thus, Popper argued that falsifying rather than verifying a theory was to be preferred in the scientific process. Similarly, he argued that induction (support by adducing confirming examples) cannot lead to definitive and final conclusions. Rather than attempting to verify by induction, Popper argued it is more effective to attempt to falsify a theory which has been deduced, just as it is more effective to seek to find one black swan when the task is to test the proposition that all swans are white. If the aim is to determine if all swans are white, verifying involves counting all the white swans. But falsifying necessitates locating just one black swan![13]

---

12. Karl Popper, *The Logic of Scientific Discovery* (London: Hutchinson, 1972), 313.

13. See Bryan Magee, *Popper* (London: Fontana Modern Masters, 1973), 23.

What is required for science, according to Popper, is the falsification of bold theories which are deduced from existing knowledge, guesses and metaphysical assumptions and ideas, rather than the reduction of empirical evidence to observation statements. In this there is the inchoate notion of what later became known as the underdetermination of theories by facts,[14] that theories are much more than the sum of the facts; theories include ideas and facts which have been selected, arranged and organised as well as assumptions and guesses.

Such theories have elements of knowledge akin to the epistemological status of religious knowledge or claims to faith. For Popper, what the Vienna Circle regarded as meaningless, and therefore not warranting the meritorious label 'scientific', were integral components of the scientific process. One such was faith. Science is predicated on the belief in the existence of regular causal laws. Popper claimed he had a 'metaphysical faith in the existence of regularities in our world (a faith which I share, and without which practical action is hardly conceivable)'.[15] He also wrote that:

> I am inclined to think that scientific discovery is impossible without faith in ideas which are of a purely speculative kind, and sometimes even quite hazy; a faith which is completely unwarranted from the point of view of science, and which, to that extent, is 'metaphysical'.[16]

Thus, Popper undermined the early Vienna Circle confidence in empiricism. He did not discount or reject

---

14. See WH Newton-Smith, *The Rationality of Science* (London: Routledge, 1981), 40–3.
15. Popper, *The Logic of Scientific Discovery*, 252–3.
16. Popper, *The Logic of Scientific Discovery*, 38.

what the Vienna Circle regarded as meaningless or non-scientific (ethical, moral, political, religious and value positions); it was not sidelined as nonsense by the standard of scientific reason adopted by the early Vienna Circle.

The scientific epistemology then, did not deliver the rock-solid knowledge the original Vienna Circle claimed. It was not the foundation of knowledge it was commonly believed to be. This is demonstrated in the following quotation from Karl Popper:

> The empirical basis of objective science has thus nothing 'absolute' about it. Science does not rest upon a solid bedrock. The bold structure of its theories rises, as it were, above the swamp. It is like a building erected on piles. The piles are driven down from above into the swamp, but not down to any natural given base; and if we stop driving the piles deeper, it is not because we have reached firm ground. We simply stop when we are satisfied that the piles are firm enough to carry the structure, at least for the time being.[17]

Popper's emphasis on theory formation, on testing bold conjectures, has another implication for science. Popper admitted a degree of idealism in the sense that he believed '*all our theories are man-made*, and that we try to impose them upon the world of nature'. He claimed that by using conventions, and theory-impregnated observations, our knowledge of the world is constructed. Yet despite this concession to an apparent idealism, in which ideas determine what is real, Popper claimed he was a

---

17. Popper, *The Logic of Scientific Discovery*, 111.

realist because the truth or otherwise of the world of facts determines if the theories are true or not.[18]

In summary then, Popper was an arch-rival of the original Vienna Circle position, a version of which I have argued resembles the dominant theory of knowledge (or epistemology) popular in the West. Such a claim is easily tested. Although some people are (justifiably) suspicious of so-called technological advances, my assessment is that a view similar to that advanced by the original Vienna Circle remains the most popular and powerful view of knowledge. Popper's criticisms certainly undermined the Vienna Circle's position and, from a sociology of knowledge perspective, it is interesting to ask why Popper's views have not filtered down into school science and social views of science, and about what comprises valid knowledge more generally.

There are more devastating critiques of knowledge than Popper's, whose position stands somewhat in the middle. For our purposes what is noteworthy about Popper is that he questioned the empiricism, positivism and the verification principles of the Vienna Circle. In particular, he challenged their repudiation of what they regarded as meaningless or nonsense claims (or faith or metaphysical claims) or values. In other words, Popper challenged the very basis of the Vienna Circle's assertion that science is based on entirely neutral and objective knowledge. This can be clearly seen in his view that science is the testing of theory-impregnated hypotheses. While facts are a part of such theories, theories are more than facts. In this respect, Popper at least touched base with the radical criticisms of scientific knowledge and yet, unlike them, still believed that science grows and should

---

18. Karl Popper, *Objective Knowledge: An Evolutionary Approach* (Oxford: Clarendon Press, 1975), 328–9.

be judged against an objective, real world of physical and social phenomena.

However, before investigating these more radical criticisms, it is possible to say a little more about the ability of science to give us the type of information which might assist us in cross-cultural understanding. Popper's challenge to the Vienna Circle, and the myriad of similar popular and powerful positions, confirms our lack of confidence in their scientific view of knowledge. It seems unable to provide the neutral, independent, absolute and objective ground by which different cultural world views may be able to communicate effectively and increasingly understand each other, and by which assessments of other cultures might be judged without being tainted by our own cultural filters.

We have already seen how the Vienna Circle's position could not help us defend the sympathetic way we believe we should approach cross-cultural understanding (U_2). Now we conclude that the Vienna Circle's view of scientific knowledge cannot really assist us to understand even the cultural phenomena which they might have called the facts (U_1). There are two reasons for this. The first is that, according to Popper, the Vienna Circle's claims about knowledge, and particularly about avoiding metaphysical claims, do not necessarily hold. Popper claimed that the very aspects which the Vienna Circle regarded as non-scientific knowledge were replete in science. Further, the very principle that was to distinguish science from drivel (the verification principle) could not be supported by the same form of knowledge which they argued distinguished science from non-science (namely, empirical evidence).

In fact, as far as Popper was concerned, scientific knowledge was impossible without metaphysics and values. For our purposes this means that the alleged neutral standpoint of science is, at least according to Popper, nonexistent in the way popularly conceived.

Even if the results of scientific theories yield such knowledge, and that is yet to be decided, the entire scientific project, and particularly its epistemological foundations, involves beliefs, faith, metaphysics and values. It is not grounded in anything which could be described as independent or neutral.

This leads to the second reason why we have little confidence in the ability of the Vienna Circle's view of science, and those akin to it, to provide a neutral ground from which cross-cultural understanding might begin. Everything about it is comprehensively western, including the faith, the metaphysical beliefs and values underlying science, and beliefs about how to determine the most valid and reliable form of knowledge. It is just this form of socially certified knowledge that is often rejected by other cultures that have alternative theories or knowledge, or epistemologies as we might call them. Recall the discussion between B and C, and D, in the previous chapter. It was precisely what comprised valid knowledge which was at issue, with D using western scientific epistemology and B and C using their own.

It is not surprising that when this western view of knowledge and scientific research has been used as the basis for cross-cultural understanding, it has often led to misunderstanding, at the very least. For example, when westerners witnessed what they described as the magical practices of some cultures, they judged them to be unreasonable or irrational. According to western standards of socially certified knowledge, they seem to be unreasonable and irrational. But who sets this standard? And why are they so powerful? Or, more accurately, why does science become the criterion by which all knowledge claims and their resultant practices are evaluated?

When the cultural beliefs, expectations, practices and values of other cultures are judged according to our standards of what is valid knowledge, western values are being imposed on others. This subjugation of knowledge which is culturally significant to indigenous people or minority groups is a form of domination. In this way, even theories of knowledge become instruments by which one culture is regarded as inferior to another. It is not only cultural beliefs and practices which can be (and often are) regarded as inferior, but the very forms of knowledge on which they are based.

An interesting facet of all this is that the dominant view of scientific knowledge may be the socially creditable and certified cultural perspective about the most valid knowledge in the West, but it is not without its critics. Moreover, some of the criticisms undermine the scientific canon to such an extent that Popper's criticism seems moderate by comparison.

A position which challenged the popular and powerful view of science even more than did Popper's was that of Thomas Kuhn, who first published his seminal work, *The Structure of Scientific Revolutions,* in 1962. In it he proposed that 'normal science' consists of a paradigm that is like a model or framework within which science proceeds. The paradigm is made up of agreements by the scientific community on what criteria are used to choose problems, the questions which should be asked, what evidence is admissible, and what a valid answer would be. Kuhn expressed this function of a paradigm in the following terms: 'one of the things a scientific community acquires with a paradigm is a criterion for choosing problems that, while the paradigm is taken for granted, can be assumed to have solutions'.[19]

Kuhn's concept of the paradigm is meant to convey the view that 'some accepted examples of actual scientific practice—examples which include law, theory, application, and instrumentation together—provide models

19. Thomas Kuhn, *The Structure of Scientific Revolutions* second edition (Chicago: University of Chicago Press, 1962), 37.

from which spring particular coherent traditions of scientific research'.[20] Ptolemaic and Copernican astronomy are examples of two competing paradigms that in their time were normal science. A paradigm in normal science then, outlines a set of questions that are to be resolved, as well as rules and standards, theories and laws, methods and goals, admissible evidence and criteria to be used for testing hypotheses.

Science is like a jigsaw puzzle, and the analogy reveals two more features that Kuhn also attributed to paradigms. Firstly, just as there are rules to solve the puzzle so there are rules which determine the nature of the solution in a scientific paradigm; a paradigm limits the range of 'acceptable solutions' to the questions or puzzles raised by it. Secondly, the steps used to find a solution are also limited by the paradigm. Kuhn illustrated his intentions here by noting that a jigsaw puzzle presupposes a picture of some sort which requires turning the parts of the puzzle and arranging them to form the solution.[21]

Adherents of a paradigm also align themselves to a set of commitments. For example, there is a commitment to the types and use of instruments and particular metaphysical conceptions. As an example, Kuhn pointed to the seventeenth-century paradigm that led physical scientists to assume 'that the universe was composed of microscopic corpuscles and that all natural phenomena could be explained in terms of corpuscular shape, size, motion, and interaction'. This paradigm 'told scientists what sorts of entities the universe did and did not contain: there was only shaped matter in motion'. Methodologically, the paradigm 'told them what ultimate laws and fundamental explanations must be like', namely, 'laws must specify

---

20. Kuhn, *The Structure of Scientific Revolutions*, 10.
21. Kuhn, *The Structure of Scientific Revolutions*, 38.

corpuscular motion and interaction, and explanation must reduce any given natural phenomenon to corpuscular action under these laws'.[22]

Occasionally, over time, crises arise and cracks appear in a paradigm. In response to anomalies in the paradigm some practitioners might choose another. This is a revolution, a revolution based on much more than strictly scientific facts or observation. In the new paradigm the solutions, the puzzles, the methods and interpretations are novel. Things that made sense before, suddenly do not; answers, puzzles, interpretations, methods and solutions are turned upside down. As Kuhn expressed it: 'though the world does *not* change with a change of a paradigm, the scientist afterward works in a *different* world'.[23] On another occasion Kuhn claimed that 'the proponents of competing paradigms practice their trade in worlds'. He continued:

> One contains constrained bodies that fall slowly, the other pendulums that repeat their motions again and again. In one, solutions are compounds, in the other mixtures. One is embedded in a flat, the other in a curved, matrix of space. Practicing in different worlds, the two groups of scientists see different things when they look from the same point in the same direction. Again, that is not to say that they can see anything they please. Both are looking at the world, and what they look at has not changed. But in some areas they see different things, and they see them in different relations to one another.[24]

---

22. Kuhn, *The Structure of Scientific Revolutions*, 41.
23. Kuhn, *The Structure of Scientific Revolutions*, 121 (emphasis added).
24. Kuhn, *The Structure of Scientific Revolutions*, 150.

Furthermore, the vital factors in any such revolution are extra-scientific. Such descriptions of changing paradigms include 'scales falling from the eyes', or the 'lightning flash'.[25] On one occasion Kuhn likened a paradigm shift to a 'conversion experience'.[26] He claimed that it was precisely because paradigms were incommensurable that the 'transition between competing paradigms *cannot* be made a step at a time, forced by logic and neutral experience'. On the contrary, 'Like the Gestalt switch, it must occur all at once (though not necessarily in an instant) or not at all'.[27]

There are several implications for value claims in Kuhn's description of the structure of scientific revolutions. The first is that, contrary to the popular view of science, there is no standard outside competing paradigms by which scientific knowledge is to be assessed. There is no such thing as an independent epistemology which leads to absolute, objective and verifiable knowledge which becomes the criterion for all claims which merit the title 'knowledge'. When science was in crisis and there were conflicting paradigms Kuhn used the term 'incommensurability' to describe the competing paradigms and the inability of practitioners of one paradigm to engage in dialogue with those of another.[28] Another way to express this is to say that there is no point external to a paradigm from which it could be evaluated. There is no Archimedean point.

This also has some implications for the hope that western science would provide some sort of external, neutral, independent, absolute, objective and intra-cultural reference point on which we could all agree and

25. Kuhn, *The Structure of Scientific Revolutions*, 122.
26   Kuhn, *The Structure of Scientific Revolutions*, 150.
27. *Ibid*, (emphasis added).
28. *Ibid*, 150.

from which we could enhance cross-cultural under-standing. In the normal stage of science, the practitioners of a particular paradigm agree; there is consensus about the type of questions to be asked, what methodology and instruments are acceptable, what instruments are to be used, what is admissible evidence, and what constitutes an adequate answer and so on. But these are based on agreements, consensus, conventions. They are just like cultures which use different paradigms. According to Kuhn, the very theory of knowledge and method which we hoped to find has eluded us again. Kuhn's analysis of science is even more devastating than Popper's.

Secondly, if all paradigms are incommensurable, if paradigm shift involves a conversion experience, if fol-lowing a paradigm is more than the sum of the empirical content of the paradigm and includes conven-tions and agreements, then the difference between adhering to a paradigm and adhering to a cultural claim has, at least, been narrowed if not abolished. If practit-ioners of conflicting paradigms are seeing the same world differently, or working in different worlds that are incom-mensurable, could the claims made by members of different cultures be also regarded as paradigms that are incommensurable?

It is not only, as Popper insisted, non-empirical issues (such as consensus and convention) which are integral to science and theory choice and which cannot be empirically demonstrated, but there is, as Kuhn emphasised, also a culture of science. Scientific paradigms contain claims which are similar epistemologically to competing cultural claims; cultural claims are similar in epistemological status to paradigms. This occurs not because competing cultural claims have been elevated to the status of empirical scientific claims; it occurs because the consensual, conventional and cultural nature of know-ledge, method and practice have been recognised as part of the scientific enterprise itself. It seems that what I have previously said of the theories of knowledge, and the beliefs, practices and values of different cultures can now be said of scientific knowledge and the culture of science (at least according to my reading of Kuhn).

What are the implications of this for cross-cultural understanding? They are considerable because members of a cultural community seem to operate in similar ways to what Kuhn called normal or ordinary science. They use conventions and consensus just like the community of scientists. In this way, cultural paradigms, the beliefs, expectations, practices and values of the members of a culture are similar to normal or routine science. In both cases a community operates within a body of knowledge which is internally consistent, self-authenticating and self-justifying. Likewise, a period of social change within a cultural community is similar to periods of revolutionary science, when conflicting paradigms compete and new paradigms are adopted on grounds which are not necessarily scientific or factual but more akin to a change in world view or religious conversion. Thus Kuhn's analysis of science is relevant to my argument. Scientific paradigms, cultural frameworks and worldviews are similar. Indeed, science is like a culture; cultures are like paradigms.

Further, some reflection unravels other implications of Kuhn's position for cross-cultural understanding. Firstly, the popular and powerful view of scientific knowledge is undermined to a degree that it is incapable of generating that neutral, independent, absolute and objective knowledge which seemed so indispensable for understanding other cultures. Secondly, not only is the popular scientific theory of knowledge incapable of giving us a neutral ground on which to compare and evaluate other cultures, it brings with it its own paradigm. As the scientific community is like a culture, then it can only proffer its own cultural paradigm. The indispensable neutral ground is seemingly unattainable; it, too, is culture bound. Yet some critics of the scientific canon go even further.

According to Paul Feyerabend, for example, there is no correct scientific method or concept of rationality by which to arbitrate between the plethora of world views. He concluded that any attempt to attribute superiority to one view is flawed since 'qualitative preferences have no inherent order'.[29] Thus, Feyerabend rejected the alleged supremacy of western science and scientific knowledge over other belief systems and world views, including over what many would regard as custom, tradition and even magic and witchcraft. 'I assert', he wrote, 'that there exist no "objective" reasons for preferring science and Western rationalism to other traditions'.[30] Science is but one of many traditions between which it is impossible to choose as 'the choice of science over other forms of life is not a scientific choice'.[31] Thus, according to Feyerabend, there is no unique scientific method. Like the Dadaists in art, who did not possess, did not want to be confined to, and opposed, previous artistic frameworks, models and programs (we might call them paradigms), Feyerabend claimed that science does not possess a program; he was opposed to the privileging of any particular method.[32]

Feyerabend adduced considerable evidence to show that scientific knowledge does not increase with the continuity, step-like progression and ascent that is often taken for granted. His point is that the history of science reveals no inner secrets which can justify the existence of a universal method which, in turn, is based on a superior theory of knowledge, such as empiricism or induction. In

---

29. Paul Feyerabend, *Farewell to Reason* (London: Verso, 1987), 155.
30. Feyerabend, *Farewell to Reason*, 297.
31. Feyerabend, *Farewell to Reason*, 31.
32. Paul Feyerabend, *Against Method* (London: Verso, 1988), 1-19, 286-287.

contrast to the popular view, all aspects of human thought and emotion enter what is called the scientific process—and do so to such an extent that there is very little (if anything) which distinguishes science from the diversity of human thought, feelings and actions in the welter of customs, conventions and traditions.

Feyerabend described himself as an anarchist and, consistent with the popular use of the term, described his conclusion regarding his philosophy as 'anything goes'. The context of this description is as follows:

> It is clear, then, that the idea of a fixed method, or of a fixed theory of rationality, reacts on too naive a view of man and his social surroundings. To those who look at the rich material provided by history, and who are not intent on impoverishing it in order to please their lower instincts, their craving for intellectual security in the form of clarity, precision and 'objectivity', 'truth', it will become clear that there is only *one* principle that can be defended under *all* circumstances and in *all* stages of human development. It is the principle: *anything goes*.[33]

Another critical approach comes from the contribution of the sociology of knowledge approach to scientific knowledge. This position insists that knowledge claims are socially constructed. As David Bloor wrote:

> Instead of defining it [knowledge] as true belief, knowledge for the sociologist is whatever men make to be knowledge. It consists of those beliefs which men confidently hold to live by. In particular the

---

33. Feyerabend, *Against Method*, 19.

> sociologists will be concerned with beliefs
> which are taken for granted or institut-
> ionalised, or invested with authority by
> groups of men.[34]

More recently, sociologists have suggested that even facts are socially constructed. According to this view, 'the study of scientific knowledge is primarily seen to involve an investigation of how scientific objects are produced in the laboratory rather than a study of how facts are preserved in scientific statements about nature'.[35] More to the point:

> the constructive operations with which we
> have associated scientific work can be defined
> as the sum total of selections designed to
> transform the subjective into the objective, the
> unbelievable into the believed, the fabricated
> into the finding, and the painstakingly
> constructed into the objective scientific fact.
> The transformational aspect of the construc-
> tivist interpretation does not refer solely to
> the moulding and shaping of things in the
> hands of scientific craftsmen . . . The trans-
> formations . . . imply a *symmetry break* in the
> sense that the natural becomes disassociated
> from the social once other selections are
> effectively ruled out, or once scientists have

34. David Bloor, *Knowledge and Social Imagery* (London: Routledge and Kegan Paul, 1976), 2–3.
35. Karin D Knorr-Cetina, 'The Ethnographic Study of Scientific Work: Towards a Constructivist Interpretation of Science', in *Science Observed: Perspectives on the Social Study of Science*, edited by Karin D Knorr-Cetina and Michael Mulkay (London: Sage, 1983), 119.

been persuaded to consider certain propositions as factual propositions.[36]

The social construction of scientific fact in 'the microworlds' of laboratories becomes the site of the creation of phenomena. In this way, the laboratory is characterised by reproduction rather than production; it is not creation that is described but the created and constructed world; the world of the laboratory, the world of scientific fact, is an artefact.[37]

With this incursion (perhaps digression) into the sociology of science I intended to show that some sociologists (at least) go even further than Feyerabend. Yet his perspective is pertinent to the topic of this book because he claimed that science in all its aspects (epistemology, methodology, findings) is on a par with other human activities such as art or even the so-called magical practices in other cultures. Thus again, my argument is that not only is the popular view of science incapable of producing the neutral territory needed for cross-cultural understanding and evaluation, but it has certain similarities with culture. Rather than being part of the resolution to some of the dilemmas of cross-cultural understanding, it has similar qualities—at least according to Feyerabend and some sociologists of science. Consequently, it is hardly likely to assist with resolving our difficulties in understanding other cultures.

The idea that what we previously called facts are socially constructed, exemplifies the position that science

---

36. Knorr-Cetina, 'The Ethnographic Study of Scientific Work', 122–3.

37. On this issue see Joseph Rouse, *Knowledge and Power: Toward a Political Philosophy of Science* (Ithaca: Cornell University Press, 1987), 100-103.

possesses similar qualities to a culture.[38] Just as cultures are social constructions, so too are facts socially constructed. Transforming the subjective into the objective, the unbelievable into the believed, the fabricated into the finding, could well be used as a definition of cultural activity, albeit incomplete because it does not seem to take into account the way the social world influences the subject, the members of a particular group.

This introduces another relevant matter. If, in some way, facts are socially constructed, what does this say about the object world which is being examined? It is often assumed that the world of objects studied in the natural and physical sciences is the raw or naked natural and physical world. We might say this world is unadulterated—in the literal sense of the word. However, the constructivist position exposes this view as defective. The natural and physical world is not pristine, or in its natural state, when humans study it. It is always 'nature-as-an-object-of-knowledge',[39] which is always encultured, that is, it has been socially influenced. Thus, as soon as it becomes the object of study, nature is no longer pristine and unadulterated. It, too, becomes influenced by cultural beliefs, practices and values.

Concluding comments

In this chapter I have discussed scientific epistemology, the form of knowledge which motivates and guides the scientific process as we know it in the West. I did this in the hope of creating a position, a place and space, from

---

38. The classic statement of the general constructionist position can be found in Peter Berger and Thomas Luckmann, *The Social Construction of Reality: A Treatise in the Sociology of Knowledge* (Harmondsworth: Penguin University Books, 1971).

39   Sandra Harding, 'After the Neutrality Idea: Science, Politics and "Strong Objectivity"', in *Social Research*, 59/3 (Fall 1992): 575.

which we can understand other cultures and have them understand us. This hope is in vain—at least if science is our hope. However, before revisiting the issues covered in this chapter, it is worth noting several things that I have not mentioned.

In this chapter I have concentrated on the epistemology of science, or the theory of knowledge on which science is based. There are good reasons for this, but in doing so I have neglected the consequences of scientific theory and technology. Science and technology have been used in some of the most unconscionable attacks on cultures, such that those who discovered the scientific theory or invented the technology would have been appalled at the use to which their work has been put.

For example, in addition to the technology used in the Nazi gas chambers during the Second World War, the dropping of the atomic bomb and in chemical weapons, there is also social Darwinism and social eugenics. Social Darwinism was the application of Darwin's theory of evolution to human societies and, in particular, the application of policies which were based on the theory of the survival of the fittest. Certain policies were justified on the grounds that the fittest would survive. Those who did not were merely the casualties of natural selection. This idea was popular in the nineteenth and twentieth centuries and, *inter alia*, was consistent with the policies of colonialism and imperialism which involved genocide and cultural destruction.[40]

Social eugenics has been used to attempt to 'improve' the genetic make-up of individuals and the community by introducing policies to improve the chances of some genes recurring and others being repressed. For example, reproduction policies which encourage child-bearing in a

---

40. Stephen Jay Gould, *The Mismeasure of Man* (Harmondsworth: Penguin, 1981).

group with desired characteristics, and policies which discouraged or prohibited child-bearing amongst groups considered socially inferior were canvassed in the earlier decades of this century. In the Unites States consideration was given to the notion of intelligence being used to encourage migrants from some countries and preclude migrants from others.[41]

There is yet another matter which I have not yet discussed. This is the elevating or valorising of western science on the one hand, and the belittling of and failure to recognise the contribution of non-western science to western science on the other.[42] In this way, western science has been privileged over its non-western counter-parts. Yet there are numerous examples in which the West has adopted and adapted aspects of non-western culture to its betterment.

For example, Sandra Harding has noted that the 'principles of pre-Columbian agriculture, that provided potatoes for almost every European ecological niche . . . was subsumed into European science'.[43] Mathematical achievements from India and the Middle East, and the magnetic needle, the rudder and gunpowder from China, are other examples.[44] The point here is not to deny the importance of western scientific endeavours, but to note that the contributions from other cultures have been belittled and discounted. Needless to say, privileging one

---

41. See Leon J Kamin, *The Science and Politics of IQ* (Harmondsworth: Penguin, 1977).
42. See Sandra Harding, 'Is Science Multicultural? Challenges, Resources, Opportunities, Uncertainties', in *Theorizing Multiculturalism: A Guide to the Current Debate*, edited by Cynthia Willett (Massachusetts: Blackwell, 1998), 344-67 and Sandra Harding, *Is Science Multicultural? Postcolonialisms, Feminisms, and Epistemologies* (Bloomington and Indianapolis: Indiana University Press, 1998).
43. Harding, 'Is Science Multicultural?' 347.
44. Harding, 'Is Science Multicultural?' 347-8

position is not conducive to cross-cultural understanding attempted in good faith.

Further, as I outlined earlier in this chapter, there seems to be little justification for the crude scientism which is so powerful and popular in the West and exemplified by early logical positivism. By this I do not mean that the findings and technology derived from western science are of necessity crude. What I mean is that the underlying theory of knowledge which is popularly held to support science is flawed. In fact, it is hard to fathom on philosophical grounds why this school view of science is so popular, particularly in the light of the critiques by Popper, Kuhn, Feyerabend and the constructivists, and many feminists and postmodernists.

A conclusion which can be drawn from this chapter is that not only does the most popular and powerful perspective of science not live up to its promise to give us the sort of neutral territory we hope for, but also, in the hands of the powerful, it has contributed enormously to the problem. The problem is that it has been privileged as the universal epistemology of discovery, and all others have been regarded as inferior. Yet my analysis in this chapter reveals how inadequate that epistemology really is. It may be the dominant one, it may have been used to aid and abet colonisation, exploitation and imperialism but, apparently, it is just one amongst many perspectives which could have been adopted for similar purposes.

Care is required here. What we are undermining here is the apparent breakdown of the fact-value dichotomy which remains dominant in the West. According to this dichotomy it is possible to arbitrate between facts but not values. Although Popper would not have agreed, one interpretation of Kuhn, and an implication of the position of Feyerabend and social constructivism, is that it is now impossible to arbitrate between facts. It is at this point that considerable care is required. Why? Because if it is impossible to arbitrate between facts, how is understanding (U_1) across cultures possible? Even knowledge about cultures seems unavailable. U_1 has been sabotaged—or so it seems. I might have been arguing that U_1 seems impossible if we cannot defend empathetic understanding (U_2), the values by which we defend that empathetic understanding (U_3) and the values by which we judge other cultures and our own (V_1). But now it is doubly problematic because even finding facts about other cultures is dubious too.

To summarise, for most of the twentieth century in the West it was considered impossible to arbitrate between competing values, and possible to arbitrate between conflicting facts. Now, it seems, both are out of reach. Does this mean that the cross-cultural understanding project has been sabotaged altogether? After all, at least when it was possible to adjudicate between facts there were agreed criteria for validity—at least for facts! In the past this has undoubtedly privileged western knowledge claims. But, if we are to expose the inadequacies of imperious western knowledge claims, finding a way of sorting facts from fiction would seem to be imperative. That possibility apparently no longer exists.

It seems that the status of knowledge is now similar to what Popper claimed of the Vienna Circle. Just as their rejection of metaphysics was a two edged sword, cutting out metaphysics of course, but cutting into science as well, so the impossibility of arbitrating between facts also cuts into the very possibility of identifying the conesquences of western actions and knowledge claims. Devoid of factual knowledge, exposing the horrendous factual consequences of colonisation and imperialism may be impossible. According to the implications of this chapter, if we do discern these things while undertaking our social science we will just be making one claim among many.

There is another related difficulty. What impact does the impossibility of arbitrating between facts have on competing factual claims encountered in cross-cultural understanding? Consider two accounts of the imprisonment of a member of a minority culture in one of the western nations. If it is impossible to arbitrate between facts, what does this mean for deciding which of the accounts comes closer to what actually happened? Even if we are very suspicious of people who claim they posses the truth, presumably we want to get as close as possible to what really happened. How can we approximate the truth, find out what really happened and whether a travesty of justice occurred, if we cannot arbitrate between facts?

This chapter has some twists and turns. I began it by asking if science could provide a neutral place from which to begin cross-cultural understanding, after which I launched into a critique of the popular view of scientific epis-temology and what counts as knowledge. The critique of Popper, Kuhn and Feyerabend and others seems devastating, particularly if facts are constructed and scientific reason is merely one form among many. In order to be crystal clear about the position I am advancing I offer the following comments.

Firstly, we are justified in concluding that the dominant epistemology of science and knowledge in the West cannot help us defend being understanding (U$_2$), with defending the values associated with being understanding (U$_3$) and with defending values (V$_1$). The popular scientific creed as we learn it in school, states that facts are objective and values are subjective. Implicit in this judgment is the view that values are always personal and private and can never qualify as possessing the same status as facts. Thus, this science could never help find the neutral position required for cross-cultural understanding.

In some forms, of course, the science dominant in the West is the reason why issues of ethics, morality, the preferable political regime and other values (such as human rights and tolerance) are merely subjective. According to this scientific view, only science yields rational and objective knowledge; by definition all other forms of knowledge are irrational and subjective. This is not only an issue for people of religious faith living in the West. Another critical issue is how the secular West can sympathetically understand the religious foundations of other cultures when what counts as knowledge differs so much.

Since 11 September 2001 this is a serious matter because terrorism is linked to the Islamic faith—or, at least, this is how some western politicians and media like to represent terrorism. Despite the fact that the vast majority of Islamic people denounce terrorism per se and repudiate it as inimical to their faith, the question should be posed: how is it possible to understand sympathetically (U_2) people of other faiths when the West is secular and what is valued as knowledge is in dispute? This is another instance where culture and religions are difficult to separate and where religion is identified as an issue in cross-cultural understanding.

Secondly, over time the dominant view of science has been used to judge other cultures, and it has judged their science and view of reason as inferior to that of the West. Thus, western scientific epistemology has been an acute obstacle to cross-cultural understanding. Moreover, not only has western science judged the factual claims of other cultures as mistaken but, in so doing, it has imposed the value of its own theory of knowledge on other cultures. Yet what in the West is regarded as the most valuable form of knowledge, is no less a value claim because it refers to science. In the West this form of scientific knowledge is valued. It concerns gaining access to the truth, what is reason and what is not, what is fact and what is value, which in turn, is associated with scientific epistemology and the scientific method.

However, this does not detract from the fact that the above involves values—in this instance western values about what and how knowledge is rendered valid. When other forms of knowledge are judged as irrational by this standard, the values associated with western knowledge are invoked. Yet, as we have seen, this western view of science is also subject to criticism.

A significant implication for ethnocentrism (E_2) seems to follow from this conclusion. I began by asking if the scientific theory of knowledge could minimise or even extricate us from ethnocentrism (E_2). However, the answer is now clearer: the theory of scientific knowledge epitomises the problems associated with E_2. Part and parcel of its very practice is the undermining of the theories of knowledge in other cultures. By claiming to be the standard, western science judges other theories of knowledge and other related claims as irrational or un-reasonable. So, is E_2 as benign as previously suggested? How readily does E_2 mutate into E_1? These are serious questions to which I will return.

My third point is perhaps the most unexpected. It is that I have grave doubts about following the critique of science to its apparent conclusion. I may have used Popper, Kuhn, Feyerabend and the sociology of know-ledge to demonstrate that there are flaws in the dominant epistemology in the West which has imposed itself on other cultures and has, at it worst, been an unmitigated disaster for cross-cultural understanding. However, this does not mean that I feel obliged to follow the critique of the scientific theory of knowledge to its end or draw similar conclusions to other critics. I abhor the imposition of the prevailing crude empiricist and positivist epis-temology in the colonialist and imperious West which has done so much to obstruct cross-cultural understanding. I regard Kuhn's work as an important challenge to the dominant western theory of knowledge. Feyerabend and the sociology of science should also be heard. But that does not mean we must abandon the search for facts any more than we need be coy about those values which advance cross-cultural understanding. In this sense, I am closer to Popper.

Fourthly, one of the reasons I advocate attempting to find out what actually happened, the truth, is because justice and truth are inextricably linked; some concept of what actually happened, or approximating the truth, is necessary when we attempt to expose an injustice. For example, if there was no attempt to get to the truth, a person wrongfully charged with sedition may be held in custody when they should have been released. In this case both what actually happened, and our values (what knowledge is valued and our sense of justice), are important. I therefore conclude that getting closer to what happened, approximating the truth (verisimilitude) or the best explanation for what happened are indispensable for cross-cultural understanding.

Thus in one sense, this chapter has not lived up to its potential—although, from the start, some of my readers may have thought my attempt to find in science a neutral, independent language was fraught with difficulties, if not futile. Western science seems to be an obstacle to cross-cultural understanding which has been used to justify the superiority of its theory of knowledge and its research findings. Our next chapter examines the view of post-modernists who are also wary about truth claims which become politically absolutist, totalising meta-narratives.

4

Can postmodernism facilitate cross-cultural understanding?

Introduction

The collection of theories known as postmodernism has been extremely influential, at least in the literary and academic world. Arguably, while originating in France, and largely in art and literary thought, the flames of the postmodernist fire have spread to the social sciences, including anthropology, cultural studies, political science and sociology. Superficially, at least, there would seem to be much in the postmodernist arsenal which would contribute to cross-cultural understanding—and so I will argue.

Postmodernists are known for their critique of the absolute stands taken, for example, by ethnocentrism (E_1); they have deconstructed even the most liberal, open, progressive and tolerant movements which are taken for granted; and they seem to espouse values which would enhance cross-cultural understanding, such as appreciating diversity and celebrating difference. They have emphasised the importance of cultural filters. In this chapter I will deal with such attempts and argue that, despite several useful concepts, there is also a tendency for postmodernism to be a loose canon which rebounds on itself. In so doing, I find the postmodernist enterprise wanting in some important areas of cross-cultural understanding, yet it offers some important steps as we approach it.

From the outset there are several noteworthy points to make about postmodernism. The first is that post-modernism is not a monolithic movement. There are many variations on the postmodernist theme. There are as many theories as there are theorists and, given that post-modernism generally espouses the avoidance of, and even condemns, generalisations as politically absolutist representations, there is a sense in which I cannot generalise about postmodernism without nailing my colours to the wall. Even generalising, that is, writing about trends for which there may be exceptions, is to swim against the postmodernist tide.

The second point is a question: if postmodernism has many voices, from which will I choose to form the basis of my generalisation? Pauline Marie Rosenau's distinction between affirmative and sceptical postmodernism is an oft-cited and helpful distinction in this context.[1] The affirmative postmodernists are inclined to be more optimistic about the future, they are not necessarily unhopeful about political change, and while most are 'non-dogmatic, tentative and non-ideological' they 'do not, however, shy away from affirming an ethic, making normative choices, and striving to build issue specific political coalitions'.[2]

The sceptical postmodernists claim that the destructive powers of modernity are so powerful and overwhelming that they do not envisage any hope for the future. They are impressed with the dark and gloomy side of modernity which, in its destruction, causes 'fragmentation, disintegration, malaise, meaninglessness, a vague-

---

1.   Pauline Marie Rosenau, *Post-Modernism and the Social Sciences: Insights, Inroads, and Intrusions* (Princeton, New Jersey: Princeton University Press, 1992), 14–17.
2.   Rosenau, *Post-Modernism and the Social Sciences*, 16.

ness or absence of moral parameters and social chaos'.[3] Rosenau also argued that there are any number of permutations in and between the two versions she has distinguished, from 'extreme to moderate'.[4]

While Rosenau's distinction is helpful, her book also provides an example of the presence of similar themes in both variations. For example, both respond to texts, to the modern subject and to notions of truth. They differ in their reactions to such themes but, if there is dissimilarity and diversity in their reactions, there is some common ground on the issues of modernity to which they are responding, including the role of the disengaged, independent self or person in modernity and the connection between truth and power.[5] In the following, I investigate these and similar themes by using Lawrence Cahoone's summary of postmodernism.[6] There are several reason for this. The first is that Cahoone's Introduction is sympathetic to postmodernism. Secondly, it nicely summarises the issues so that, even if not all postmodernists would identify with Cahoone's description, they would probably agree that the issues raised are important to them. However, before we start, let us consider the transition from modernism to postmodernism.

3.   Rosenau, *Post-Modernism and the Social Sciences*, 15.
4.   Rosenau, *Post-Modernism and the Social Sciences*, 16.
5.   On the latter see Michel Foucault, 'Truth and Power', in *The Foucault Reader: An Introduction to Foucault's Thought*, edited by Paul Rabinow (Harmondsworth: Penguin, 1991), 51–75.
6.   Lawrence Cahoone, *From Modernism to Postmodernism: An Anthology* (Malden, Massachusetts: Blackwell, 1996).

Modernism and postmodernism

The Enlightenment and the industrial revolution increased confidence that the living conditions of human beings could be improved by technology. It was hoped that the application of science and the attendant new inventions would transform the way humans lived and worked, and lead to the betterment of life. Associated with this view was an increasing confidence in scientific knowledge. This does not only refer to scientific discoveries as such, but the type of knowledge that was used in science and produced by it (previously called the scientific theory of knowledge or scientific epistemology). As we have seen, this belief in the scientific method of hypothesising and testing is usually known as positivism. Empiricism was another part of this scientific theory of knowledge. This view insists that only things which are amenable to sensory perception can be the subject of definite knowledge. Consequently, the methods of science generated knowledge which was considered accurate, certain and secure. From the combination of the new technological discoveries such as electricity, and the knowledge used in science and gained from it, belief in progress developed and with it belief that living conditions would improve.

To some extent, even the First World War did not dent the confident spirit of progress popular in the West. It was, after all, regarded as the war to end all wars. However, by the Second World War, belief in progress was under question following the use of technology in the gas chambers, the increasing use and destructiveness of weapons, and the technological developments leading to the atomic bombs that were dropped on Hiroshima and Nagasaki in August 1945. Despite these concerns, at least in the West there was great interest in the space program and in the nuclear arms race that characterised the Cold War.

Other factors which questioned the progress of modernism also emerged. Malnutrition in large proportions of the world's population, the extent of poverty in otherwise rich and developed nations (such as the United States and Australia) and environmental concerns (such as pollution, the greenhouse effect and the emission of ozone-depleting gases, and the dangerous meltdown and consequent leakage of radioactivity in nuclear power stations), to name just a few, damaged confidence in science, technology and progress. The decline of confidence led, among other things, to the diagnosis that optimism had been undermined to such an extent that a new period had emerged, the postmodern era.

The postmodern era

Early in one of the first and most influential statements of postmodernism *The Postmodern Condition: A Report on Knowledge,* we find this rather enigmatic statement: 'Simplifying to the extreme, I define *postmodern* as incredulity toward metanarratives'.[7] What does a disbelief in metanarratives mean? What is a meta-narrative? One of the features of modernism which most disturbs the postmodernist is the power and force of stories (the narrative) which are all encompassing, or which are so dominant or ubiquitous that they are used to control, justify or legitimate. The metanarrative might be an explanation which has become so widely used or popular that it is no longer questioned, or a cultural perspective which is so widespread that it becomes the basis of everyday action. Ideas such as progress, freedom, justice and scientific knowledge come into this category.

---

7.   Jean-Francois Lyotard, *The Postmodern Condition: A Report on Knowledge* (Minneapolis: University of Minnesota Press, 1984), xxiv.

When the postmodernists refer to metanarratives they might be referring to something as specific as a political view that is not questioned, or taken for granted. Liberalism, democracy, capitalism, fascism, Leninism and Stalinism exemplify the metanarrative. A metanarrative, the big socially accepted and validated story, might justify a country's decision to limit its intake of migrants because they will (according to this view) be a drain on the economy. The metanarrative might involve stories about how and why things happened in the past, including the dominant stories of the powerful majority about how a country was colonised, why a country went to war, the stories of valour and glory which tend to valorise the dominant group and devalue indigenous or minority views. The varied but racist, ethnocentric and xenophobic stories of the past in Australia, Canada and the United States, which eulogise the experience of the white colonisers, and depreciate or ignore the stories of indigenous people, exemplify the sort of metanarrative to which the postmodernists (and I) would object.

However, the word metanarrative also refers to broader views such as what counts as knowledge and why. So the grand narrative of science is also an example of a metanarrative. For example, social Darwinism, the application of Darwin's theory of natural selection, or the use of cultural variations in intelligence scores in order to restrict or exclude migrants from certain countries, would also be considered metanarratives.

Metanarratives also include the very beliefs and values on which a society or culture is built. One such belief is scientific knowledge itself. Here the issue is not so much the technology which ensues from science (although that is not exempt from becoming a metanarrative), but the dominant view that science can discover truth which is objective and valid for all time. If it is not scientific knowledge, it is not regarded as socially valid knowledge in most western cultures. If a view or perspective is not scientifically verifiable, it is not the truth. Any claim to truth would be a metanarrative.

Postmodernists often use the word privilege to express their objections to metanarratives. The problem is that scientific knowledge is privileged in the sense that it is elevated to become the standard by which all other knowledge claims are assessed. This privileging is what the metanarrative does. It arrogates to itself a general, universal and total claim which is questioned by postmodernists. For postmodernists, claims to truth that are regarded culturally or socially as the truth or right are totalising, and any repression and oppression that follows from this they find problematic. In other words, from the view that it is possible to derive the truth there arises political absolutism that is totalising in the sense of being authoritarian and tyrannical. The argument is that if cultural or social groups claim they possess the truth, they will want to foist their version of it on those whom they believe do not share it.

For at least some postmodernists, it is not only that truth is impossible to attain, it is also that there is no one reality in which the truth is to be found. What appears real is merely a fabrication, a fiction, a fantasy; what appears total is only the denial of the variegated nature of what is constructed as real. In this way there is a similarity between the way postmodernists object to the notion of truth and the way a text is interpreted. Just as there is no absolute or total truth which reads the physical or the social world, so there is no one authoritative and valid interpretation of a text. In the modern past the author of a text was privileged in the sense that it was thought that there was a principle message which the reader sought or should seek; in postmodernism it is the reader who can be privileged in the sense that the reader has the opportunity to interpret, to assign meaning to the text. In this way a text is mediated by the reader, there is a diversity, even an uncertainty, of meaning which is celebrated.

However, the text is not exclusively the written word. The text could also be an event. More accurately, an event is a text in that it is a story which could be experienced, told, narrated. In this way, an event could be anything from an international incident or flashpoint, to more mundane things such a football match. The story, the small, local narrative, the instance, is entirely different from the grand or metanarratives repudiated by post-modernism. The text and the incident are open to inter-pretation; in the mediation of the story there will be a variety of renditions. Plurality, diversity and multiplicity result and all possibilities are valued, perhaps even considered valid. In this, however, it seems that it is the reader and the listener, not the author or storyteller, who is valorised and whose interpretation is privileged.

Contrary to the metanarrative with its one voice, the many perspectives from which a text can be interpreted allow the texts to speak with diverse voices and from many perspectives. The result is the realisation for the postmodernist that what may have been considered a metanarrative is fractured and fragmented. In place of metanarratives there is, thus, a vast array of competing, contradictory perspectives which not only defy and belie the metanarrative but enrich it and are a cause for celebration. It is this diversity which is the reason post-modernism tends to eschew the pictures and portrayals of the metanarratives which universalise.

In summary, whenever metanarratives are represented, they are re-presented in ways which accord with them. The representations reinforce and confirm the absolutist and totalising portrayal which, when heard or read as texts and interpreted by privileged readers, are consistent with the metanarrative, or even integral to it. In reality, however, for postmodernism, stories and experiences are fragmented, fractured and characterised by diversity.

If postmodernism seems to undermine metanarratives and valorise the isolated text and reader, it may be anticipated that it would elevate the individual, that its position enhances the status of the discrete person, that it dignifies the subject. However, it is not that straightforward since the subject includes the social construction of the consumer self, and the obsessive individualism[8] with which one is besieged during elections and in advertising commercials. It is to the subject that the media appeals when (re)presenting metanarratives about social problems and their causes, or hysteria about the increase in crime, the demand to increase penalties, and the demand for an increasingly punitive society. It is this wooing of individuals as if they are independent when they are not, it is this feting of individuals as if they are autonomous when they are treated as automatons, which exemplifies the post-modernist concern with the subject. Consequently, for the postmodernist the subject is not the disengaged, rational self often projected as the norm.

Postmodernism and cross-cultural understanding

As such, postmodernism gives cross-cultural understanding some important analytical tools. As postmodernists have emphasised cultural filtering, challenged dominant metanarratives, identified and privileged small narratives, questioned absolute truth claims, detected the link between what counts as truth and power, questioned taken-for-granted binaries such as object/subject and criticised the related notion of the independent, disengaged subject, they can make, and have made, a

---

8. For an interesting, although not necessarily postmodernist, account of individualism see Anthony Elliott and Charles Lemert, *The New Individualism: The Emotional Costs of Globalization* (London: Routledge, 2006).

contribution to understanding other cultures. Even critics of postmodernism have acknowledged this point. For example, Ben Agger commented that the 'most politically engaged version of American postmodernism is multiculturalism'.[9] In other words, postmodernists have supported multicultural policies. In the following, I highlight five more characteristics of postmodernism sympathetic to postmodernism and, where relevant, relate them to cross-cultural understanding.

Presence and representation

Lawrence Cahoone suggested that typically there are five objects of postmodernist criticism. The first is the criticism of 'presence or *representation*'.[10] We have seen how representations are indicative of a metanarrative. The postmodernist, however, also draws our attention to the possibility that many of the representations of our culture, and others, and the connection between them, are part of a totalising metanarrative. Our understandings, including those of our relations to other cultures, are never independent; they come to our attention through being mediated by our cultural language and symbols. There are no true presentations and there are only re-presentations. If alternative representations could challenge the existing metanarratives associated with misunderstanding, namely, ethnocentrism and racism, then cross-cultural understanding may be enhanced. For example, if postmodernism could expose the social mechanisms by which a particular negative or pejorative image of a certain social group is constructed and conveyed, then

9. Ben Agger, *Critical Social Theories: An Introduction* (Boulder, Colorado: Westview Press, 1998), 69.
10. For this point and the remaining four, I rely on Cahoone, *From Modernism to Postmodernism*, 14–17.

that could be a step in the direction of understanding another culture.

Origins

The second perspective to which postmodernism provides an alternative is the alleged modernist preoccupation with ascertaining the origins of an idea or cultural practice. As Cahoone stated, postmodernism 'denies the possibility of returning to, recapturing, or even representing the origin, source, or deeper reality behind phenomena, and casts doubt on or even denies its existence'.[11] There is nothing that is authoritative, and certainly nothing that is authoritative that can be revealed, by seeking the origins of the text. So, for example, an 'author's intentions are no more relevant to understanding the text than any other set of considerations; they are not the "origin" of the text and have no "privilege" over other factors'.[12]

Cahoone's point about origins does not mean that postmodernists are opposed to historical or in-depth analyses. The point about origins is that there is no underlying, hidden, arcane or mysterious reality which, if plumbed, will help explain the text, including the cultural text. The intentions of the authors of our cultural meta-narratives are no more authoritative than that of anybody else and should not be privileged. This is particularly true, according to Cahoone, in the case of socially constructed 'modern philosophies of the self (eg existentialism, psycho-analysis, phenomenology, even Marxism)'.[13]

---

11. Cahoone, *From Modernism to Postmodernism*, 15.
12. *Ibid.*
13. Cahoone, *From Modernism to Postmodernism*, 14.

A more tangible example relevant to cross-cultural understanding may be helpful. Modern thought usually emphasises the concept of human nature, the idea that there are intrinsic and innate rights or abilities with which we are born and which, in the modern era, have been used in political philosophy to derive and defend certain political rights (such as the freedom of the individual). Consider, for example, the idea of human nature that features, however differently, in the four modern philosophies of the self mentioned in the paragraph above. The postmodernist is less likely to see some metaphysical, pre-social or innate human trait, than to explore the social function of human nature and how it has been constructed.[14] The questions then become: What social function does the idea of human nature serve? How has it been used to dominate and oppress?

Undoubtedly, in cross-cultural relations the idea of human nature has proved destructive—or more accurately, the imposition of a privileged perspective about human nature has been destructive. This is particularly so in the sense that the dominant, white, western and patriarchal view of human nature has prevailed over alternative views, including those of other cultures. In this way, the view of human nature as possessing innate qualities from which certain rights follow has been used to legitimate and sanction patriarchal relations and defend and perpetrate the decimation of cultures with differing views of human nature. So in postmodernism the significant issue is not some putative underlying, original, authoritative, metaphysical reality of human nature, but about the social function which this concept serves. This is relevant to cross-cultural understanding because we can ask the same question about a whole range of issues including the following: what social

---

14. Paul Rabinow, 'Introduction', in *The Foucault Reader*, edited by Paul Rabinow (Harmondsworth: Penguin, 1991), 3–7.

function does white racism serve? what social function is served by policies which take indigenous children away from their parents? what social function is served when indigenous beliefs are ridiculed as legitimating what are regarded by the dominant groups as spurious land claims?

Unity

The next postmodern critique which Cahoone noted is that of unity.[15] Cahoone's point is that, where modernism adopted metanarratives, postmodernism privileged the little perspectives which have been ignored, drowned-out, belittled or discounted; where modernism saw unity, postmodernism sees plurality; where the modernist saw the whole, the postmodernist sees the parts; what the modernist aggregates into a constructed unity, the post-modernist disaggregates into diversity. In relation to cross-cultural understanding the fracturing of the socially constructed whole, the fragmenting of the unity, is a prerequisite for exposing dominant views. The implication is that it is only as the many stories are heard from different cultures, and within cultures, that experiences can be understood. It is only when what is regarded as one monolithic understanding of culture is shattered into its many facets that it will be possible to understand in any sense of the word.

Denial of transcendental norms

The fourth object of postmodern criticism is the modernist assertion that there are no timeless, universal and perennial norms and values.[16] For the postmodernist

---

15. Cahoone, *From Modernism to Postmodernism*, 15.
16. Cahoone, *From Modernism to Postmodernism*, 15-16.

there are no norms and values which are independent of, and beyond, a particular time and place. The postmodernist denies the idea of transcendent norms and values. This would seem to be of great assistance to cross-cultural understanding. After all, ethnocentrism invokes transcendental values like God, or truth, or goodness, or natural rights which are, according to postmodernism, bound by time and place.

In postmodernism, the claims made by ethnocentrism can be shown to depend on a particular culture or epoch; they are not independent. Thus, if a person claims that a cultural practice or skin colour is inferior to their own they are invoking standards which have no transcendental or universal validity. Such values are time and culture bound, despite claims to the contrary. The denial of timeless and universal norms and values shakes the foundations of the ethnocentrist's appeal to transcendental values. In that, the cause of cross-cultural understanding would appear to be advanced.

Constituted otherness

Finally, postmodernism is more than the denial of presence, origin, unity and transcendence. It adopts a method of analysis; it uses the method that Cahoone described as 'constitutive otherness'. He wrote:

> What appear to be cultural units—human beings, words, meanings, ideas, philosophical systems, social organizations—are maintained in their apparent unity only through an active process of exclusion, opposition, and hierarchization. Other phenomena or units must be represented as foreign or 'other' through representing a hierarchical dualism

in which the unit is 'privileged' or favored,
and the other is devalued in some way.[17]

In other words, there is a connection between cultural units that are regarded as absolute or are totalising, and 'the others' or 'the other'. How? Because for one to be regarded as superior another must be inferior, for one to be included in the dominant perspective others must be excluded, for one to be at the top of the hierarchy another must be relegated to lower places, for one to be accepted others must be rejected.

There are many examples of constituted otherness. For example, the wealthy maintain their privilege by representing themselves as devoid of the qualities which constitute the poor others. The wealthy are hardworking and thrifty while the poor are portrayed as indigent spendthrifts. Employers and business organisations extol the virtues of free enterprise and how it has worked for them, while portraying employee groups and trade unions as hostile to free enterprise, even though both may be in favour of reforming capitalism rather than being totally opposed to it. Business organisations and free enterprise groups represent themselves as being involved in the generation and distribution of wealth which will inevitably filter down, and berate those who are not appreciative when it is distributed unevenly. I am not attributing such views to postmodernists, but they do exemplify the use of the notion of the constitutive other—the privileging of certain perspectives over others, as indicated by the inclusion of some and the exclusion of others.

This method of analysis is also useful for understanding cross-cultural relations. For example, racists try to portray themselves as open and tolerant while ethnic

---

17. Cahoone, *From Modernism to Postmodernism*, 16.

groups are presented as divisive. Some opponents of multiculturalism present themselves as advocating equality while policies for indigenous people are por-trayed as perpetuating inequality, as discriminating against the majority. Some powerful groups and political parties portray their policies as inclusive, while denying that they exclude cultural and other minority groups. Colonisers and their descendants may portray their actions as justified violence, while any resistance by the colonised, no matter how small and unsuccessful, is represented as unjustified violence and militancy. There are many other examples of social distortions but the above will suffice.

Constitutive otherness is also significant because it is one of the reasons that postmodernists criticise and attempt to overcome popular and powerful dichotomies or dualisms (which are also known as binaries such as right/wrong, good/bad, objective/subjective, fact/value, reason/faith). This usually involves the socially approved appreciation of one side of the dichotomy or dualism, and the depreciation of the other side. For example, in the distinction between the objective and subjective in western culture, the valorising of what is considered objective includes the privileging of certain forms of knowledge which are socially constructed as superior. These privileged forms are absent in the subjective knowledge of the 'other'. Another example is the popular view that only that which can be seen is true (seeing is believing). This empiricism by its inclusion of sensory data excludes all other forms of knowledge. In this way subjective knowledge, knowledge about ourselves, religious knowledge and the beliefs, stories and cultural practices of other cultures, are represented as the inferior other.

Thus, regardless of which dualism is used, there is inclusion and exclusion, there is valorising and discounting, appreciating and depreciating, privileging and devaluing, and self-justification and denunciation of 'the other'. The political consequences of this are profound. For inclusion is a political act; excluding the other can only be done by groups which have the power to do it. It means asserting one view as superior, and its alternative as inferior. Culturally this does not merely happen by coincidence or chance, or by the survival of the fittest ideas in a social form of natural selection which should be accepted because it is natural or right.

In this process, one side of a dualism is socially privileged as another is, to varying degrees, repudiated. When a dualism is activated in social and cultural contexts it means that there are oppressors and the oppressed; it means there are repressors and those who are repressed. It means this process is dictated by those who are more powerful. Whether the dualism is male/female, employer/employee heterosexual/homo-sexual, White/Black, First World/Third Word, urban/rural, literate/preliterate, post-industrial/pre-industrial, Eurocentric/Afrocentric, or the colonialist's pers-pective/the colonised's perspective, the second is marginalised by the power of the first. The binaries may masquerade as innocuous descriptions, but I would argue that they are actually the result of powerful social mechanisms which allocate social favour to the first part of the binary and discredit the second.

One might argue that our preferences or leanings are choices we should make as individuals. However, most sociologists would argue—and here postmodernists would agree—that social priorities are not only socially constructed but involve the social selection of one side of a dualism over the other. If one is selected others are omitted; if one is included others are excluded. There is a powerful social and political process through which this selection occurs; there is nothing natural about it (despite appearances to the contrary). We might learn that the process of selection and omission, inclusion and exclusion, are as natural as the river or the tree which was always just there. Closer analysis, however, reveals that such social things are not accidents of time or place, but that inclusion necessitates exclusion, selection presupposes omission, and that social and political mechanisms which involve power and those who wield it are operating. Identifying or exposing such social processes of construction is sometimes known as deconstruction.

Postmodernism: summary

It would seem then that postmodernism has the potential to offer a great deal to cross-cultural understanding. The critique of the metanarrative, of the total and absolute forms of knowledge, the emphasis that such knowledge is not independent but conditional on social processes of inclusion and exclusion which are represented in ways which support the dominant and powerful, have paved the way for greater recognition of cultural diversity. After all, in seeing the plural where others emphasise the singular, by emphasising diversity where others see a much vaunted and prized unity, postmodernists would seem to be advocating the recognition of cultural differences. They seem to give expression to the misperception of other cultures by the dominant culture. They seem to include what others have excluded. Highlighting such social practices, and then deconstructing them, could enhance cross-cultural understanding.

Furthermore, by emphasising that there are no origins other than those which are socially constructed, and that there are no transcendent values, postmodernists have swept away the norms and standards used with such force (if not violence) by the political absolutists (defined as those who impose their will on others), including those who are committed to ethnocentrism and racism. The emphasis on fragmentation and fracture instead of on the social monolith, on diversity rather than on imposed unity, on pluralism instead of political absolutism is a much needed starting point for recognising cultural differences that is required for cross-cultural understanding.

Postmodernism: several comments

Postmodernism and action

The idea of the constituted otherness alerts us to the privileged and the repressed parts of a story, a narrative. As Cahoone noted:

> Once we become aware of the constitutive otherness in the text, we see that the text itself, despite its own intentions, alerts us to the dependence of the privileged theme on the marginalised element. The repressed eventually returns to haunt us.[18]

In a narrative it is possible to descry the way in which the included, privileged and selected account depends on the parts of the story that have been excluded or repressed. However, postmodernists do not always draw the same conclusions from this aspect of their position. Cahoone noted this as he continued from the quotation above:

> Social disenfranchisement, marginalisation of sexual and radical groups, is the moral and political case of this pattern [of exclusion or repression]. Some postmodernists wish to remove such repression, while others, seeing in that wish a longing for an impossible

---

18. Cahoone, *From Modernism to Postmodernism*, 17.

authenticity, admit there is no escape from repression and hope only to render repressive forces more diverse and fluid, so that none becomes more monopolistic and hence excessively onerous.[19]

Consider firstly the second group of postmodernists identified by Cahoone, namely those who admit there is no escape from repression.[20] The seeming fatalism and pessimism here is in stark contrast to the postmodernist enthusiasm for their position overall and the manner in which they derive it. If it is possible to deconstruct the social constructions, to see through the tangle of power and knowledge, to do all the postmodernists claim to be able to do, it is difficult to comprehend why the same forces could not be put to undermining repression rather than making it more 'diverse and fluid'. However, evidently this is impossible for some postmodernists because to remove oppression is to advance 'an impossible authenticity'.

In the postmodernist literature, authenticity is challenged because it necessitates a consistent, coherent, logical, plausible and rational approach. Such consistency is reproached as being merely 'logocentric'; a rational approach which, *inter alia*, carefully calculates the most efficient means or method to achieve an end or goal is symptomatic of the very modern notion of self and the social which the postmodernists abjure. Authenticity is then impossible for them because it has all the hallmarks of modernity. So the idea of removing repression is surrendered.

---

19. Cahoone, *From Modernism to Postmodernism*, 17.
20. The distinction Cahoone made between those postmodernists who wish to address repression and those who claim there is no hope is similar to the one Rosenau made between the affirmative and sceptical postmodernists.

In response to this, one is tempted to ask if consistency, logic, plausibility and rationality are inadequate to the task, would their opposites help? Would an inconsistent, illogical, implausible and irrational approach be of any benefit? To this the postmodernist might respond by saying: 'That is the very problem. The social criteria for authenticity are totally inadequate; it is the cause of much of the problem with modernity'. The socially constructed criteria for what is here called authenticity, a consistent, coherent, logical, plausible and rational approach, could be considered to have been hijacked by the powerful. But does it have to be that way? Are there other criteria which might expose such repression? Are there other criteria which could become an essential analytical tool to remove repressive forces?

Thus we can agree with postmodernists and others that the criteria for the social construction of authenticity are fraught with difficulties because they buttress the modern repressive project. But that does not eliminate altogether the possibility of other standards which counter, expose and undermine such criteria. This is precisely what the postmodernists are chary about, namely criteria which might merit our recognition and allegiance as true or right or correct. Of course, that is what they allow for themselves; postmodernists of this ilk speak as if their diagnosis and position is true, right and correct, while denying the same status to other positions. The point here is that some postmodernists can criticise and diagnose but their very position seems to render them inert, stalled and stymied. We will consider this again later, but for the moment the point is that they advocate an approach based on the impossibility of attempting to eliminate repression while their alternative is to 'render repressive forces more diverse and fluid, so that none becomes more monopolistic and hence excessively onerous'.

This approach to politics and power is also difficult to follow; more seriously it has some of the features of philosophical quietism, appeasement and tinkering on the edges of oppressive power. Apart from anything else, the language defies the usual meaning of words. What does 'to render repressive forces more diverse and fluid' mean? Repressive forces can be diverse and fluid (arguably even made to become more diverse and fluid). Repressive forces seem to be able to camouflage themselves in many ways. Nonetheless, repressive forces are always repressive, as any number of historical examples attest (for example Nazi Germany, Stalinist Soviet Union). It is seems incredible that anyone who has lived in the last half of the twentieth century could believe that making repressive forces more diverse and fluid, 'so that none becomes more monopolistic', would prevent them from becoming 'excessively onerous'.

Furthermore, the position does not deal with what we might call the causes of the monopolisation of power. The problem here is that in order to achieve their ends in the competitive jostling for power, individual power groups may combine to form power blocs. There are many examples of this which, in turn, have led governments to introduce anti-trust or anti-monopoly legislation and create regulatory authorities with the power to penalise those agencies which collude (to set prices). This is also a reason for ensuring that legislation deregulates and casts previous government monopolies to the forces of the market, and to attempt to protect consumers by legislating for a minimum number of competitors.

With such an inadequate notion of power and how it operates, it seems that postmodernism cannot tackle the very forces which construct the constituted other, the very forces which render united that which it sees as fragmented, which render as a totality that which it sees as fractured. It fails to recognise that repressive forces are constitutionally incapable of allowing opposition, and that they tend to forge alliances with other repressive forces.

The time has come to consider the other group of postmodernists Cahoone identified, namely, those who advocate the removal of repression. While agreeing with the intention, one wonders on what grounds post-modernists would defend such an objective, because as noted previously, any value position which might be involved is apparently rejected. If there are no such things as transcendental values such as truth and rationality, how can there be such transcendental values such as justice and freedom on which we depend to expose repression?

The point here is about values. If there are no transcen-dental values how, and on what basis, do we decide that justice is preferable to injustice, freedom to repression? How do we decide between different forms of justice (for example, western or non-western)? It might be argued that transcendental values are not being invoked by post-modernism here, that the values by which repression is determined are culture-bound. That would be consistent with the postmodernist claim about transcendental values, but it does not overcome the problem of how we can detect repression outside our own culture and society.

It is also relevant here to recall a postmodernist aim to identify the other in the distorted representations. But if the constituted other (say from another culture) is repressed, how can this repression be detected by post-modernists without some notion of what constitutes repression and non-repression, freedom and justice, notions which transcend their culture? Without the criteria which can establish such values we would seem to be locked into a cultural prison, so rendering us incapable of making a diagnosis. Thus, the second group of postmodernists to whom Cahoone referred seem to deny what is required of their position; they criticise absolute or transcendental values as politically absolutist and totalising, yet such values seem to be essential to their own diagnosis and prescription. Moreover, to add to the tension, such values are invoked by default when they identify the repressed and constituted other.

A fundamental tension in postmodernism

This leads to the criticism that postmodernism seems to allow and arrogate to itself what it denies and disallows of everyone else. In particular, postmodernism denies the existence of transcendental, absolute values when they are used by others. Yet they invoke such values in their own diagnosis of repression and injustice (by necessity in my view). It might be countered that postmodernism does this in a more modest way, cognisant of the dangers of positions which are totalising. However, this does not change the way it operates and raises the question of whether it is any less culture-bound, limited and totalising than any other perspective.

It also raises the question of whether postmodernism is a metanarrative. It will be recalled that the metanarratives of modernity are particularly odious and reprehensible to postmodernists, largely because they result in political absolutism, they are authoritarian and totalising or, we might say, totalitarian. Metanarratives are, thus, inherently political devices; they exclude and repress the smaller narratives, or the narratives of minority or less powerful groups. Many who would be labelled modernists would agree with this postmodernist diagnosis—as I do. Nonetheless, does its own diagnosis, do postmodernism's own explanations and criticisms, resemble totalising metanarratives? Does postmodernism have the features of a metanarrative?

The evidence suggests that postmodernism can operate like a metanarrative. It does diagnose, criticise and explain in ways that are seemingly all-encompassing. The diagnosis might differ but the nature of the diagnosis, criticism and explanation would seem to possess all the characteristics of a metanarrative. The metanarrative might be that the extent of human difference, the multiplicities, has been repressed, but that does not change the all-encompassing, universal and hence, seemingly metanarrative quality of the claim.

I have a mixed reaction to my conclusion that postmodernism is a metanarrative while simultaneously condemning the metanarratives of modernism. One reaction is that it is inevitable. Diagnosing, criticising and explaining demand generalisations, which I define as trends to which there may be exceptions. Conclusions are summaries of discerned trends. Even if the diagnosis is the identification of a trend where modernity has homogenised heterogeneity, reduced the multiplicities of human activity, expression, practice and thought to one dimension, to a monolith, that remains an overall, encompassing observation—and one for which credible evidence can be adduced. My other reaction is that if postmodernists were to be reflexive about their position they may conclude that it has the potential to be a metanarrative.

The argument here is not merely about inconsistency, although the postmodernism which I have adapted from Cahoone does seem to criticise others for adopting a transcending and totalising view when they seem to have one of their own. However, as valid as that objection is, it is only part of the point I am making here, which is one of power and the exercise of power. If the postmodernists arrogate to themselves a position which they regard as accurate, when they claim that others are not only inaccurate, but that it is also impossible to be accurate, then they are exempting themselves from the criteria and standards of criticisms they impose on others. More than inconsistency is at stake here since, according to their own standards, a view which claims to be overarching is totalising in the sense of being politically absolutist.

Yet, paradoxically, postmodernism has been used to defend multiculturalism. This has been noted by those who have distanced themselves from postmodernism. For example, Ben Agger claimed that 'postmodern difference theory underpins what is typically called multi-culturalism'.[21] By multiculturalism, Agger meant 'the academic and curricular manifestation of certain key postmodern tenets regarding narrativity, new social movements and the trinity of class/race/gender'.[22] Post-modern multiculturalism of this variety maintains that class is not the only way in which exploitation occurs. Race and gender also feature. Clearly they do. Undoub-tedly, evidence can be adduced that people with a different skin colour from the most powerful group, experience economic and social discrimination and exploitation simply because of their skin colour. Likewise, women, in addition to their class position, are dis-criminated against and exploited because they are women.

However, according to Agger, postmodern multi-culturalists are disinclined to the suggestion that class, race and gender are linked to broader structures of op-pression. Instead, they prefer to regard them as 'aspects of identity that influence ("inflect") experience, which can then be narrated by the person who occupies that particular subject position'.[23] Such narratives tell of individual experiences and personal characteristics (such as income, education achieved and employment) which are often the variables sociologists use to explore social issues.

---

21. Agger, *Critical Social Theories*, 56.
22. Agger, *Critical Social Theories*, 56.
23. Agger, *Critical Social Theories*, 71.

However, rather than linking such variables and personal experience of inequality to broader social categories such as class, race and ethnicity, and the social institutions which legitimate and adversely affect their position, Agger argues that postmodern multiculturalists tend to emphasise the experience and the narrative. They retain class, race and gender as separate entities because if one or all are elevated to provide an all embracing explanation, the narrative is lost in the totalising generalisation (of class, race or gender). Agger explained that his:

> argument against postmodernism multi-culturalism is that class, race and gender are typically treated not only as analytically separate but that this analytical separation underlies an identity politics necessarily fragmenting the working class, people of colour and women into separate and even competing interest groups. This produces a neoliberal agenda that leaves the large structures of our society intact but simply attempts to improve the lots of individuals within these various multicultural factions.[24]

Agger does not deny the importance of policies and programs which improve the conditions of different groups (such as affirmative action programs). His argument is that to refuse to address the broader structural issues while emphasising narratives is consistent with, and supportive of, a political agenda which deflects and diverts attention from the broader structural issues. In this way, postmodernism may not be inherently right or left, conservative or radical, but the implications of the position may defend an obsessive and

---

24. Agger, *Critical Social Theories*, 101.

possessive individualism in liberal democracies without tackling the underlying structural causes of the problem it identifies.

Concluding comments

Despite the shortcomings identifiable in postmodernism, in this chapter I have been alert to the promises it holds for cross-cultural understanding. I have noted its accent on difference, and the emphasis on the sheer multiplicity of actions, beliefs, expectations and values against the metanarratives which, in turn, convert social diversity into homogeneity which is absolute and totalising. This is a salient observation and a diagnosis shared by other political and social theorists, several of whom we meet in forthcoming chapters.

The notion of the constituted other was also invoked as a probing analytical device. The constituted other is the voice repressed or excluded. It a significant concept because it provides a method for identifying those whose voice is excluded from every narrative. Stories are not merely told; their content is selected. As it provides an opportunity to challenge what we have heard, to ask questions about whose story we have heard and what has been included (and why), and whose story has been excluded (and why), the concept of the constituted other is indispensable to cross-cultural understanding. It certainly challenges the stories we have heard, the perceptions we have learnt, our socialisation. Further, it facilitates an awareness that even as we approach under-standing there may be powerful cultural stories which limit our entrée into cross-cultural understanding. If understanding is hearing the stories of our cultural inter-locutors as they would like them to be heard and under-stood, then a prerequisite for cross-cultural under-standing is that our version of their story should be challenged. What has been excluded in our account of their story should be included.

Without undermining the importance of its diagnosis, the emphasis on diversity, the critique of metanarratives and the recognition of excluded others, the other observation I make in this chapter is that postmodernism does not realise its potential to approach cross-cultural understanding. The explanation for this is that it rejects the possibility of some of the preconditions of such understanding. Without being able to defend values there would appear to be little justification for an empathetic approach, or for the values which would attract us to such understanding in the first place. The postmodernist accent on pluralism may have exposed the diversity repressed in modernism, but at the cost of defending it. Despite the fact that it denounces the one-dimensional nature of the metanarratives, postmodernism seems hamstrung because it avoids at all costs the suggestion that there may be values which are sufficiently robust to form the basis for such criticism.

In a nutshell, postmodernism condemns meta-narratives, but recoils from stating the value position on which such condemnation rests; it is coy about the values with which a narrative might be defended and alter-natives justified. This leaves it open to the criticism that, bereft of stated values, postmodernism is incon-sistent, at least, and capricious at worst. Further, its opposition to ascertaining origins and representation also evokes criticism of its rejection of the existence of a reality against which actions can be measured. The position is reminis-cent of the breakdown of the fact-value dichotomy. Not only is it impossible to arbitrate between values, it is impossible to arbitrate between facts. This leads to the difficulties outlined in the previous chapter, namely, how can we determine acts of repression if the truth about such injustice is always elusive because there is no reality or truth to which we can appeal?

Critics of postmodernism may also be open to the charge that they are ignoring the differences among postmodernists, putting them into our procrustean bed. According to this criticism, making generalisations about them resembles the authoritarian metanarrative they reject. However, by rejecting the possibility that there are values which transcend cultures, but which repudiate tyranny and defend policy, which appreciate, celebrate and encourage diversity, they are stymied. Absolutism about values is always authoritarian for the postmodernist. For the postmodernists, relativism about values defends pluralism and values which seem to include what is commonly called tolerance. Absolutism about values imposes; relativism about values liberates.

This position is two sides of a coin with enormous currency in the social sciences, and in social and political theory. On one side of the coin the link between absolute values and repression is forged and on the other side the link between relativism in values and freedom and liberty is advanced. This coin exemplifies the main argument against political absolutism, on the one hand, and for relativism, on the other. It is one of the main arguments adduced to challenge oppression and advance crosscultural understanding, multiculturalism and tolerance. Its validity and viability will be examined in the next chapter.

Pauline Marie Rosenau's summary of postmodernism reflects some aspects of the analysis in this chapter:

> The post-modern view—there is no truth, and all is construction—is itself the ultimate contradiction. By making this statement postmodernists assume a position of privilege. They assert as true their own position that 'there is no truth'. In so doing they affirm the possibility of truth itself. Few postmodernists

escape the dilemma, but those who try (Derrida and Ashley are examples) relativize everything, including their own statements. They say even their own views are not privileged. They warn their readers that the views they express are only their own and not superior to the opinions of others. But even this relativist position, once stated positively, implicitly assumes truth. It assumes truth in the statement that what they are saying is not more veracious than any other position. There is no logical escape from this contradiction except to remain silent.[25]

In conclusion, postmodernism's contribution to cross-cultural understanding is its diagnoses of modernity which can, in turn, be regarded as step on the way to cross-cultural understanding. It emphasises diversity and the excluded other, exposes heterogeneity in the socially constructed homogeneity, and contributes to a helpful deconstruction of the dominant social explanations which are inimical to cross-cultural understanding. However, their suspicions of cross-cultural values seriously attenuate the possibility of cross-cultural understanding as U_1, U_2 and U_3. In other words, without a value position about why we should understand another culture (U_1), why we should be understanding (U_2), and the values associated with U_2 (U_3), understanding another culture is difficult, if not impossible. Thus I conclude that in diagnosing some of the barriers to understanding other cultures, postmodernism proffers some improvements, but it also has reinforced some old and new quandaries. In the next chapter we look at another one.

---

25. Rosenau, *Post-Modernism and the Social Sciences*, 90.

5

Do absolute objective values lead to political absolutism and intolerance? Does relativism lead to understanding and tolerance?

Introduction

The spectre of relativism has been raised in almost every chapter thus far. In Chapters 1 and 2, I introduced the view that there is a connection between the impossibility of claiming that one value is better than another or others, on the one hand, and democracy, tolerance and (at least by implication) multiculturalism, on the other. If we can't say one value is better than another, so the argument goes, then we should be accepting of them all; we should be tolerant, at least.

The other side of the relativist–tolerance link is the connection between value absolutism and intolerance and associated undemocratic and anti-liberal political values. Here the issue is the nexus between believing that it is possible to defend and justify values, and at the same time foist them on others. Again, if we can say that one value is better than another, we will want to impose our values on others.

In this chapter we examine this two-fold connection between value relativism and tolerance, and value absolutism and intolerance. In order to demonstrate that aspects of this connection are extremely powerful and popular—and why—it is useful to refer briefly to representative selections from the literature. After clarifying the terms, I discuss both sides of the relativist–absolutist coin and their alleged implications, paying particular attention to whether they can facilitate or imply cross-cultural understanding.

The conclusion drawn from the analysis in this chapter is straightforward, although it might seem rather protracted. This, in turn, is itself a consequence of the need to slowly deconstruct the dominant defence of tolerance and the values associated with multiculturalism, and defend the position which is usually regarded as opposed to tolerance, multiculturalism or cross-cultural understanding. My conclusion is this: what I call value relativism is constitutionally incapable of justifying tolerance, cross-cultural understanding, and multiculturalism. Despite the fact that it is usually thought to lead to intolerance, value absolutism has the potential to justify tolerance and cross-cultural understanding. So, the popular view cannot deliver; the unpopular view has the potential. That might be the conclusion, but how do we get there? It is helpful to return to two words mentioned previously although this time without the descriptive 'value'.

How the terms are often used

Let's begin with two seemingly straightforward terms, relativism and absolutism. If it seems that, compared with the previous chapters, we are travelling one step forward and two steps backwards, that I am retreating to simpler concepts and terms (relativism instead of value relativism) then you have detected my method. However, the terms we have used for other purposes, and with other connotations in previous chapters, now require fuller explication. Clarity is essential if we are ever to unload the freight of these loaded terms. To change the metaphor, if we are ever to deconstruct their meaning, we need to know how they were constructed in the first place. In this regard, one of the first things we notice is that relativism and absolutism are used in a plethora of ways; they have different meanings, connotations and implications.

Firstly, relativism is sometimes used as an alternative for a plurality, or diversity of cultural expressions (previously called descriptive relativism). Secondly, in Chapter 2 we discussed cultural relativism, a relativism between cultures arising from the belief that our cultural filters make it difficult to perceive, let alone understand, another culture. Thirdly, relativism is sometimes used to theorise about the physical and social world, concepts and cultures. In this sense, they are relative because there is no underlying neutral language, criterion or standard which can be used to compare or measure contrasting theories about the physical or social world, or concepts or cultures. There is nothing that builds a firm foundation from which we can compare various positions; there is no agreed standard of measurement.

The relativism which arises because there are no agreed standards can also be applied to ethics, morality, religious beliefs and values. Value relativism claims that we have no neutral language that we can use to judge values; there are no external standards by which we can measure or compare the validity of values. It is this position that is a prime concern in this chapter. Relativism is also used as a synonym for tolerance and multi-culturalism. If someone is a relativist in this sense they usually advocate tolerance, respect for others and may even celebrate diversity, heterogeneous beliefs, cultures and values. So there are many uses of the term although, as confusing as it sometimes is, the meaning can usually be discerned from the context.

For the purposes of this chapter I suggest that we put to one side descriptive relativism (that is, the sheer diversity of views) and concentrate on disentangling its other meanings and uses. To that end I would like to ask two questions. One is about the respective meanings of relativism; the other is about what is said to follow from the position.

The first question is: What is the essence of relativism? It is that, as in the third sense just mentioned, there are no neutral criteria or standards from which to judge different cultural and conventional perspectives. It is this lack of criteria and standards that is central to most forms of relativism (except those relating to the descriptions of diversity, which claim to only count the differences).[1] A number of beliefs are considered to be conventional or merely social constructions because there are no neutral, independent, context-free criteria or standards by which to evaluate them.

The second question is what are the consequences of this lack of neutral criteria? This is an important question and addressing it consumes most of the remainder of the chapter. One answer is that there is a profound implication which is drawn, irrespective of its validity or otherwise, and which is found in the relativism which advocates tolerance and multiculturalism. If we confine this implication to values, it seems to proceed using the following steps. The first is: because there are no independent criteria for our cultural perspectives and conventions, it is impossible to arbitrate between values. Therefore, secondly, if it is impossible to arbitrate between them it is impossible to claim that one value is preferable to another. The third step proceeds as follows: it is precisely because we cannot arbitrate between values that we should be tolerant and implement multicultural policies.

---

1. Although some would argue that if there are no agreed criteria to decide what an adequate or accurate description looks like, then this too bears the hallmarks of relativism in the third sense mentioned.

In a nutshell, there are so many values between which we cannot decide so, therefore, we should be tolerant of them all.

So far in this chapter I have outlined the essence of value relativism relevant to this book, and noted an implication that is drawn from it. It is also possible to analyse the opposite of value relativism, that is, value absolutism. Of particular interest are the political implications that each seems to contain: tolerance for value relativism; intolerance for value absolutism. However, I defer that analysis in favour of reinforcing some of the issues already discussed and clarifying some terms. I hope to show that there is more to such terms than meets the eye. Implicit in each are a set of assumptions; there are all sorts of issues tangled up in the way the terms are used. So explicating the implicit is the task; disentangling the connections, and the reasons for them, is the aim which, in turn, necessitates further clarification.

Further clarification of terms

Firstly, a point about alternative words or terms you may have encountered. There are other terms which seem almost synonyms for those I have chosen. For example, you may be wondering why I refer to values instead of ethics or morality. Sometimes these terms are used as adjectives to describe a type of relativism or absolutism. So there is ethical relativism or ethical absolutism, moral relativism or moral absolutism. However, we are concerned about values, and particularly those required to facilitate cross-cultural understanding. In a culture which may be loosely described as western, money and the acquisition of material possessions is a value. In addition, there are other things that are valued, such as means or methods for reaching a goal (for example, education, employment and income). There are also cherished political values that include the political institutions and process, and parliamentary democracy. But it is because of cross-cultural understanding that I emphasise values.

There may also be other terms you have seen which are used as substitutes for relativism and absolutism. Two are subjectivism and objectivism. For our purposes, subjectivism usually refers to the view that things like our ethical or moral standards, or values, are merely personal or private preferences. This is because reason cannot supply interpersonal or intersubjective criteria which could be used to set standards for ethics or morals. Objectivism claims that there are interpersonal or even extrapersonal, valid or objective standards which can be use to sort out claims about ethics, morality and values. According to ethical objectivism, it is possible to arbitrate between conflicting ethics, morals and values by using their objective standards.

So far so good; the twin set of opposites—objectivism/subjectivism, absolutism/relativism—have similar meanings. However, the risks of terminological confusion are increased when the terms are not used with their opposite. When this occurs, the distinction is usually drawn between relativism and objectivism (rather than relativism and absolutism). One reason that objectivism is preferred to absolutism is that, at least for some, the latter implies imposing one's views on others; it connotes intolerance rather than the theory of knowledge on which it is based. It is just this sort of conflating, of merging theories of knowledge and their alleged political implications that I am trying to disentangle. As what I am about to consider is usually known as value relativism, for consistency I will juxtapose it with value absolutism. I am sensitive to the possibility that my readers may confuse value absolutism with political absolutism, but this is precisely the conflation and the confusion that I am attempting to distinguish and clarify. Before that though, I will summarise the discussion thus far.

A summary and some examples

In the following I do not use relativism to refer to descriptive relativism or pluralism or diversity. Rather, it refers to the view expressed in Chapter 3 that it is impossible to arbitrate between competing and conflicting values. This position is usually defended on the grounds that there are no external, universally valid criteria which could be used to weigh up conflicting values. Value positions are like Kuhn's paradigms in abnormal or revolutionary science. Each value position may be internally coherent, self-justifying and self-validating. However, there are no external, universally recognised criteria for adjudicating between conflicting value positions. It is, therefore, impossible to rank them, or say which are preferable outside the culture in which they prevail. In short, it is impossible to arbitrate between conflicting values because no external, independent reasons can be given.

This inability to adjudicate between competing values is an implication of a perceived inadequacy of reason and reasons in value conflict. Others conclude similarly. For example, Charles Taylor mentioned what he called 'a rather facile relativism' in which '[e]verybody has his or her own "values" and about these it is impossible to argue'.[2] In the context of what she calls 'the abandonment of general social theory', Linda Nicholson noted that this 'only poses the possibility of relativism in so far as it is accompanied by the abandonment of the idea of a belief

---

2.   Charles Taylor, *The Ethics of Authenticity* (Cambridge, Massachusetts: Harvard University Press, 1991), 13.

in cross-cultural, mediating criteria of truth and validity'.[3] She continued: 'A plethora of claims about social life becomes problematic only when there are no means to decide among those which are in conflict'.[4] Value relativism, then, refers to the impossibility of arbitrating between competing values because there are no external, cross-cultural, neutral or independent standards which can be applied.

The position which is usually at odds with value relativism is value absolutism. I wish to emphasise that this could mean imposing values on others but I do not intend to use it in this way (as I repeatedly state later in this chapter). In popular parlance, and even in the social sciences, the term itself evokes thoughts of political absolutism, tyranny and totalitarian regimes. However, what the value absolutist claims is much more modest and has nothing to do with imposing one's views on others. The value absolutist claims that, at least in principle, there are criteria by which to arbitrate between conflicting values. They may be hard to find, but for the value absolutist there are methods for sorting and ranking opposing positions so that the values which are most important, and which merit allegiance, are discernible. So the value absolutist believes there are benchmarks or standards which give reasons as to why a particular form of justice is preferable to its opposite, or a society in which freedom is valued is preferable to a dictatorship.

In practice, of course, the value relativist may agree with the value absolutist about which form of justice is superior to another, or which form of freedom is preferable. The value relativist and the value absolutist

---

3.   Linda Nicholson, 'On the Postmodern Barricades: Feminism, Politics and Theory', in *Postmodernism and Social Theory: The Debate over General Theory*, edited by Steven Seidman and David G. Wagner (Oxford: Blackwell, 1992), 84–5.
4.   Nicholson, 'On the Postmodern Barricades', 84–5.

may both support tolerance, multiculturalism and pluralism. They may even be in the same or similar advocacy and support groups. The salient difference is that they have different reasons for their positions.

As we shall see, on the one hand, value relativists prefer pluralism because there is no method to arbitrate between competing values. They therefore conclude that tolerance is better than intolerance, and multiculturalism is preferable to ethnocentrism. Value absolutists in the sense used here often agree with value relativists about tolerance and multiculturalism but do so for different reasons: unlike value relativists they believe that it is possible to defend tolerance and multiculturalism against their opposites. It is the unsettling of such links between theories of knowledge about values (namely, value relativism and value absolutism) and the alleged political implications which follow (for example, tolerance) which is the topic of this chapter. It is to such issues that I now turn.

The relativist-tolerance nexus

That there is a link between relativism and tolerance and related values (such as multiculturalism) is easily demonstrated by the literature, although the formulations are sometimes different, disguised or even oblique. While disagreeing with the position, Craig Calhoun noted that: 'Relativism of some sort seems a necessary starting point in the project of taking difference seriously—and opening to new knowledge and understanding'.[5] In other words, relativism is linked to taking differences seriously. Again Calhoun noted: 'It is commonly assumed that the approach to cross-cultural understanding, the antidote to

---

5.   Craig Calhoun, *Critical Social Theory: Culture, History, and the Challenge of Difference* (Oxford: Blackwell, 1995), 73.

ethnocentrism, is simply to suspend judgment. This is sometimes made into the ground of a thoroughgoing relativism'.[6]

The point here is not so much about suspending judgment (which, as difficult as it is, would in some ways seem to be a pre-requisite for cross-cultural under-standing). I cited this quote because of the link Calhoun observed between the antidote for ethnocentrism (that is, tolerance and multiculturalism) and relativism; relativism supplies the grounds for the critique of ethnocentrism. As external, independent criteria cannot be adduced for values one way or another, pro or con, judgment must be suspended. We should be tolerant. In this way relativism justifies the critique of ethnocentrism (E_1) and defends tolerance.

There are other commentators who have recognised the link we are discussing here. For example, Brian Fay wrote of the view which states that:

> because we have no independent basis for criticising the way others think or act, our attitude should be one of tolerance and appreciation rather than the judgmentalism that has so often marred human thought and practice. In this way relativism is meant to guard against chauvinism. In this way relativism encourages multiculturalism.[7]

This is fairly explicit; because there are no agreed external standards by which to judge we should be tolerant.

The link between relativism and tolerance can also be discerned in postmodernist writings. It is true that the subject matter is couched in slightly different language but, nonetheless, many postmodernists seem to take the

---

6.   Calhoun, *Critical Social Theory*, 80.
7.   Brian Fay, *Contemporary Philosophy of Science: A Multicultural Approach* (Oxford: Blackwell, 1996), 3.

view that relativism leads to tolerance and the appreciation of diversity. Certainly, the argument for tolerance is based on the view that in the postmodern world we are bereft of standards and values which could be used to arbitrate between the diversity of conflicting values.[8] Sometimes the standards required are likened to foundations which are the basis on which our ethical, moral and value edifices are constructed. In deconstructing them even the foundations crumble.

For example, in *The Postmodern Condition: A Report on Knowledge*, Lyotard forged the connection between what I am calling value relativism and tolerance (even if the word relativism is not used). For example, in the Introduction Lyotard wrote that 'Postmodern knowledge is not simply a tool of the authorities; it refines our sensitivity to differences and reinforces our ability to tolerate the incommensurable'.[9] Incommensurability, which is due to relativism, connotes the impossibility of arbitrating between competing 'little' narratives,[10] the 'heterophonous' local knowledges[11] or the 'multiplicity of worlds of names, the insurmountable diversity of cultures'.[12] Even if the links are obscure or camouflaged by different language they are, nonetheless, detectable.

Other examples can be adduced. The 'abandonment of foundationalism', Steven Seidman argued, 'raises the

---

8.   Pauline Marie Rosenau, *Post-Modernism and the Social Sciences: Insights, Inroads, and Intrusions* (Princeton, New Jersey: Princeton University Press, 1992), 114–15, 139.

9.   Jean-Francois Lyotard, *The Postmodern Condition: A Report on Knowledge* (Minneapolis: University of Minnesota Press, 1984), xxv.

10. Lyotard, *The Postmodern Condition*, 60.

11. Lyotard, *The Postmodern Condition*, 66.

12.   Jean-Francois Lyotard, *The Postmodern Condition: Explained to Children: Correspondence 1982–1985 (Sydney: Power Publication)*, 42.

specter of relativism'. He continued, 'the abandonment of epistemic and moral certainty [that is, the abandonment of foundationalism] does entail relativism, if by that we mean a heterogeneity of standards of truth and moral rightness'.[13] I would call 'heterogeneity of standards' value relativism; there are diverse standards of truth and moral rightness due to not having the wherewithal to establish independent epistemic and moral criteria. Between the diversity of standards we cannot arbitrate.

Until this point Seidman offered no link with tolerance of other political values. But he continued, arguing that, while relativism 'may imply a degree of social flux and conflict that some may judge unacceptable. This course is preferable ... to the repression of difference and diversity that is implied in the quest for foundations and disciplinary order.'[14] According to Seidman, relativism implies social flux; the quest for foundations (what might be called value absolutism) implies the repression of diversity. Here we can see the links between relativism and tolerance and what I have called value absolutism and political repression; one is implied by the other. Particularly relevant to our analysis is the nature of the connections exemplified by the words entail and implied. Before analysing these links we will turn to the other connection about which we are concerned and to which Seidman alluded.

---

13. Steven Seidman, 'Postmodern Theory as Narrative with Moral Intent', in *Postmodernism and Social Theory: The Debate over General Theory*, edited by Steven Seidman and David G Wagner (Cambridge, Massachusetts: Blackwell, 1992), 74.
14. Seidman, 'Postmodern Theory as Narrative with Moral Intent', 75.

The absolutist–tyranny nexus

The other side of the relativist–tolerance coin is the link between value absolutism, on the one hand, and the imposition of beliefs and values, on the other. Opponents of value absolutism argued that if it is possible to find criteria for ranking values more or less objectively, then those who make this claim are bound to want to foist their own values on others. This might range from unsolicited overtures, manipulative proselytising in a busy street, to bombing an abortion clinic or imposing restrictions on immigration from certain cultures and nations, or to using even more violent means such as torture, the threat of death and even genocide.

For those who see a link between absolutism and tyranny, how power is abused is not the only consideration. Also crucial is the so-called truth which motivates the imposition of thought; truth, it is alleged, has a compelling quality. After all, if it is the truth then everyone should accept it and, if they do not, it should be imposed on them! As Hannah Arendt, the political philosopher who escaped the Nazis and lived in the United States after the Second World War wrote: 'the modes of thought and communication that deal with truth, if seen from the political perspective, are necessarily domineering'.[15]

Of course, some people may believe and act as if the truth they claim to possess should be a mandatory belief for all others (for example, dictators, religious extremists). However, I neither believe that the connection between so-called value absolutism and imposition is valid, nor do I wish to do anything other than gently persuade those with whom I disagree. However, the notion that the truth

---

15. Hannah Arendt, 'Truth and Politics', in *Philosophy, Politics and Society*, edited by Peter Lasslett and WG Runciman (Oxford: Basil Blackwell, 1969), 115.

about values is by its very nature tyrannical, that it obliges acceptance, and dissent should be met with some sort of threat of force so that opponents acquiesce, is one of the most popular views in the social sciences and humanities. We noted it in Steve Seidman's views. He highlighted what he believed was 'the repression of difference and diversity that is implied in the quest for foundations and the disciplinary order', that is, in the quest for truth.

The alleged, innately compelling nature of any truth claim is certainly a concern for most postmodernists. In fact, despite their variation on other issues, their diagnosis of the truth is that it is totalising, oppressive, a denial of the diversity and fragmentation of modernity, and highlights the underlying yet repressed other whose voice is muted by the privileged. According to some postmodernists, at least, this diagnosis of repression is based on a privilege claim to the truth of some kind, thus exemplifying the very connection being addressed here.[16]

An example of the link

The relativism–tolerance/absolutist–tyranny nexus can be found in perhaps the most powerful and popular view of science in the twentieth century which, in a previous chapter, was described as logical positivism. The influence of this view has been pervasive in the West, particularly in the social sciences after the Second World War. You will recall that the logical positivists asserted that only statements which meet certain conditions can be called knowledge. The conditions include verification of the statement; if it cannot be scientifically verified it is not knowledge. As we saw in Chapter 3, metaphysical beliefs (for example, about God) and values could not be verified

---

16. This I regard as a continuing theme in Lyotard. See Lyotard, *The Postmodern Condition*, xxiii–xxv, 12–13, 27, 66–7, 81–2.

by scientific (positivist) and empirical means. So, as they could not be sensed, they were nonsense.

However, the Vienna Circle were progressive thinkers and believed that their logical positivism was an antidote to the metaphysical and absolutist perspectives which they considered had afflicted Europe in the first three decades of the twentieth century. Here we can see the absolutist–tyranny nexus. They believed that the various non-scientific and value absolutist views (including nationalism) contributed to the First World War and other problems in Europe at the time. Value absolutism led ineluctably to political absolutism.

They also claimed that, while factual statements could be verified, statements about values could be neither verified nor refuted. While the members of the Vienna Circle expressed what I would call the fact–value dichotomy and its alleged implications differently, they were value relativists. Moreover, they related this value relativism to their endorsement of progressive, increasingly reformist, democratic, liberal and, for several members, socialist objectives. One of their members, Hans Feigl, advocated what he called a 'scientifically oriented humanism',[17] which is consistent with many of the values upheld by those who appreciate diversity, plurality of cultural expression, and cross-cultural understanding more generally. Thus, value relativism entailed political tolerance; value absolutism led to political absolutism. In their work we see the two sides of the absolutist–intolerance/relativist–tolerance coin.

---

17. Herbert Feigl, 'No Pot of Message', in *Inquiries and Provocations: Selected Writings, 1929–1974* (Dordricht: D Reidel, 1981), 19.

A similar link was observed by Ernest Gellner[18] in his criticism of positivism in the context of post-Second World War decolonisation. According to Gellner's analysis, while positivism supports colonialism, what he called 'subjectivism' indicates respect and tolerance. Previously we noted the similarities between subjectivism and relativism. They are observable here. Thus, according to Gellner:

> Positivism is a form of imperialism, or perhaps the other way around, or both. Lucidly presented and (putatively) independent facts were the tool and expression of colonial domination; by contrast, subjectivism signifies intercultural equality and respect.[19]

The latter highlights the value relativist–tolerance nexus. Gellner noted the connection in postmodernism 'between two sets of events, between political liberation and cognitive subjectivity'. He explained:

> Clarity and the insistence on—or rather the imposition of—an allegedly unique and objective reality is simply a tool, or perhaps, in some versions, the preferred tool, of domination. The objectivism aspired to or invoked by traditional, pre-modern social science was covertly a means of imposing a vision on men, which constrained those dominated to accept their subjection.[20]

---

18. Ernest Gellner, *Postmodernism, Reason and Religion* (London: Routledge, 1992), 26.
19. Gellner, *Postmodernism, Reason and Religion*, 26.
20. Gellner, *Postmodernism, Reason and Religion*, 27.

Further clarification and some consequences

In the preceding section, we looked at the links between relativism–tolerance / absolutism–tyranny and the position of the Vienna Circle, as well as the observations of Ernest Gellner. I argued that the links are popular and, more importantly, justify tolerance, multiculturalism and cross-cultural understanding on the one hand, and on the other are a reason for abjuring absolutism because it entails imposing one's views on others. We also noted Brian Fay's observation that relativism encourages multi-culturalism, and Steven Seidman's view that relativism implied social flux and conflict which was preferable to the repression of diversity implied by the search for foundations. In a nutshell, relativism is used to justify and defend tolerance. There are several points to be made here about the relativist–tolerance side of the coin.

Firstly, to be clear, in the foregoing I had a particular form of relativism in mind. I was not referring to the relativism which is a descriptive or empirical claim about the sheer variety of cultures, cultural norms, beliefs and values. Nor was I was referring to cultural or conceptual relativism, as defined and examined in Chapter 1 and 2, which allegedly locks us into our cultural and conceptual worlds. Whatever, I am not using relativism in that way.

Secondly, in using the term 'value relativism' I have attempted to describe a position about the very epistemic status of values. Undoubtedly, there are some similarities between cultural relativism and value relativism— because values are inextricably connected to cultures— but the latter more accurately describes what I have in mind. Value relativism, in the sense used here, is a view about the status of values as knowledge and how values are different or similar to other forms of knowledge. It is about how values rate or rank compared with other forms of knowledge, such as scientific knowledge. Value relativ-

ism makes claims about the certainty, or rather the uncertainty, of values.

Value relativists are more than pessimistic about the
possibility of justifying our values. According to them,
there are no standards or benchmarks to which we can
appeal when seeking to defend or justify values. By
justifying, opponents of value absolutism mean offering
cogent, rational arguments using cross-culturally independent and neutral criteria and standards. To defend
this view, value relativists often compare conflicts about
values with conflicts about so-called facts. Many value
relativists argue that it is a relatively straight-forward
matter to arbitrate a disagreement about whether rainfall
for this year was below or above average. It is simply a
matter of obtaining the numbers.

According to the fact–value dichotomy, disagreements
about facts are theoretically resolvable. For the value
relativist however, it is much more difficult, indeed
impossible, to arbitrate between the values of two people
who, for example, hold opposite views about abortion or
migration, or on what grounds we should tolerate those
cultural expressions and practices which we find distaste-
ful or offensive. There are no reference points outside our
frameworks to which we can appeal. There are no
equivalents to facts when it comes to values. The external,
independent criteria which could allow us to arbitrate
conflicts between facts, particularly in science, are simply
absent when it comes to values. They are of a different
order.

Although it may come as a surprise, the third point is
that value relativists are not bereft of values. As we have
seen, value relativists are often committed to values such
as openness to other cultures and the appreciation of
diversity and tolerance. Simply because they do not
believe it is possible to arbitrate between values does not
mean they are not committed to some values.

For example, some logical positivists and their followers claim that all values are expressions of emotions, or are deep commitments to worldviews that cannot be verified by the scientific method, but which remain important to those who hold them.[21] In this way, value relativists are usually not nihilists (in this case those who believe there are no valid ethical, moral and value principles).

Likewise, Steven Seidman argued that the relativism he describes does not 'amount to surrendering to nihilism'.[22] As with other supporters of relativism, Seidman has his own value position. He wrote:

> I can maintain both that the epistemology of postmodernism projects ceaseless social heterogeneity and conflict and that in practice heterogenous interests, values, worldviews, and lifestyles negotiate a coexistence which does not depend on the metadiscursive efforts of a moral and intellectual elite.[23]

So here we have someone who is committed to 'the epistemology of postmodernism', someone who adopts a relativist position who quite happily states his allegiance to social heterogeneity and negotiating. He is not a nihilist as far as values are concerned.

But this does bring into sharp relief the very point which is central to this chapter: I recognise that value

---

21. For example, whatever else may be said about them, the Vienna Circle were certainly not nihilists on values. They were implacable defenders of progressive and reformist governments and democracy. See Chapter 3.
22. Seidman, 'Postmodern Theory as Narrative with Moral Intent', 75.
23. Seidman, 'Postmodern Theory as Narrative with Moral Intent', 75.

relativists espouse various value positions, that they are not usually nihilists. But the intriguing and salient question is: how do they defend the value positions to which they adhere and how consistent is their position? In a nutshell, the issue with which I am concerned here is not whether value relativists uphold and defend various values. They usually do—and in so far as they are values of tolerance I usually agree with them. Germane to this chapter, however, are the grounds on which they attempt to defend such values and their consequences. More particularly, is the link they make between value relativism and tolerance consistent with their position? Can value relativism be used as a cogent and defensible argument for tolerance or anything else?

Just before the above questions are addressed, it is worth asking why we need to defend tolerance. Surely its value is axiomatic? I agree, but it is not axiomatic to some people and it is certainly not axiomatic for the person who adopts the ethnocentric or racist position. Seidman may be confident that these differences are negotiated, but the conflict in many so-called liberal democracies over migration, multiculturalism and the treatment of indigenous peoples and nations would seem to require more than negotiation. Do people who are ethnocentric or racist really want to negotiate? Yet there may be others who adopt more moderate positions and want a debate. Without reasons, how can we defend our views against those who disagree with us?

There is also another group for whom reasons may not be necessary including, for example, those who insist that conventional reasons are merely constructions, that reasons are merely about a particular form of written logic which is logocentric, which establishes criteria for justification when neither the criteria nor the need for justification are any more than social conventions connected with the abuse of power. Again, there is no doubt in my mind that there have been, and are, circumstances in which this diagnosis is quite accurate. Such reasons or justifications only serve to enhance power, and those who parrot them as shibboleths, glibly stating their so-called objective reasons, are merely stool pigeons, irrespective of their unctous intonings!

But if reasons are not offered, and particularly if they are not offered in a sequential, step-by-step manner to justify and defend a position, there is a possibility that any, even contradictory, reasons will be used. The possibility of a capricious response is dangerous because it is a way to exert power over the constituted other.

As my reader may have realised by now—and certainly will in the next chapter—I agree that many of the explanations given for a whole range of social beliefs and phenomena are distortions and smokescreens which legitimate the ideologies of the dominant and the privileged. The social function which popular and dominant reasons and explanations for social phenomena fulfil is worthy of in-depth inquiry. However, the matter in hand is the need for reasons and their adequacy or lack thereof. How is it possible to negotiate without giving reasons for what we espouse and advocate? As soon as we say, 'because we think this should or shouldn't happen' we are invoking reasons. They seem inevitable.

Thus, there is no reason to be chary about providing reasons or explanations for things. They are essential. What is also essential is that the socially constructed, the culturally bound and, therefore, the particular and culturally relative nature of social things, is analysed and any inconsistencies between social reality and rhetoric (the description and the reasons) are exposed and the social function of the dominant reasons is uncovered.

But there's another point to be teased out here, namely, how can we sort out the reasons for espousing certain values? How can they be ranked? To this you might be thinking: 'well, the value relativist claims that it is impossible to sort or rank values into a hierarchy, to say that one value is preferable to another. So why criticise them for something they claim not to do?'

At this stage I'm willing to agree with you at least in part; I won't criticise value relativism for saying it is impossible to arbitrate between values. But I would like to pursue the issue of consistency though; if value relativists claim it is impossible to arbitrate between values, then how can they maintain that tolerance is better than intolerance?

At this point the work of James Flynn is relevant.[24] Over three decades ago, Flynn challenged what he called ethical relativism (which is similar to value relativism). He found this ethical relativism in the work of the American pragmatist philosopher William James (1842–1910) and wrote the following:

> James' argument is as persistent as it is fallacious. American social scientists right up to the present day formulate vulgarized versions of it (quite independently of any knowledge of James). Time after time, we open their books to read something like this: 'Ethical relativism means that our values are no more objective than anyone else's; therefore, we should respect the values of others as much as our own. In a word, we should be tolerant.[25]

This, of course, is exactly what the link between value relativism and tolerance asserts. The language is slightly different: ethical subjectivism instead of value relativism and objectivity rather than value absolutism (but, as these have been explained previously in this chapter, that

---

24. James Flynn, *Humanism and Ideology: An Aristotelian View* (London: Routledge and Kegan Paul, 1973).
25. Flynn, *Humanism and Ideology*, 77.

should not disturb you). Nevertheless, Flynn discerned the prevalence of the link between views which insist that tolerance follows from value relativism (or, as he said, ethical subjectivism).

Flynn, however, not only agreed that the view is popular in some circles but he also diagnosed the ways in which it is flawed. In fact, he wrote of the view outlined in the above quotation: 'These arguments are of such immense contemporary influence that they deserve a special name: perhaps, the "tolerance school fallacy"'.[26] In the light of the above discussion, Flynn's assessment remains valid even though it was made over three decades ago.

The reason why the relativism-tolerance connection is fallacious is embedded in the discrepancy between what value relativism means, and what the value relativist does when making the connection with tolerance. This is particularly the case for value relativists who promote appreciation of diversity, tolerance and multiculturalism. In stating, 'there are no absolute values, therefore we should be tolerant of others', or 'because our values are no more objective than anyone else's, therefore, we should be tolerant', the value relativist is making an 'ought, should or must' statement. In other words, for the value relativist of this ilk a normative conclusion or action is believed to follow from the fact that values are not, and cannot be, absolute or objective. This should come as no surprise; such an analysis merely explains the inner dynamics operating in the value relativist–tolerance nexus. Further, it simply reiterates what I argued previously, namely, that some value relativists are committed to tolerance and they are not necessarily nihilists.

But for the moment please put the spotlight on the 'ought', the 'should', the 'must', the normative element

---

26. Flynn, *Humanism and Ideology*, 77.

which is said to follow from value relativism in the relativism–tolerance nexus. The spotlight reveals that tolerance is something good, a value high on any hierarchy of values and that it is superior to intolerance. We have reached the critical point in uncovering the fallacy. It is this: in saying that tolerance is superior to intolerance, in advocating tolerance, the value relativist asserts that one value (tolerance) is more valid than another (intolerance). Yet this is precisely what the value relativist rejects. I endorse wholeheartedly the conclusion but it does not follow from value relativism.

Let's try to pinpoint my objection in another way. Recall that the value relativist who advocates tolerance states that it is precisely because we cannot attain absolute or objective knowledge of values that we should be tolerant; if it is impossible to arbitrate between values then they have the same rational status—one is not to be preferred to another—so we should be tolerant. But here again there is a problem: if we cannot say that one value or set of values is to be preferred over another, it is impossible to conclude that tolerance is better than intolerance. The premise renders their conclusion untenable.

This leads to another interesting observation about the nature of the connection, namely, that in concluding that tolerance is preferable to intolerance, the value relativists are acting as if absolute or objective knowledge about values is possible. They seem to have decided in favour of a particular value, in this instance tolerance, when their value relativism denies any such possibility.

You will recall that several pages back we engaged in a little (albeit contrived) conversation over the possibility or otherwise of ranking values, of claiming that one was preferable to another, that tolerance, for example, was preferable to intolerance. I was reminded that it was not fair to criticise value relativists because they did not rank values (because they claimed it was impossible) as long as they were consistent, and did not say that one value was preferable to another. I could have argued there and then that the value relativists were misguided and that it was possible to arbitrate between values. But that was not my response. You will recall that I agreed that provided the value relativist was consistent and did not prefer one value to another, I would not criticise them for being value relativists. Now you will see why I responded in such a way.

I do not think the value relativists are consistent. They argue that because it is impossible to arbitrate between conflicting values we should be tolerant. Accordingly, tolerance is preferable to intolerance. So then they do rank values. This leads to another observation. You will recall that in our conversation I indicated that, at that point, I would not criticise value relativists for claiming it was impossible to rank values in order of priority. However, now you will see why I mentioned it. Why? Because, despite their disavowal, and irrespective of what their point entails, they often do rank values; tolerance is preferable to intolerance (a position with which I agree).

The absolutist–tyranny nexus

There are more things that could be said about the relativist–tolerance connection but they can wait until we have explored the absolutist–tyranny nexus. You will recall that this connection is usually an accusation or an allegation made by those who adhere to the relativist–tolerance nexus. The relativist argument is that to claim values are absolute or objective is to impose them on others. That is, in claiming that it is possible to demonstrate that some values are valid, that some are preferable to others, that it is possible to rank values and therefore arbitrate between conflicting values, it appears value absolutists wish to impose their values on others.

Just as value relativism is connected to tolerance, so value absolutism is linked to the imposition of values against individual will and, ultimately, to authoritarianism and tyranny.

Again, the argument sounds compelling. We certainly know of people and groups who believe their values are valid not only for themselves and their partisans but for everybody else.[27] They have no scruples about imposing them on others. For example, those who adopt ethnocentric and racist positions, colonialists and imperialists (past and present) assert that their own values are superior and impose them on others. The experience of indigenous people in Africa, the Americas, and in Australia and New Zealand is to this day characterised by the dominant values and knowledge claims of those who do not even question the correctness of their own value position. Even if they do not regard their values as universally valid (in the literal sense), these people believe and act as if their own values are more valid than those of the people they are oppressing. Thus, because we can identify those who are value absolutists and who impose their values on others, it would seem as if the value absolutist–tyranny link is at least empirically or descriptively accurate.

However, that we can point to some examples does not prove the validity of the connection. Opponents of value absolutism charge it with a different point; descriptive or empirical accuracy is not the salient issue here. They are alleging that there is something intrinsic in the nature of value absolutism which renders its protagonists ready and willing to impose their values on others. You will recall it from a previous discussion. According to this view, the truth of values is compelling; it demands to be imposed.

---

27. See Flynn, *Humanism and Ideology*, 30–52.

But here an obvious question arises: what is it about value absolutists that compels them to impose their values on others? The answer that I would like to offer is this: there is nothing inherently tyrannical about claiming that it is possible to arbitrate between values; such a view does not necessitate imposing values on others.

There are, at least, two reasons for this. The first is that value absolutism is a theory of knowledge in the same way that value relativism is a theory of knowledge. In both cases the theory is about knowledge of values. Both positions turn around (and take opposite positions on) whether or not it is possible to claim that some values are preferable to others. Neither is a political doctrine. Neither is intrinsically about tolerance or intolerance. Neither is about imposing views on others against their will, nor are they about being respectful and tolerant; they are about the possibility of one value being preferable to another. Just as value relativism is not a doctrine about tolerance, so the value absolutism I am analysing is not a doctrine about intolerance.

In a previous chapter, I used the word epistemology to describe theories of knowledge. Both value relativism and value absolutism are epistemologies of values. In fact, to make their status clear it is helpful (if not cumbersome) to call them epistemological value relativism and epistemological value absolutism (hereafter e-value relativism and e-value absolutism).[28] This highlights the point I am making here, namely that neither position inherently advocates or holds political values such as tolerance and

---

28. At one time I would have been reluctant to use such an abbreviation. However, abbreviations such as 'e-mail' for electronic mail, and 'e-business' for electronic business, are so common that I do not anticipate my readers will have any difficulty reading 'epistemological' when they see the 'e-'.

tyranny. They are about the philosophical status of values.

Thus, to derive tolerance from e-value relativism is to extract something from it which it is constitutionally unable to provide (because the e-value relativists claim it is impossible to arbitrate between competing values); to derive intolerance from e-value absolutism is to confuse an epistemological position with a political position, to presume that all e-value absolutists wish to impose their views on others, which is clearly not the case. There are e-value absolutists who are ethnocentric and there are e-value absolutists who advocate the same tolerance as e-value relativists.

Political values which are derived from either position, or connected with them, are implied, or arise subsequently, from additional steps in an argument. My argument here is that there is a huge and unwarranted logical jump between e-value absolutism and tyranny, and e-value relativism and tolerance. Political absolutism (such as colonisation, imposing powerful and privileged views on others and oppressing dissidents) does not of necessity inhere in e-value absolutism any more than tolerance is inherent in e-value relativism.

This leads to the second reason for suggesting that e-value absolutism does not lead to, or justify, political absolutism. The reason is that if e-value absolutists ranked values such as freedom, justice and tolerance at the top of their hierarchy of values, and acted accordingly, they would have a warrant for supporting policies which implement those values and oppose those that inhibit them. Such e-value absolutists would advocate and support policies such as multiculturalism and oppose the incarceration of political dissidents. Unlike the e-value relativist, the e-value absolutists are in a position do this. They are at least being consistent when they say that freedom, equality and tolerance are preferable to their opposites. So it is possible for e-value absolutists to be as opposed to political absolutism as any e-value relativist, with the difference being, of course, that the e-value relativists cannot defend their choice of ultimate value positions because such a defence would treat values as if there was (at least potentially) some way of arbitrating between epistemological value positions—which is precisely what they deny.

We can now state the issues addressed so far concisely and precisely. We have seen that there is a distinction between a theory of knowledge and political values to which we might subscribe. There is a significant distinction to be made between an epistemology on the one hand, and the political values which may follow on the other. If we apply the distinction to each we see that there is an enormous difference between e-value relativism and political tolerance; likewise between e-value absolutism and political absolutism.

Concluding comments

I hope that I have not been too repetitive over the past few pages. It is tempting to summarise my argument again just to clinch it. Some of you, though, may be wondering why I have emphasised the above issues, made distinctions, analysed the grounds for political deductions drawn from epistemological positions, and assessed the political implications drawn from them. You may be asking: so what? What's the relevance of what I've been arguing to cross-cultural understanding? The following I trust will answer those questions.

Firstly, as I've argued, it is important to be able to defend tolerance. Some may disagree. They might claim that it is self-evident that tolerance is better than intolerance, justice preferable to injustice, and multi-culturalism of whatever brand preferable to assimilation, colonialism, ethnocentrism or racism. Again, I agree with their conclusions, but there are numerous competitors to those values. There are some individuals and groups in the social and political realm who try to exclude competition to the pluralistic and tolerant values to which we are committed, and may be downright hostile to them. Others defend their values; it is important that we can defend those to which we are committed. And that seems to be impossible if we use e-value relativism.

Secondly, it is important to be able to defend our values with reasons. In Chapter 7 we will see that justification of our values may involve more than just rational or cognitive justification. Reason in the sense of a broad rationality may involve more than merely marshalling cognitive assent or, put differently, there may be affective as well as cognitive reasons for upholding our values. However, in the social and political realm it is so-called rational reasons, cognitively derived, that are the currency. Not to use that currency means to exclude oneself from the marketplace of ideas. That may allow others to have much more influence than is warranted.

Thirdly, I said in the last paragraph that tolerance was preferable to intolerance. However, there may be times when it is necessary to begin to ask which tolerance is preferable to intolerance. Are western versions of tolerance all the same? Are some superior to others? The ability—albeit with modesty—to defend values would seem imperative. Moreover, as I will argue in the next chapter, it may be necessary on some occasions to defend intolerance, not in the sense of being ethnocentric or racist, but in the sense that it is necessary to be intolerant and critical of political and social conditions which are repressive.[29] However, as we have seen, e-value

---

29. This does not detract from an overall commitment to tolerance, although in the next chapter the meaning of tolerance will be explored and qualified. The point is that tolerance by definition need not tolerate intolerance! See Chapter 6.

relativism renders it impossible to argue for any value. Both tolerance and intolerance are possible; it cannot arbitrate between them. If tolerance were advocated by e-value relativists we could ask why. If intolerance were thought to be necessary for some reason (perhaps of a neo-Nazi group in order to guarantee tolerance for a repressed minority) we could legitimately ask the same question.

Hence, if defending values is as important as I have suggested, and if it is important to defend tolerance against intolerance, then such a defence will not come from e-value relativism. As argued, and despite the popularity of the view, e-value relativism is not an antidote for intolerance. Central to e-value relativism is the view that tolerance can no more be defended than intolerance; if it is impossible to arbitrate between values then the consistent e-value relativist cannot argue that tolerance is preferable to intolerance. In other words, the popular defence of tolerance, cross-cultural under-standing and the values associated with liberty and equality is indefensible from e-value relativism and moreover, advocating the above values contradicts its basic tenants. If we are to defend these values it will not be from e-value relativism.

The same argument can be mounted about understanding in cross-cultural understanding—with significant implications. If it is impossible to arbitrate between values, how can the argument that under-standing is preferable to misunderstanding be advanced? It cannot. In this way, e-value relativism subverts our attempts to understand, whether it be in the sense of being empathetic (U_2) or defending the values by which we defend the sympathetic understanding of other cultures (U_3). If it is impossible to defend one value against another, there are no rational grounds for arguing that accurate information is preferable to inaccurate information, or that being sensitive is preferable to being insensitive. Thus, e-value relativism has implications for the very project of cross-cultural understanding.

There is another point of here concerning tolerance itself: tolerance has many meanings. As we shall see in the next chapter, tolerance is used to mean that something is tolerable, or that something should be tolerated. As such, tolerance can be narrow and niggardly. But, if we cannot say that overall, tolerance is preferable to intolerance, we are not really in a position to argue that broad tolerance is preferable to limited tolerance, that tolerance which extends freedom is preferable to tolerance which is counterproductive and which some claim is repressive. Without being able to arbitrate between values, the critique of how tolerance may have been used to constrain freedom is undermined; the criticisms of the social function of tolerance to curtail some beliefs and practices that could or should be tolerated are eroded. In summary, if it is impossible to arbitrate between values then it is impossible to argue about tolerance itself and whether one form of tolerance is preferable to another.

My point is that e-value relativism has closed these alternatives. If it is impossible to arbitrate then debate is futile. The very position which in much popular and academic discourse is linked with tolerance, and is claimed to support multiculturalism, cross-cultural un-derstanding and tolerance, is feckless. The argument— that it is precisely because we cannot arbitrate between values that we should be tolerant and not impose our values on others—might appear plausible, but it is flawed. The irony is that the one position that, at least, provides the preconditions for the debate to continue (e-value absolutism) is falsely condemned because it is confused with political absolutism, imposing values on others.

Yet e-value absolutism, as I call it, simply says that it is possible to arbitrate between conflicting values. By itself, it says nothing about imposing views on others; it says nothing against intolerance. To such a proposition some may respond: 'But if someone believes they are correct surely they will want to foist their views on others?' I concede that there are those—there have been many —who believe they have some monopoly on rationality and the justification of value positions and, as it were, have held the gun at the heads of dissenters to induce agreement. The heinous nature of such actions stands condemned.

However, as we have seen, e-value absolutism is about knowledge and whether one value can be argued to be preferable to another. Further, it is plausible that some e-value absolutists will say that freedom of opinion is preferable to tyranny of thought, that except in extreme situations tolerance is preferable to intolerance, that justice is preferable to injustice. They do not wish to impose their views on others. If some do, it is because they defend illiberal and undemocratic values, not because they argue that it is possible to arbitrate between values (that is, not because of their epistemological position). And, a least with e-value absolutism it is possible to engage in the debate about values, something seemingly denied in e-value relativism. Without it, being understanding (U_2), the values we use to defend such an understanding (U_3) and the values required to assess our cultural values (V_1) are impossible to defend. In brief, without e-value absolutism, genuine cross-cultural under-standing is difficult, if not impossible.

Hopefully, by now, you will be clear about my argument. You may disagree with me, although I hope I have been convincing. The next chapter continues one of the themes of this chapter, namely tolerance. There, however, the issue is not about whether it is possible to defend tolerance or not, but about the nature of tolerance and the social function that value relativism performs in legitimating a particular view of tolerance which is limited and limiting.

6

Is tolerance enough?

Introduction

In the previous chapter I examined some political implications of certain theories of knowledge. In analysing e-
value absolutism and e-value relativism I argued that the
political implications often derived from them do not
follow from their positions. Tolerance, no more than intolerance, can be deduced from e-value relativism, and
political absolutism is not the only conclusion that can be
derived from e-value absolutism. If we are to defend
cultural or political values which are aligned with freedom, equality and tolerance, we are more likely to use an
argument similar to e-value absolutism.

But having explored the inadequacy of the defence of
values, it is now timely to ask about a key value in cross-
cultural understanding, namely tolerance. In fact, in
everyday parlance and in official documents, citizens of
western countries with multicultural policies are exhorted
to be tolerant. Even if the word tolerance is not used, it
motivates much of what is written.[1]

But what is tolerance? As used in everyday language,
is it suitable for use in understanding another culture?
Does it give us the necessary intellectual and social space?

---

1. For example, see National Multicultural Advisory Council,
    Multicultural Australia: The Way Forward (Belconnen,
    Australian Capital Territory: National Multicultural Advisory
    Council, 1997), 6, 11.

Or is it a miserly, niggardly and parsimonious way of approaching cross-cultural understanding? What are the social functions of the contemporary discourse about tolerance? The chapter proceeds by examining a critique of the dominant discourse of tolerance.[2]

My argument in this chapter consists of several parts. Firstly, I will argue that the recent criticisms of the discourse on tolerance are justified on the grounds that it is limited, that it puts an undeserved gloss on current policy and practice, and diverts attention from salient issues. I also argue, contrary to some critical analyses, that the very notion of tolerance has an emancipatory potential which is worth retrieving.

Before beginning, though, I will say a little more on how this relates to cross-cultural understanding. This topic is relevant because many who are committed to cross-cultural understanding believe that they are tolerant. In fact, the western world regards itself as being tolerant. Western nations operate immigration programs, many citizens come from other countries and reside with full citizenship, and citizens from diverse backgrounds attend community festivals. Tolerance is part of cross-cultural understanding, or so it is alleged! How can one be committed to understanding other cultures, to cross-cultural understanding, without being tolerant? A logical implication of a commitment to cross-cultural understanding is to be accepting, to appreciate diversity, to celebrate difference or, in a nutshell, to be tolerant. In fact, so enmeshed are the terms that it is difficult to determine

---

2.   In order of appearance in the chapter: Preston King, *Toleration* (London: George Allen and Unwin, 1976); Ghassan Hage, *White Nation: Fantasies of White Supremacy in a Multicultural Society* (Annandale, New South Wales: Pluto Press, 1998); and Herbert Marcuse, 'Repressive Tolerance', in Robert P Wolff and Barrington Moore Jnr, and Herbert Marcuse, *A Critique of Pure Tolerance* (London: Jonathon Cape, 1969), 95–137.

which comes first, commitment to cross cultural under-standing or to tolerance. In either case, the link to cross-cultural understanding is forged.

However, what is the consequence if we find that western nations, which are so fond of promoting their cross-cultural understanding, have a rather limited view of tolerance? What happens if those people who have migrated do not feel that they are understood? What happens if they feel that are merely tolerated? What happens if the way tolerance is used and understood, the way it is socially constructed, is circumscribed within clearly defined and sanctioned limits? What then happens to our pretensions of tolerance?

My point is this: if tolerance is constrained and limited in some way, then so is any cross-cultural understanding which follows. In fact, it may not be understanding at all. It may be closer to ethnocentrism (E_1), irrespective of what is espoused. But in the previous chapter, the problem was an inadequate defence of tolerance. Here, the salient issue is whether the prevailing understanding of tolerance is adequate, or if there are elements which minimise rather than maximise the extent of socially approved tolerance.

The discourse of tolerance: the meanings of the term

The word 'tolerance' has a long history and, even in everyday language, has several nuances.[3] There is a variety of similar words: tolerate, tolerable and tolerance, not to mention toleration. Consider tolerate. We might hear someone say: 'I can't tolerate loud music' or 'I can tolerate watching the football and netball on television,

---

3. For a helpful introduction see David Heyd, editor, *Toleration: An Elusive Virtue* (Princeton, New Jersey: Princeton University Press, 1996) and Catriona McKinnon, *Toleration: A Critical Introduction* (London: Routledge, 2006).

but I can't tolerate watching the basketball or the baseball'. Implicit in such statements is the idea of limits and, in the above examples, limits of acceptability. Using an analogy from some occupations which use precise measuring instruments, we could say that loud music and watching basketball and baseball are outside our tolerance limits, while watching football or netball is within our limits of tolerance.

We might say, 'The weather is tolerable' or 'His cooking is tolerable' or 'The address (speech) was tolerable'. Usually the first is taken to mean (perhaps even translated) as: 'The weather may have been hot but it was within a range that I find comfortable'. The second might mean, 'He almost burnt the sausages to a frazzle but they were still edible'. If the address (speech) was tolerable it may mean that, while it was not an arresting, riveting, stimulating address, listening to it was not a burden.

In all three instances there is a sense that the weather, the cooking and the address were within a range that was acceptable but not necessarily ideal. Thus tolerance may refer to accepting an action, a form of behaviour, a belief or system of belief, which falls between the lower and upper limits of comfort, within the limits of acceptability. There are several points inferred by the above discussion that are worth noting.

Tolerance involves a range and limits

The first point is that tolerance implies limits; a range. It is like a perimeter within which the loud music, the weather, the sausages or the address are confined. If they remain within it we tolerate them; if the music becomes much louder, if the weather gets hotter, if the sausage is burnt to charcoal or the address is monotonous, then they move outside the perimeter and become intolerable.

Tolerance: (largely) a response to external influences

Secondly, in the first point *our* reaction to the music, the weather, the sausages and the address was important while, in this second point, the direction whence they came is pertinent. At issue were our reactions. I described as tolerable the loud music which was heard, the weather which was felt, the sausage which was tasted and the address which was heard.

But the emphasis in this second point I want to make is that, in a real sense, the loud music was unsolicited, the person had no influence over the weather, the cook burnt the sausages and the invited speaker presented the address. They were things that happened to the person who tolerated them. It was as if these things came from outside to a place and space over which we think we have control, that is, ourselves. The point here is that we have little or no control over these things and whether or not they are within the bounds of our tolerance.

We set the tolerable limits—the thresholds

The third point is that, while we may have little or no control over external influences and, although we may be influenced by physiological factors (such as sensitivity to loud noise) or cultural factors (such as learned gender stereotypes), we are largely responsible for setting our own limits of tolerance. Nonetheless, we know the upper threshold of acceptable noise, we know from experience the range of comfortable weather, we know what is undercooked and overcooked, and we know whether a speaker is acceptable or painfully and embarrassingly boring.

Tolerance is not neutral

This brings us to a fourth point, namely, that the determination of what is tolerable and what we tolerate is not neutral like the tolerances of an instrument in a tool-making or engineering project. The tolerance of fish to heavy metals and that of plants to certain chemicals are not neutral either. The worlds tolerable and tolerate, and their opposites, are not neutral; they are something we decide for a reason or purpose we determine and measure, even if what makes us intolerant is external.

This brief examination of tolerance levels leads to certain conclusions:[4] (1) words such as tolerable and intolerable presuppose limits; (2) that the source of the influence which we judge to be tolerable or intolerable is external; (3) that, we believe we have the right to say what we can tolerate because we receive and mediate the external influences which come unsolicited into what we regard as our place and space, and that, at least in some instances where we can, it is the individual who decides and controls the thresholds of what is tolerable or intolerable to them; and (4) such limits are not neutral like precision instruments which measure within objectively defined limits of tolerance. The critical question which follows is: are these conclusions applicable when we explore the meaning, use and practice of tolerance of other cultures? If they are, the results could be surprising.

If they are relevant, the questions which arise include the following. When other cultures come into our sphere of influence, how many people from different cultures, and their beliefs and practices, is tolerable? How extensive is the range? Is it narrow? Is it broad? Is it possible for us to regard ourselves as tolerant and

---

4.   McKinnon, *Toleration*, 13–16 outlines 'six essential structural features of toleration'. McKinnon's features are formulated differently from those in the text but they are helpful as features about which '(most) contemporary theorists agree'.

inclusive while those whom we are tolerating regard us as narrow and restrictive? Is there a spatial correlation between the extent of my tolerance and my proximity to the other people? And what about collective tolerance? It may be appropriate for one person to believe they have a right to decide what arrives in their place and space, but what if a large group, or an entire nation, believed that? Do we really have control in and over our borders in such a way? Does it operate this way: the closer the external influence the narrower the range of what is tolerated?

These questions have the potential to challenge some cherished views about tolerance. Overall, most people regard themselves as tolerant, as open and accepting. But our questions alert us to the possibility that tolerance has limits, and that there are thresholds within which we are prepared to tolerate and beyond which we are not. If such questions are applicable, tolerance is not something about which we can be neutral, which in turn raises the issue of the implications of tolerance and the interests it serves. This also prompts a question about the consequences of advocating or promoting tolerance.

Tolerance as neither changing individuals nor social structures: Preston King

While adopting a different approach, Preston King's[5] analysis suggests that some of the above questions and the analysis are relevant to tolerance. He began his analysis in a manner which dovetails with one of the matters raised above, namely, that people set their own limits of what they will tolerate. But the issue for King was not merely tolerance of specific beliefs and practices. It is about tolerance per se, and so he discussed the implications of advocating or promoting a policy of

---

5.   King, *Toleration.*

tolerance. For King, the establishment of limits or thresholds highlighted the power we have to do so.

When we make concessions to the beliefs and practices of others so that we are tolerant, or advocate that others should also be so, we are employing powers we possess. As King maintained: 'if one concedes or promotes a power to tolerate, one equally concedes or promotes a power not to tolerate'.[6] Those who advocate tolerance have the power to do so. Thus, King continued: 'Tolerance presupposes a liberty of action in regard to those matters or persons which are tolerated'.[7]

The introduction of power into this analysis is quite disarming, although it was implicit in the previous discussion about establishing limits and thresholds, levels of tolerance. However, in contrast to the above discussion, King's point is political rather than individual. At the political level, those who advocate and promote tolerance, or assert that others should also be tolerant, are asserting their power to do so. It is a disarming, if not confronting and disturbing suggestion, largely because those who normally advocate tolerance, may not see themselves as being particularly powerful. They may even be offended by the suggestion. Nonetheless, King's point is incisive. As we have seen, tolerance is about establishing limits of what is acceptable or not, the very possibility of which presupposes the power to do so—and no less so at the broader political level.

Furthermore, advocating a policy of tolerance may be counterproductive because it has not addressed the implicit power to be intolerant. 'Where we empower an agent to be tolerant, we empower him equally to be intolerant'.[8] King insisted that those who claim they are tolerant, or who advocate tolerance, have the power to do

---

6.   King, *Toleration*, 9.

7.   *Ibid.*

8.   *Ibid.*

what they will, whereas the beneficiaries of the policy, those to whom tolerance is conferred, do not. Those of whom we should be tolerant do not have the same clout; otherwise they would not have to be tolerated. Tolerance may be recommended but not necessarily exercised; both are possible for the proposer and their agents, but not for its beneficiaries.

Thus King made the distinction between 'two classes' of those who propose tolerance.

> On the one hand, there are the poor, the oppressed, the unfortunate, who, hard-pressed as these always are, beg for indulgence. On the other hand, there are the wealthy, the powerful, the fortunate, who, the better to protect their advantage, make marginal concessions to those over against whom it is held, and so invite the observers and recipients to sing paeans of praise to their selflessness, generosity, nobility, as reflected in this wonderfully publicised disinclination (at points) to act against (what they will normally perceive to be) the imbecile vulgarity of the mass, the folk, the workers, the dreadful poor and, in sum, all those who occupy inferior positions in whatever hierarchies there be.[9]

King's distinction presses his point about an implication of, or perhaps a rationale for, the power dimension of those who are in a position to propose tolerance, and the beneficiaries of such advocacy. According to King, the beneficiaries 'beg for indulgence', and, while he may not be literally correct on this point, they certainly are entitled to demand what is afforded to other groups (namely

9.   King, *Toleration*, 10–11.

recognition and tolerance). As well the proposers and those they are attempting to persuade make small concessions in order to appease those who seek to be accorded tolerance. As a result, the proposers and those they have persuaded experience the cosy warming of the cockles of their hearts because they have smiled so benevolently when, according to the proposers, they did not have to be so magnanimous. It is in their power to be tolerant. They are in a position to bestow tolerance; they are also in a position to remain intolerant.

King also argued that tolerance is an inherent part of the liberal tradition. Thus, tolerance 'is certainly consistent with the effective protection of the narrow interests of those affluent few who occasionally or consis-tently espouse it'. He cautioned that if tolerance 'is not handled carefully, is not kept in its proper place, we might discover too late in it a philosophical wolf in sheep's clothing, a formidable Beast in Beauty's guise'.[10] He continued:

> Thus we must fold back the layers of fur, disengage the magicality that envelops the thing, to seize it coldly, nude. Tolerance, it should be plain, has its points. But to recommend it meaningfully is always to recommend it upon condition. It should be no part of anyone's purpose, and is certainly not ours, to provide cheap comfort to that species of smug 'liberal' (for whom *every* party seems fated to reserve a niche) who is content with his advantage, and so capitulates before the urge but also unsettled by it; who seeks to justify his advantage, and so capitulates

---

10. King, *Toleration*, 11.

before the urge for such more self-display as
that advantage alone allows him.[11]

According to King, the need for tolerance is to be found
in inequalities. While there are disparities in power, with
their concomitant hierarchies of what counts as important
knowledge and language, cultural beliefs and practices,
there will be a need for tolerance. While there is inequality
there will be a need for powerful groups, and they and
their beneficiaries may feel the need to extend their favour
of acceptance to other groups lower on the social pecking
order.[12]

Thus, King detected a link between the need for
tolerance and inequality that can only be overcome by
more democratic institutions on the one hand, and
associated notions of rights on the other. The connection
he made is clear: 'The promotion of toleration basically
presupposes an inequality, but an inequality that has to
be accepted. The promotion of democracy basically presupposes an inequality, but one that can and should be
removed'.[13] This distinction has implications for tolerance:

> Where one perceives a lack of toleration, and
> encourages it, what one is basically en-
> couraging is a change of *attitude*. Where one
> perceives a lack of democracy, and en-
> courages it, what one is basically encour-
> aging is a change of *structure*. Thus, a pre-
> dominant feature of a commitment to
> toleration is the concern with psychology,
> while a predominant feature of the commit-

---

11. King, *Toleration*, 11.
12. King, *Toleration*, 11–12.
13. King, *Toleration*, 15.

ment to democracy is a concern with
institutions.[14]

Whether democracy as we know it still holds the
potential for changing structures and institutions is a
moot point. But King not only continued his theme about
the link between unequal power relations and the
necessity for tolerance, but advanced it by emphasising
the consequences of advocating tolerance compared to
increasing levels of democracy. Advocating tolerance
does not address structural imbalances, the inequalities in
institutional power whereas, according to King, advocating democracy does. Again, whether democracy can
deliver on this is debatable. But this does not detract from
his diagnosis: to advocate tolerance is to promote a
change of individual attitudes; to advocate democracy is
to change institutions.[15]

King's analysis is useful for several reasons. The first
point concerns the rather provisional manner in which I
introduced the problem of tolerance. There, I did not
presume that my analysis of 'tolerable' and 'tolerate' was
relevant to the tolerance required for cross-cultural
understanding.[16] King's analysis suggests that such an
analysis is pertinent. In fact, his analysis has raised the
stakes considerably. He did this by emphasising the
power dimensions of advocating tolerance so that
individual citizens decide how tolerant they will be.
King's point is that if they have the power to invoke more
tolerant thoughts and deeds, they have the power not to
so invoke. Thus, advocating tolerance is not a neutral act
like specifying tolerance of measurements.

Secondly, King's analysis invites the question: what
social function does tolerance perform? Or, as asked
above: in whose interests are policies of tolerance

---

14. King, *Toleration*, 15.
15. King, *Toleration*, 12.
16. There I was merely clarifying the implications of the terms.

advocated? One interest, of course, flows from the gushy, unctuous benevolence of those who deign to be tolerant. Yet as King explored the power imbalances, he identified other groups who benefit, and the resultant social function performed by advocating tolerance. Those on whom tolerance is bestowed benefit (at least according to those who grant it). Those to whom tolerance is recommended are able to change their attitudes, or not change them; their freedoms have not been diminished in any way. By being given a choice—to increase the breadth of their tolerance—their freedoms have been recognised and exercised. Moreover, the need for structural change which, according to King, is necessary to render tolerance irrelevant, is circumvented.

A third issue arises from King's suggestion about rights. The extension of tolerance is, as indicated, something that springs from those who espouse tolerance; it is accorded to others who are not in a position to demand the right to live according to their cultural practices and beliefs. If they possessed that right, tolerance would be irrelevant. They could act and believe however and whatever they wanted without needing to demean themselves by seeking permission from those prepared to be tolerant.

Tolerance as fantasising control: Ghassan Hage

These issues are explicated in what is, arguably, one of the most damning critiques of tolerance. In *White Nation, Fantasies of White Supremacy in a Multicultural Society,* Ghassan Hage demonstrated, inter alia, how power relations are implicated in policies of tolerance and multiculturalism in Australia. He agreed with Preston King that 'when those who are intolerant are asked to be tolerant, their power to be intolerant is *not* taken away. It is, in fact, reasserted by the very request not to exercise it'.[17] In his section on tolerance Hage argued that tolerance is much espoused in Australia. He then systematically exposed this tolerance for what it is. We might say he deconstructed the adherence to tolerance as a shallow platitude and demonstrated the social mechanisms whereby tolerance is used to assert and reinforce existing power inequalities.

Hage argued that tolerance in the Australian context of multiculturalism 'is not . . . a good policy that happens to be limited in its scope'.[18] Rather it is a 'strategy aimed at reproducing and disguising relationships of power in society, or being reproduced through that disguise. It is a form of symbolic violence in which a mode of domination is presented as a form of egalitarianism'.[19] In Australia, tolerance may seem to be the extension of equality but, as articulated and practised, it disguises power relationships only to distil and concentrate them even more.

Put differently, the strategy denies the distance between the person advocating tolerance and the person to whom we offer that tolerance. Australians pride themselves on their mateship, on levelling hierarchies and reducing social distance. Using different terminology, but I hope making a similar point, at times some people talk as if there is only a benign, horizontal axis of equality, including equality of respect. They talk as if there is a level playing field. However, this is belied by the very need for tolerance. The discourse of horizontal equity, including the presumption of exclusivity and openness, of mateship, camouflages the vertical axes of inequality, the hierarchies of power, wealth and acceptability.

Using the metaphor of social distance, it seems as if the social distances between those who advocate tolerance, and those of whom we should be tolerant, is compressed

---

17. Hage, *White Nation*, 85.
18. Hage, *White Nation*, 87.
19. *Ibid.*

and masquerades as close proximity. But nothing really changes the power relationships that cause the social distance; it is only a mirage of proximity but it fulfils an important social function. As Hage suggested, 'To tolerate is not just to accept, it is to accept and position the other within specific limits of boundaries. This concern with limits and boundaries emphasises, above all, the *empowered spatiality* that is part of tolerance'.[20] Tolerance provides a way of controlling the influence of the other who, as indicated previously, influences our space from beyond. Yet, as Hage insisted, at the individual level, at least, this influence is illusory. So apparently tolerant comments such as a person saying they would not object to more migrants, or they do not object to people speaking other languages, are uttered 'by those who *fantasise* that it is up to them whether people speak Arabic on the streets or not, whether more migrants come or not, and that such happenings are dependent on their capacity for tolerance'.[21]

It may seem that there is a tension in Hage's analysis. On the one hand, the very language or discourse of tolerance indicates a control of the other, deigning 'to give them some space' as they influence our space. On the other hand, this influence is a fantasy of megalomania; it is imagined that the other is present within our sphere of influence. Despite this fantasy, at one level we do not have control over other people. We cannot prevent them acting according to their cultural beliefs and practices any more than they can us.

But Hage's point concerns the person who advocates tolerance. His argument is that there are assumptions implicit in the language of those who advocate tolerance which make it sound as if they are allowing, or giving

20. Hage, *White Nation*, 89.
21. Hage, *White Nation*, 88.

permission for, others to come to Australia, or to speak their mother language on the streets. According to Hage, there is no doubt that those who allow, who are tolerant, are acting as if they possess power, as if they can deign by their prerogative to allow others to do certain things.

However, wrote Hage, the irony is that they do not have control. The belief is a fantasy. The language of tolerance and permission exposes their longing which is denied in reality; they want to assert their control but cannot. The very advocacy of tolerance implies that they are desperate to control the external space whence come those beliefs and practices which they condescend to tolerate. Further, in this respect the degree of tolerance or intolerance does not matter. In both, the main concern is to control the space that exceeds their tolerance thresholds. It is just that the tolerance levels are different. Thus:

> those who engage in practices of intolerance
> do not do so because they are uncommitted to
> tolerance, but because they feel that someone
> has exceeded their own threshold of tolerance
> and that they are entitled to put them back
> where they belong, within the limits and
> boundaries of tolerance they have set for
> them.[22]

According to Hage, the distinction that is often made between tolerant and intolerant people is not really the striking issue. Both 'equally claim the capacity to manage national space . . . Both are about realising a vision of national space through tolerance and intolerance, through the inclusion and exclusion of others'.[23]

Moreover, the reason for wanting to manage national space is because people sense they are losing control over it (even though they did not have that control in the first

---

22. Hage, *White Nation*, 92–93.
23. Hage, *White Nation*, 93.

place). Thus, when white Australians use the expression 'you're one of us now', or 'you're an Australian now' to those who came to this country, they are expressing their sense of loss of control. Hage wrote that when Australians say such things,

> [i]t allows the White Australians who engage in this form of acceptance to live in a fantasy space where the Australianness of the ethnic other appears as if it is under their control at a time when the migrant is inexorably becoming Australian independently of their will.[24]

The analyses by King and Hage challenge what they saw as an essentially liberal agenda. What both elucidated is the social function of tolerance. Tolerance has a context which is firmly grounded in a political and social agenda which is more about changing attitudes than changing structures, which is more about urging others to be tolerant while not diminishing their right to be intolerant. It is about determining the levels of personal tolerance threshold, and maintaining these in the face of the cultural beliefs and practices of others. It is about advocating tolerance and openness by deigning to permit others to express themselves, but only in ways which do not challenge existing tolerance thresholds. It is about fantasising that individuals possess power which, in fact, exposes their sense of loss of control and power. While Hage insisted that 'it is better for the state to advocate tolerance than intolerance' he argued that tolerance is a policy which supports and buttresses the white fantasy of ownership and control of the nation which is *'unable* to

---

24. Hage, *White Nation*, 103.

foster strategies aimed at going "beyond tolerance"', as understood, practised and limited.[25]

Repressive tolerance: Herbert Marcuse

Hage's argument is not the only one which suggests that tolerance has a social function which is limiting, which seeks to curtail and contain perimeters of tolerance. In the mid-1960s Herbert Marcuse wrote a stinging indictment of tolerance. While largely aimed at the United States, to which he migrated after Hitler's usurpation to power, it is also pertinent to the West more generally. Marcuse's argument is relevant to this chapter for several reasons.

Firstly, while critical of tolerance as practised, Marcuse argued in favour of tolerance. In this way his position differs from Hage's, who argued that tolerance is not a good policy incompetently implemented and administered, but a policy which is a 'strategy aimed at reproducing and disguising relationships of power in society, or being reproduced through that disguise'.[26] I suspect Marcuse would endorse Hage's analysis, including his misgivings about tolerance and its social function. However, as we shall see, Marcuse advocated tolerance, albeit a form of tolerance in stark contrast to the one practised in the United States at the time, and the one King and Hage were addressing.

A second difference is that, in some extreme circumstances, Marcuse countenanced the possibility of the non-toleration of some beliefs and practices as the only way to achieve more thorough and genuine tolerance. This is an issue significant to our discussion (although not to Hage's). Both issues are canvassed early in Marcuse's article entitled 'Repressive Tolerance':

25. Hage, *White Nation*, 97.
26. Hage, *White Nation*, 87.

The conclusion reached is that the realization of the objective of tolerance would call for intolerance toward prevailing policies, attitudes, opinions, and the extension of tolerance to policies, attitudes, and opinions which are outlawed or suppressed. In other words, today tolerance appears again as what it was in its origins, at the beginning of the modern period—a partisan goal, a subversive liberating notion. Conversely what is proclaimed and practised as tolerance today, is in many of its most effective manifestations serving the cause of oppression.[27]

My discussion of Marcuse's view of tolerance begins with his diagnosis of tolerance, and then proceeds to his prescription that includes his statement of the conditions that necessitate intolerance toward some policies.

A crucial issue for Marcuse is that tolerance operates to curtail freedom rather than extend it. Repeatedly he claimed that tolerance as 'proclaimed and practised' is 'repressive', which gives rise to the oxymoron that is the title of the article.[28] This repressive tolerance tolerates practices which perpetuate the existing social and economic structures but is intolerant of any dissent; 'the political locus of tolerance has changed: while it is more or less quietly and constitutionally withdrawn from the opposition, it is made compulsory behaviour with respect to established policies'.[29] Furthermore, 'Tolerance toward that which is radically evil now appears as good because it serves the cohesion of the whole on the road to

---

27. Marcuse, 'Repressive Tolerance', 95. See also Rodney Fopp, 'Herbert Marcuse's "Repressive Tolerance" and his critics', in *Borderlands*, 6/1 (2007).
28. Marcuse, 'Repressive Tolerance', 95–8, 104–9, 112.
29. Marcuse, 'Repressive Tolerance', 96.

affluence or more affluence'.[30] In this context there are two forms of tolerance:

> (1) the passive toleration of entrenched and established attitudes and ideas even if their damaging effect on man and nature is evident; and (2) the active, official tolerance granted to the Right as well as to the Left, to movements of aggression as well as movements of peace, to the party of hate as well as that of humanity. I call this non-partisan tolerance 'abstract' or pure inasmuch as it refrains from taking sides—but in doing so it actually protects the already established machinery of discrimination.[31]

According to Marcuse, tolerance is not always a policy in collusion with the dominant interests, in which debate is regimented and dissent stifled. Tolerance once possessed a 'civilizing function attributed to it by the liberal protagonists of democracy, namely, the protection of dissent'.[32] Subsequently, the liberal function of tolerance has been altered:

> The tolerance which was the great achievement of the liberal era is still professed and (with strong qualifications) practised, while the economic and political process is subjected to an ubiquitous and effective administration in accordance with the predominant interests.[33]

So, unlike Hage for whom tolerance was not simply a good policy gone awry but a bad policy, Marcuse

---

30. Marcuse, 'Repressive Tolerance', 97.
31. Marcuse, 'Repressive Tolerance', 99.
32. Marcuse, 'Repressive Tolerance', 131.
33. Marcuse, 'Repressive Tolerance', 129.

advocated tolerance although, of course, he gave it a completely new twist. He believed that tolerance could still become 'a liberating and humanising force' although the conditions for this 'have still to be created'.[34] However, there are several more aspects of Marcuse's argument that are worth emphasising, particularly as they relate to the topic of this chapter and cross-cultural understanding.

Firstly, the context and focus of Marcuse's analysis are societies which are organised democratically. While critical of such societies,[35] he recognised that democratic societies permit alternative ideas. For Marcuse, it was axiomatic that liberal democratic nations are more tolerant of diverse ideas than totalitarian regimes such as the former Soviet Union. Marcuse recognised this and made the point several times in his article.[36] For example, he argued that democratic freedoms (such as freedom of assembly and speech) are a precondition for restoring tolerance even though currently they are an 'instrument for absolving servitude'.[37] Thus, he maintained that:

> With all its limitations and distortions democratic tolerance is under all circumstances more humane than an institutionalised intolerance which sacrifices the rights and the liberties of the living generations for the sake of future generations.[38]

Nonetheless, he continued: 'The question is whether this is the only alternative.'[39] As we shall note, Marcuse's answer was negative.

---

34. Marcuse, 'Repressive Tolerance, 124.
35. Marcuse, 'Repressive Tolerance', 118.
36. Marcuse, 'Repressive Tolerance', 105–6, 111.
37. Marcuse, 'Repressive Tolerance', 98.
38. Marcuse, 'Repressive Tolerance', 113.
39. *Ibid.*

Secondly, what concerned Marcuse about liberal democracies with mixed economies was that, under the veil of openness to competing ideas, the espousal of real freedom, and tolerance of dissenting ideas and groups, debate is stifled, and the ideas of dissenting groups are muzzled, if not gagged altogether.[40] Yet this occurs under the guise of associated values such as impartiality and neutrality. Thus, it seems as if the propaganda machines are fair, presenting both sides of an argument, or that both sides in a debate are represented. According to Marcuse, however, this is merely a disguise for the relentless pursuit of the powerful ideas which have become popular. Particularly salient is that the impartiality espoused is really a brazen policy of partiality; it is intolerance masquerading as tolerance. It is this which Marcuse found objectionable.

Thirdly, despite the chimera of neutrality and impartiality, Marcuse argued that tolerance requires a re-examination of what constitutes violent and non-violent action. He was opposed to the perpetuation of violence,[41] but observed: 'Even in advanced centers (sic) of civilization, violence actually prevails: it is practiced by the police, in the prisons and mental institutions, in the fight against racial minorities'.[42] His point seems to be that certain forms of violence are tolerated and others are not. The problem is that non-violence is 'normally not only preached to but exacted from the weak'.[43]

While historically, he argued, there is a difference between violence perpetrated by the oppressed and the

---

40. Marcuse, 'Repressive Tolerance', 97, 108.
41. As Marcuse maintained: 'This discussion [about the distinction between violent and non-violent action] should not, from the beginning, be clouded by ideologies which serve the perpetuation of violence'. Marcuse, 'Repressive Tolerance', 116.
42. *Ibid.*
43. *Ibid.*

oppressors, ethically 'both forms of violence are inhuman and evil'.[44] Thus violence is always problematic but particularly so if the violence of the oppressors is tolerated but not the oppressed. Why? Because the violence of the oppressors serves 'the cause of actual violence by weakening the protest against it.'[45]

Despite Marcuse's seemingly radical position, there appears to be some variance between Hage and Marcuse. Hage certainly claimed that any kind of tolerance is preferable to intolerance, but recognised its social function in the power of those who are tolerant in order to retain control over the space they believe belongs to them. He exposes the intoning of those who call for tolerance but use it as a bastion of their own privileged knowledge and position. One conclusion which we could draw from this is that Hage seemed to reject tolerance as a political objective worthy of realisation. Marcuse came to a different conclusion. He was critical of tolerance which is used to repress rather than liberate but, nonetheless, regarded it as a goal worth realising and practising, and one which has the following features.

Firstly, contrary to the claims of passive and active (abstract or pure) tolerance,[46] tolerance should be more like what Marcuse claimed was characteristic of the beginning of the modern period. This early advocacy of tolerance had 'a partisan goal, a subversive liberating notion and practice'.[47] As Marcuse stated: 'The tolerance which enlarged the range and content of freedom was always partisan—intolerant towards the protagonists of the repressive status quo'.[48] Against the tolerance which

---

44. Marcuse, 'Repressive Tolerance', 117.
45. *Ibid.*
46. Marcuse, 'Repressive Tolerance', 99.
47. Marcuse, 'Repressive Tolerance', 95.
48. Marcuse, 'Repressive Tolerance', 99.

purports neutrality and impartiality Marcuse suggested a tolerance which is not '"closed"',[49] one in which the evaluation of alternatives is not precluded or regarded as merely utopian.[50] Consequently, the tolerance that Marcuse advocated extends rather than limits freedom.[51]

Secondly, whereas the tolerance of the past has been indiscriminate, Marcuse advocated what he called a 'discriminating' tolerance.[52] Existing forms of tolerance in western liberal democracies, according to Marcuse, tout tolerance of most perspectives and positions. There is a place for such a tolerance; it is 'justified in harmless debates, in conversation, in academic discussion; it is indispensable in the scientific enterprise, in private religion'.[53]

However, 'where freedom and happiness themselves are at stake'[54] this indiscriminate form of tolerance is unjustified when it enters the political domain. Instead, some behaviours, ideas, views and policies cannot be tolerated. The tolerance which is consistent with freedom 'cannot protect false words and wrong deeds which demonstrate that they contradict and counteract the possibilities of liberation'.[55] For Marcuse, the tolerance required of freedom necessitates increasing tolerance of the left of politics in order to restrain the right. In this way the inequality of freedom, which previously favoured the right, can be offset.

Thirdly, Marcuse did not advocate a complete denial of freedom to the Right. He was specific:

---

49. Marcuse, 'Repressive Tolerance', 132.
50. Marcuse, 'Repressive Tolerance', 114, 107, 95.
51. Marcuse, 'Repressive Tolerance', 102.
52. Marcuse, 'Repressive Tolerance', 102, 120, 133–4, 136.
53. Marcuse, 'Repressive Tolerance', 102.
54. *Ibid.*
55. *Ibid.*

Tolerance would be restricted with respect to movements of a demonstrably aggressive or destructive character (destructive of the prospects for peace, justice, and freedom for all). Such discrimination would also be applied to movements opposing the extension of social legislation to the poor, weak, disabled.[56]

To the accusation that such discriminating tolerance would deny the freedom '"to the other side"', Marcuse claimed that:

there are issues where either there is no 'other side' in any more than a formalistic sense, or where 'the other side' is demonstrably 'regressive' and impedes possible improvement of the human condition. To tolerate propaganda for inhumanity vitiates the goals not only of liberalism but of every progressive political philosophy.[57]

In case one thinks that Marcuse's proposal involves one elite being displaced by another, it should be recognised that, while Marcuse explored the idea, he rejected it uncategorically.

He certainly recognised that the record of the then current elite, who comprise a 'non-intellectual minority of politicians, generals, and businessmen', 'is not very promising'.[58] He also appeared to recognise that his proposal has an 'antidemocratic, "elitist" sound —understandably because of their dangerous radical implications', [59] However, he opposed such options:

56. Marcuse, 'Repressive Tolerance', 133-4.
57. Marcuse, 'Repressive Tolerance', 134.
58. Marcuse, 'Repressive Tolerance', 135.
59. Marcuse, 'Repressive Tolerance', 136.

the alternative to the established semi-democratic process is *not* a dictatorship or elite, no matter how intellectual and intelligent, but the struggle for a real democracy. Part of this struggle is the fight against an ideology of tolerance which, in reality, favours and fortifies the conservation of the status quo of inequality and discrimination.[60]

The discriminating tolerance which Marcuse advocated, the suspension of the rights of those who are intolerant, is 'justified only if the whole of society is in extreme danger'.[61] He argued that American society was in such an emergency situation, yet one which had become 'the normal state of affairs'.[62] Whether he was correct in his diagnosis is another thing. His point is that he regarded his proposals as warranted by the extreme situations that he believed existed at the time. Nonetheless, he rejected the usurping of one elite over another; he advocated the struggle for a real democracy.

Concluding comments

In Chapter 5, I concluded that at least e-value absolutism had the potential to demonstrate that tolerance, presumed essential for cross-cultural understanding, was preferable to intolerance. In this way, this chapter has taken e-value absolutism at its word: tolerance is preferable to intolerance. But is the taken-for-granted understanding of tolerance, the one used every day in conversations, in the media, by politicians, adequate to the task of cross-cultural understanding? Is the tolerance espoused conducive to understanding other cultures or a hindrance? Does it limit or circumscribe the extent of under-

---

60. Marcuse, 'Repressive Tolerance', 136 (emphasis added)
61. Marcuse, 'Repressive Tolerance', 123.
62. *Ibid.*

standing? If it does, what social function does this form of tolerance fulfil? What social purpose does it serve?

In this chapter I have used the work of King, Hage and Marcuse to argue that tolerance as understood in western liberal democracies is limited and restricted in a number of ways. Just as individual people have limits beyond which they cannot tolerate loud music, weather extremes and so on, tolerance in the social and political realm has very definite limits. Further, between the limits there is an upper range that is tolerable, but go beyond this and we will be intolerant.

Perhaps an illustration will convey the point. At one time my main form of recreation during holidays was camping. One of the very helpful devices I discovered was an extendable tent pole. Irrespective of the slope of the ground, or how soft it was, I could extend the pole to the desired height. This was very helpful. Tolerance is like those poles (although, as with all metaphors, they have limits too). People who are tolerant are inclined to regard the range and limits of their tolerance like the extendable tent pole. They are flexible and tolerant to the upper limit of the pole. They regard people who uphold ethnocentric values (E_1) as having a shorter tent pole or as being less extendable. Moreover, when they decide to be more tolerant, as when they encounter a member of another culture, they congratulate themselves on extending the limits of their tolerance to an ever greater height.

This linear aspect of tolerance has a corresponding spatial aspect in the sense that the reason for tolerance thresholds is the influence of another person. The very presence of this external influence demands a reaction and a judgment about whether the behaviour or belief fits within our existing limits, whether our tolerance frontier should expand or contract.

Preston King argued that the call for policies of tolerance is, in fact, a call for people to be more tolerant.

There is no corresponding plea for political and social structures to change. Here, a social function of tolerance as commonly understood can be identified, namely, it limits tolerance to individual behaviour rather than changing structures or institutions. In this way, the dominant view of tolerance is reinforced: individuals are ethnocentric or racist, institutions are not; individuals are intolerant, structures are neutral.

Yet it is quite clear from the experience of indigenous and minority peoples in the West that the education system, institutionalised religion, and the judicial system have been, or are, ethnocentric and racist. Indigenous people speak of the inequalities they experience in the health, economic and political systems. What this means is that in the West policies advocating tolerance are directed at individual citizens. Yet at least some social groups are being forced to tolerate policies and practices that the remainder of the population regard as intolerable —and these policies and practices are inherent in the very institutions in which the majority find their safety and security. This situation explains Marcuse's oxymoron. Tolerance is repressive because the dominant groups are urged to be tolerant while the minority and less powerful groups are supposed to tolerate unjust and racist structures.

The relationship between the individual and the broader social structures of tolerance were also identified by Hage. His argument is that white Australians fantasise that they have some say in how many people migrate to this country, that levels of migration somehow depend on their levels of tolerance and degrees of generosity. Simultaneously, though, this fantasy exposes the deep psychological need to control the national space known as Australia. In this way, tolerance fulfils the social function of enabling white Australians to feel they are in control of migration to Australia or what language is spoken in the street, when clearly they do not have such control—or at least, not directly.

This is of critical importance to cross-cultural understanding. Tolerance, you will recall, is usually regarded as essential to multicultural policies of cultural diversity and understanding. Yet, if tolerance really has a social function to quell debate, to limit change, to support existing inequalities, to control space (no matter how unsuccessfully), what does this say about the role of tolerance in genuine cross-cultural understanding? It would appear that tolerance as usually understood and practised in the West is a policy so allied with existing and inequitable power imbalances that it is incapable of yielding any sort of sympathetic understanding (U_2).

It might be thought that we are being sympathetic when we are being tolerant, but this seems unlikely, if not impossible, particularly if tolerance is allowing dominant groups to exercise power over less powerful groups. How is it possible to understand (U_2), to be understanding, when we are fantasising about control or when tolerance involves control? In this situation it is difficult to envisage how any sort of genuine empathy (U_2) is possible. The use and abuse of power, even if unacknowledged, is likely to clutter, if not sabotage, the process of understanding at all levels (U_1, U_2, U_3). It is just as likely to influence our understanding of facts (U_1), as to impede empathy (U_2) and intrude on the very values with which we defend sympathetic understanding (U_3) and our cultural values generally (V_1).

In one sense, this is a very disappointing conclusion. Tolerance is probably the key value advocated in multicultural societies and is certainly evident in public documents. In fact, it is seen as a condition of multiculturalism. Without tolerance it is difficult to envisage it. Yet, the critique by King, Hage and Marcuse cuts deep and is sustained. All claimed that tolerance is preferable to intolerance. Yet they argued that tolerance as socially understood and constructed fulfils social functions that are at odds with the rhetoric.

In such circumstances, it would seem that E_2 is inevitable. This form of ethnocentrism we have described as rather benign. The reason for this is that whenever we study another culture, or attempt to communicate with people from other cultures, it is unavoidable that we see the encounter from our cultural perspective. We may even concede the point in an effort to rid ourselves of some of the cultural filters we inevitably use. Until this point, E_2 has been largely understood by emphasising what appear to be the epistemological implications of something we take for granted; it is simply impossible to be free of our cultural filters and understand a member of another culture. We acknowledge their presence in order to be less distorted in our communication and understanding, not that we can be totally free from them. But our intentions are sympathetic (U_2) and we earnestly desire to be tolerant and we are committed to being understanding (U_2).

Now though, it seems that tolerance is more about a begrudging acceptance in the context of controlling social space, changing individuals and preserving ethnocentrism and racism in our institutions and, in general, stabilising and supporting our repressive society which claims to be open and tolerant. It is not merely about epistemological difficulties but also about the social positioning of the other.

At this point, it is possible to discern a power dimension in our attempts at cross-cultural understanding. The very value most people believe is integral to cross-cultural understanding is seen to be concerned with the maintenance and reproduction of uneven power relations. This leads to a very interesting, if not challenging, question: if tolerance performs social functions as alleged, how is it possible to be sympathetic

(U_2) and how is it possible to avoid the more malign attributes of E_1? Consider the first part of the question, namely, if tolerance performs the social functions as alleged, how is it possible to be understanding (U_2)? We tend to think of being understanding as being sympathetic or empathetic, as aligning ourselves with another culture's perspective, to be fair in the way we approach problems, particularly sensitive ones. Many who advocate tolerance would include such values in their own armoury. At the very minimum, we regard ourselves as being tolerant.

Yet we have seen that tolerance is about protecting national space, about calling for individuals to be more tolerant, rather than clamouring for radical changes in ethnocentric and racist institutions. According to this diagnosis, tolerance is repressive. If these functions are pervasive how do we avoid them? Can we deny their influence in our attempts to be tolerant and understanding? At the very least, our attempts to be understanding would seem to be severely undermined by the social functions tolerance performs.

Identifying the problem may assist at the personal level, but how can we really understand (U_2) if we benefit in some way from the very institutions which the person we are attempting to understand has experienced as ethnocentric, racist and violent? The question is: does the analysis of tolerance as outlined in this chapter sabotage our best and most sincere efforts to be understanding (U_2)? The answer would seem to be affirmative unless, of course, we were able to find a path by which we could limit and counteract the effect of this repressive tolerance. I think such a path can be discovered, but not before we answer the second question above, and then some more.

The second question was: if tolerance performs the social functions as alleged, how is it possible to avoid the more malign attributes of E_1? The force of the question is similar to that above. If the social functions of tolerance are so political, how is it possible to prevent the slide from E_2 to E_1? The former, you will recall, results from our own cultural filters influencing what we see, how we interpret, and the values by which we judge. At first glance, there may seem nothing sinister here. After all, the people with whom I'm engaged in cross-cultural understanding presumably encounter the same problem. On that score, we are similar.

But what the analysis of tolerance demonstrates is that tolerance is about space, and power and repression. If these colour my cultural filters, then how will I be different from the bigoted defenders of ethnocentrism (E_1) who perceive, interpret and judge using values from the rigidity of their cultural centre? In the context of the critique of tolerance, at what point does E_2 slide so close to E_1 that they are difficult to distinguish? At the very least there would appear to be a power dimension in E_2 previously only attributed to the most rabid forms of ethnocentrism (E_1). But if arguing for tolerance means that institutional power is invoked yet disguised as goodwill, if tolerance as espoused is repressive, if tolerance is claimed to facilitate cross-cultural understanding while exonerating the very institutions which act violently against members of minority groups, how can it facilitate a genuine approach to cross-cultural understanding? In this sense, tolerance has contributed to the problem.

But that, in my view, does not lead inexorably to the conclusion that it should be abandoned altogether. In practical terms, the conclusion reached is that approaching cross-cultural understanding necessitates such a critique in order to be vigilant whenever appeals to tolerance are made. It is also imperative to use the critique to develop a notion of tolerance which is both critical and facilitates cross-cultural understanding. That is why Marcuse's position is so helpful; he outlined another scenario which renders possible the participation of those voices previously not tolerated. He believes that tolerance includes the ability to be intolerant of any attempt to curtail such full participation.

The suggestion that tolerance should be critical and intolerant may be alarming. The retort might be that we should be impartial and neutral in weighing up competing claims. King, Hage and Marcuse demonstrated that the social function tolerance performs is not impartial or neutral. Nonetheless, Marcuse in particular showed how both are used in the defence of repressive tolerance. If such a view has merit, approaching cross-cultural understanding while advocating neutrality will exacerbate the difficulties, not resolve them. The social function of neutrality is the topic of the next chapter.

7

Do relativism, neutrality and impartiality impede cross-cultural understanding?

Introduction

In the previous chapter I concluded by saying that if tolerance is to be used as a motivation for cross-cultural understanding it will, of necessity, be a different kind to that analysed and criticised by King, Hage and Marcuse. All three, albeit in different respects, regarded versions of tolerance as practised in western liberal democracies as an instrument of political power which is closer to political oppression and repression than cultural pluralism.

When analysed, tolerance as practised is not the accepting, inclusive, open political virtue it might seem to be. In fact, Preston King, Ghassan Hage and Herbert Marcuse mounted an impressive array of arguments against it. We might summarise these arguments by saying that, for King the call for tolerance is more about changing attitudes than changing structures, which are rendered immune from change by such a call; that for Hage tolerance disguises the power relationships which attempt to control national space; and for Marcuse tolerance in western liberal democracies is repressive.

Yet there is an irony in their analyses. If they are valid, then they are at least one explanation of the social function performed by tolerance, namely, to assert and control and repress while espousing the opposite. But what of the alleged neutrality and impartiality of tolerance? You will recall that Marcuse, in particular, noted the function performed by the seeming neutrality and impartiality of tolerance. Is that part of its social function? There are also problems with the defence of tolerance. Moreover, in the light of e-value relativism and e-value absolutism some pertinent questions arise: if e-value relativism is so inadequate as a defence of values (including tolerance), why is it so popular? Why is it used so much? What are the social functions of e-value relativism? Such questions are investigated in this chapter.

Another concern I address in this chapter arises from the problems we have found with tolerance. What is the corrective to repressive tolerance and its usual defence? What is the antidote if tolerance and its epistemological defences are flawed, yet are still used in ways which distort and subvert liberal rhetoric? More specifically, if we adopt Marcuse's notion of discriminating tolerance where will the discrimination begin? If we are to be tolerant yet avoid the repressive pitfalls, from whose perspective are we to begin our assessment? Marcuse certainly said we should create a climate conducive to the freedom of the repressed. But does our assessment include their perspectives? Further, if we do factor in their perspective, to what extent do we do use their standpoint? Do we regard it uncritically or are we permitted some evaluation?

Such questions are central to any approach to cross-cultural understanding. The critique in the previous chapter alerted us to the problems associated with liberal notions of tolerance. It does that very well. But if we decide there is a form of tolerance worth pursuing, one which, in Marcuse's terminology, is discriminating, which advocates tolerance to those who previously experienced intolerance, there remains the issue of whose perspective we should adopt in order to begin searching for the tolerance we do want. Germane here is the issue of the extent to which we should adopt it in preference to other standpoints, and the competing, powerful and intolerant opposition. In other words, if we accept the criticism of tolerance yet decide that Marcuse's discriminate tolerance is preferable to intolerance and is a political goal worth pursuing, then where do we start? From whose perspective do we begin? If the loudest voices I hear are of the most powerful and are inextricably linked to the cause of intolerance, repressive tolerance or controlling space, whose voice should I hear in order to advance cross-cultural understanding in the sense of adhering to a policy of discriminating tolerance?

In the last two decades there has been a resurgence of interest in these and similar questions. A number of marginalised voices have combined to emphasise and use the standpoints of those whose voices have been ignored, or whose protests have been muzzled or shouted down by stronger voices. Such marginalised voices include those of women, people who have been colonised, the descendents of people who were slaves, people of the so-called Third World, and people who are gay or lesbian. Within each group there is also diversity, so that for example, there are women who have a variety of skin pigmentations and sexualities. The virtue of beginning with such voices, particularly as proposed by Sandra Harding,[1] is that it is based on a critique of both relativism and neutral objectivity while, simultaneously, proposing an objectivity which is more adept at hearing the standpoints of voices hitherto unheard, or protests previously drowned-out.

This chapter begins by outlining the social function that e-value-relativism performs in creating a power vacuum which gives the pretence of tolerance and

1.   Sandra Harding, 'After the Neutrality Ideal: Science, Politics and "Strong Objectivity"', in *Social Research*, 59/3 (1992): 567–87.

diversity, but which in turn allows the powerbrokers to dictate their terms. I will return to aspects of Marcuse's work to explore this theme and also introduce the work of Sandra Harding, including her views on objectivity. My argument in this chapter is that if we are to understand others, including people from other cultures, it is essential to start from their standpoint. This makes it feasible, and I dare say possible, to overcome the minimalist notions of objectivity which reduce understanding to either condescension at best, or ethnocentrism at worst. A prerequisite for cross-cultural understanding is, I argue, hearing the voices of others previously unheard. The argument begins with the social function of e-value relativism which attempts to disentangle Marcuse's use of the terms impartiality, neutrality and objectivity.

The social function of neutrality

If impartiality refers to the equal treatment of ideas in the administration, the media and policy, neutrality is a conesquence of the fair treatment of conflicting ideas. However, competing ideas or knowledge claims of the more powerful and those of the less powerful are not treated equally. We might say that when ideas or knowledge claims are played out in what is purportedly the free and fair exchange of competing ideas, the conesquence is that the hierarchy is maintained. When the superior and inferior and often dissenting positions have engaged in this way and the hierarchy of knowledge still remains, the inferior position has been neutralised and its potential to assert, or even usurp, a position higher in the hierarchy of knowledge has dissipated. Marcuse called this the 'neutralization of opposites'[2] or a 'spurious neutrality'.[3]

---

2.   Herbert Marcuse, 'Repressive Tolerance', in *A Critique of Pure Tolerance*, Herbert Marcuse, 'Repressive Tolerance', in Robert P

We can now see Marcuse's use of 'objectivity' at work. He agreed that 'impartiality to the utmost' and the 'equal treatment of competing and conflicting issues is indeed a basic requirement for decision-making in the democratic process', as it is for 'defining the limits of tolerance'.[4] However, he continued, in the current social, economic and political arrangements, 'in a democracy with total-itarian organisation',[5] such impartiality or 'objectivity' may fulfil a very different function, which is:

> to foster a mental attitude which tends to obliterate the difference between true and false, information and indoctrination, right and wrong. In fact, the decision between opposed opinions has been made before the presentation and discussion gets under way—made, not by a conspiracy or a sponsor or a publisher, not by any dictatorship, but rather by the 'normal course of events', which is the course of administered events, and by the mentality shaped in this course.[6]

Marcuse's point is that objectivity, impartiality and neutrality, while different in some respects, perform a crucial social and political function; they create the impression or pretence of objectivity. In fact, if objectivity is about truth, about some form of certain, valid knowledge which can withstand critical examination, then

---

Wolff and Barrington Moore Jnr, and Herbert Marcuse, *A Critique of Pure Tolerance* (London: Jonathon Cape, 1969), 111, 125, 127.

3. Marcuse, 'Repressive Tolerance', 127.
4. Marcuse, 'Repressive Tolerance', 111.
5. *Ibid.*
6. *Ibid.*

Marcuse described this objectivity as 'spurious'.[7] For, 'If objectivity has anything to do with truth, and if truth is more than a matter of logic and science, then this kind of objectivity [in western liberal democracies] is false, and this kind of tolerance inhuman'.[8]

This means that what is considered objective is not. It may sound as if Marcuse wanted it both ways; that there is, and there is not, a sense in which values and political and social ideas such as tolerance are objective. Indeed, Marcuse did state that values can be objective but in the above he emphasised that what masquerades as objectivity is not objective at all; it is a distortion. It is the socially or politically approved version of truth, it is promoted as objective, but what is claimed as true and, therefore, objective is at variance with reality. So, even though the impression of truth and objectivity is given, the political practice belies it.

We might call this political objectivity, that is, the objectivity promoted by some socially accredited claims of powerful and established interests. Further, it may also appear as if impartiality and neutrality are practised, but the rhetoric and practice disguises the real authoritarian characteristic of repressive tolerance. Such political oppression is also legitimated by being shrouded in the valued goals of impartiality and objectivity. In summary, Marcuse repudiated the socially certified version of truth which limits tolerance while simultaneously espousing it. He rejected the impartiality and neutrality which purportedly champion objectivity; their use is a giant ruse to create the impression of objectivity while generating the very opposite.

Thus, Marcuse opposed the much vaunted claim of objectivity as always being neutral and impartial; used in this way it becomes a charade for repressive tolerance.

---

7.   Marcuse, 'Repressive Tolerance', 112.

8.   *Ibid.*

Does this mean that Marcuse rejected the notion of objectivity altogether? Before we answer that question it is worth asking the following: if Marcuse exposed the political consequences of objectivity-as-neutrality, does its opposite, e-value relativism, also perform a social function?

The answer is yes. This is discernable in Marcuse's view that impartiality and neutrality have their origins in an epistemology. The reason that impartiality and neutrality are so socially powerful and popular, Marcuse argued, is because it is believed that truth as such cannot be found. Marcuse dissented from this view but he alluded to it when he wrote that the 'pure toleration of sense and nonsense is justified by the democratic argument that nobody, neither group nor individual, is in possession of the truth and capable of defining what is right and wrong, good and bad'.[9]

Notwithstanding the so called democratic argument the issue Marcuse highlighted is also epistemological. According to Marcuse, the reason that no-one is in possession of the truth about what is right and wrong, good and bad is because of the e-value relativism which says that no such view is possible.[10] The socially creditable position is that it is impossible to say that one view is right and another wrong; it is impossible to arbitrate between values. This position we know as e-value relativism. In rejecting it, Marcuse exposed its social function which is paradoxical: epistemologically no value

9.   Marcuse, 'Repressive Tolerance', 108.
10. I recognise that it is not only relativism about values that is at issue in this context. In some instances it is relativism about facts. You may delete the 'value' in e-value relativism. However, as values play an integral role in politics, I retain the term here and in the next few pages.

is right or wrong which, in turn, obscures the fact that only the socially certified view is correct.

So, for Marcuse there is a powerful institutionalised view about what is objective and what is objectively true. In this oppressive climate, in which e-value relativism is touted as the dominant epistemological position, it is impossible to say that one value position is preferable to another. This creates both an illusion of impartiality and neutrality, and a vacuum in which the powerful are able to usurp what are promoted as valid and powerful political and social ideas and values.

Put differently, Marcuse claimed that socially, im-partiality and neutrality are used in two different ways. One use is epistemological; it is about how we decide what counts for knowledge. The dominant conclusion in the West is that there is no definitive and absolute claim about right or wrong, good or bad, true or false, because we do not have the means available to decide such things. The other use is political; a power vacuum is created by the powerbrokers because it is (allegedly) impossible to arbitrate between values, and so the dominant interests usurp that power. While masquerading as neutrality and impartiality, understood both epistemologically and politically, 'a mentality is created for which right and wrong, true and false are predefined wherever they affect the vital interests of the society'.[11]

Marcuse's point is that even theories of knowledge are socially licensed and certified, and perform social func-tions. In the light of his argument he might seem to be opposed to objective knowledge. However, while Marcuse opposed the political limitations of repressive tolerance that does not make him an e-value relativist, as the following demonstrates.

> Tolerance of free speech is the way of
> improvement, of progress in liberation, *not*

---

11. Marcuse, 'Repressive Tolerance', 109.

because there is no objective truth, and improvement must necessarily be a compromise
between a variety of opinions, but because
there *is* an objective truth which can be
discovered, ascertained only in learning and
comprehending that which is and that which
can be and ought to be done for the sake of
improving the lot of mankind. This common
and historical 'ought' is not immediately
evident, at hand: it has to be uncovered by
'cutting through', 'splitting', 'breaking
asunder' *(dis-cutio)* the given material—
separating right and wrong, good and bad,
correct and incorrect.[12]

Here, Marcuse made it clear that he is, as we would
say, an e-value absolutist. His objection to repressive
tolerance did not lead him to abandon tolerance
altogether, any more than his rejection of objectivity-as-
neutrality caused him to jettison objectivity. Further,
unlike many of his contemporaries, his obvious opposition to political absolutism did not lead him to e-
value relativism, even though he indicated the social
function it performs.

Marcuse is not the only one who has pointed out the
social function of e-value relativism and e-value
absolutism. Sandra Harding, writing in the feminist
tradition, is another.[13] However, more than Marcuse, she
addressed the question of whose voice should be heard if
we are to overcome some of the epistemological and
political conundrums outlined above and, I would add, be
understanding. I turn to her perspective now.

---

12. Marcuse, 'Repressive Tolerance', 103–4.
13. Harding, 'After the Neutrality Ideal', 567–87.

Harding's critique of relativism and objectivity-as-neutrality

Harding's argument is, at least in part, a response to the absolutist-relativist debate mentioned in previous chapters. Although in Chapter 5 I stated that I prefer to retain the dichotomy between absolutism and relativism, Harding followed general usage and largely referred to objectivity and relativism. Nonetheless, this should not be too off-putting because Marcuse used objectivity (rather than absolutism) and the sense does not really change.

Like Marcuse, Harding noted that neutrality is attached to objectivity in both the natural and physical sciences and the social sciences.[14] She identified the problems associated with objectivity-as-neutrality, including the depoliticisation of contentious social issues so that they are no longer part of the political debate. These important contentious issues have been resolved, or are considered resolved, because they have been reduced to technical and scientific issues assigned to socially accredited experts.

According to Harding, a social science committed to objectivity-as-neutrality is unable to challenge that which masquerades as objective. Out of the political arena, and without challenge, controversies have been normalised with the result that 'scientific neutrality ensures that "might makes right"'.[15] Furthermore, she noted how 'feminist and postcolonial critics recently have pointed to the inadequacy of neutral objectivism to identify the androcentric, Eurocentric, and racist assumptions in many of the most widely accepted scientific claims'.[16]

Harding argued that objectivity-as-neutrality 'operationalises objectivity too weakly'.[17] There are many

---

14. Harding, 'After the Neutrality Ideal', 568–9.
15. Harding, 'After the Neutrality Ideal', 569.
16. Harding, 'After the Neutrality Ideal', 574.
17. Harding, 'After the Neutrality Ideal', 579.

reasons for this but they centre on the presence of distorting cultural assumptions in the social sciences which, because of the alleged neutrality, escape detection.[18] The neutrality ideal effectively precludes the possibility that powerful cultural assumptions and biases are uncovered and, further, neutrality cannot ensure that the requisite values are galvanised into action. Moral and political values such as fairness, honesty and detachment might suggest that minority groups are treated in a balanced way, and the perspectives of those on the margins are taken seriously. However, such values operate to silence smaller, dissenting voices.[19]

According to Harding, the voices of peoples of different colour, and the colonised, do not feature in the sciences and social sciences in the same way as the dominant voices, even in academic journals, books and conferences. The most socially powerful perspectives are, with scientific and social scientific backing, not neutral and they exclude some voices. 'Thus the sciences are left complicitous with the projects of the most powerful groups in society. The neutrality requirement is not just ineffective at maximising objectivity; it is an obstacle to it'.[20]

Many, including some postmodernists, have abandoned objectivity because of this purported and nominal neutrality. Harding resisted this temptation but her alternative, unlike others, was not to resort to relativism. Her reasons seem to be twofold.[21] Firstly, Harding noted that relativists act as if they were objectivists. The e-value relativist critics of racism or ethnocentrism do not believe or act as if their positions

---

18. Harding, 'After the Neutrality Ideal', 577-9.
19. Harding, 'After the Neutrality Ideal', 580.
20. *Ibid.*
21. Harding, 'After the Neutrality Ideal', 577–88.

are merely perspectival or partial. Second, Harding noted that even relativism originated in a particular time and place. It, too, can be relativised. It can be shown to have its origins in nineteenth-century Europe as anthropologists became aware of the myriad ways of thinking and behaving in the cultures they described. There is, thus, neither justification for relativists to privilege their own position nor any warrant to accept it.[22]

As indicated, Harding's alternative to the political constraints associated with neutrality, and what I would call e-value relativism, is to maximise objectivity, to defend a strong objectivity against the weaker objectivity-as-neutrality which she exposed as defending existing inequality and injustice.[23] Her argument is that it is possible—indeed, essential—to strive for 'the *least* possible partial and distorted' results of social scientific research,[24] to increase 'the production of less partial and distorted accounts of nature and social relations' and promote those values such as 'fairness, honesty, detachment' and 'advancing democracy' which are required to maximise objectivity.[25]

In order to do this it is necessary to begin from outside the institutional sites of bias and distortion. Harding suggested starting from the lives of the most marginalised. This, in turn, is based on a social and political theory, one which is concerned with the connec-tions between the centre and margins.[26] Accordingly, the rich are located in the centre because the poor are on the margins; the socially constructed patriarchy is valorised as socially constructed female gender stereotypes are

22. Harding, 'After the Neutrality Ideal', 576–7.
23. Harding, 'After the Neutrality Ideal', 573.
24. *Ibid*, (emphasis added).
25. Harding, 'After the Neutrality Ideal', 580.
26. Harding, 'After the Neutrality Ideal', 581–2.

devalued; the dominant culture is privileged as sub-cultures are excluded and marginalised.

Maximising objectivity demands that we hear people on the perimeters, that research begins from their pers-pective and not those of the centre. In Kuhnian language, this requires a paradigm shift in all aspects of research. According to Harding, what constitutes the research program, the problem to be investigated, the questions asked, the evidence received, must begin from the perspective of those on the margins, not the centre.

In this, Harding went further than Marcuse. Un-doubtedly, Marcuse believed that the voices of members of groups previously not tolerated should be tolerated. He advocated listening to their story from their previously repressed viewpoint. However, Harding urged that not only should those on the margins be heard, but they should be the starting point of our research. For our purposes this means the starting point of our under-standing. Several points are worthy of emphasis.

Firstly, the accounts are not fundamentally about the lives of the marginalised.[27] Harding did not advocate generating ethnosciences of those on the margins. Her aim was to research the science of their experiences and their causes. Thus by sciences Harding meant 'systematic causal accounts of how the natural and social orders are organised such that the everyday lives of marginalised people end up in the conditions they do'.[28] Hence, explanatory accounts remain integral to science. The salient point is that they begin with the very people and groups whose life conditions are to be explained rather than the pretensions to objectivity of those who claim to be neutral.

27. Harding, 'After the Neutrality Ideal', 582.
28. *Ibid.*

Secondly, Harding distanced herself from what she called interpretative approaches. By this she seems to refer to those approaches which merely describe the personal perspectives of people whose life conditions are under scrutiny. She acknowledged that standpoint theory (of which Harding's is representative) is 'persistently misread as a kind of "perspectivalism" that generates relativistic interpretations of nature and social relations'.[29] Harding rejected any suggestion that her work is relativist in this way. Thirdly, starting from those on the margins does not entail taking their accounts as incorrigible.[30] As this word will be used in the final chapter it is important to clarify Harding's use it.

Incorrigible here means that the perspectives of those on the margins are not 'irrefutable grounds for knowledge'.[31] Starting from the standpoint of those on the margins is not the last step in obtaining a less partial and distorted account, but it is an indispensable first step. But even here the aim is not to obtain a personal account which may be regarded as one interpretation among many, but to begin the process whereby we acquire a 'causal, critical account of the regularities of the natural and social world and their underlying causal tendencies'.[32] In this sense, it is a science, an explanatory account.

One might think that the accounts, or explanations, of those on the margins should be taken as the only account. Harding opposed this suggestion. She claimed that 'to start from marginal lives is not necessarily to take one's problems in terms in which they are expressed by

---

29. Harding, 'After the Neutrality Ideal', 583.
30. Here incorrigible does not mean incapable of reform—its dictionary usage. It appears to be a technical term derived from corrigible, and here means not necessarily correct or absolute.
31. Harding, 'After the Neutrality Ideal', 585.
32. *Ibid.*

marginalized people'. This is as 'true of researchers who come from such groups as for those who do not'.[33]

Her reason is that it is possible that no-one is totally resistant to the 'dominant ideology' including those who are on the margins. This is another reason why their account should not be regarded as incapable of correction, that is, incorrigible. According to Harding, 'the dominant ideology restricts what everyone, including marginalised people, are permitted to see and shapes everyone's consciousness'.[34] As she explained:

> African Americans, too, have argued that African Americans should be satisfied with their lesser places in the social order. Women, like men, have had to learn to think of sexual harassment, not as a matter of 'boys will be boys', but as a violation of women's civil rights. Marital rape was a legal and, for most people, conceptual impossibility until recently. Western feminists, like the rest of Westerners, are only beginning to learn how to conceptualise many of our 'problems' in anti-Eurocentric terms.[35]

Thus, Harding acknowledged the influence of the social order and its adverse consequences for marginalised people. Nonetheless, to start with the standpoints of those on the margins is a totally different project from attempting to be neutral and then purporting to be objective. The latter does not even purport to understand (U_2) and, further, it abjures personal and political commitments as subjective intrusions which allegedly distort but,

---

33. Harding, 'After the Neutrality Ideal', 582.
34. Harding, 'After the Neutrality Ideal', 582–3.
35. Harding, 'After the Neutrality Ideal', 583.

according to Harding, ignore the corrosive distortions of their neutrality.

Some may respond that Harding is committed to a standpoint that contaminates her research. For example, logical positivists will claim that her research results will be subjective. Even some who are critical of a crude scientism may still argue that, at best, what Harding advocated will yield contrary views between which we cannot arbitrate. However, Harding argued that stand-point theory, as she called her position,[36] rejects such epistemological relativism. Rather than merely repeat her position, it is worth exploring the issue of commitments.

It is often thought that commitments distort research. In a sense, Harding would agree—but with a different twist. The commitment to objectivity-as-neutrality has resulted in the perpetuation of distortions which ignore those at the margins while defending and legitimating the very structures which cause their poor life conditions. We have noted the view that our cultural filters influence our perceptions and understanding. Our cultural filters are very much like our commitments. They reflect our com-mitment to those things we cherish and value. We are committed to our values, the value of cross-cultural understanding, and approaching the task with empathy (U_2). One way or another, by default or with full aware-ness, everyone is committed to various values, including those committed to ethnocentrism, cultural relativism and cultural pluralism. This leads to two very significant points. The first concerns the inevitability of our commit-ments and our allegiances; the second regards an up side to what is usually regarded as the down side of our com-mitments.

So, to the first point which arises from the inevitably of our commitments. It is obvious that if our commitments are inevitable then the crucial issue cannot be whether we

---

36. Harding, 'After the Neutrality Ideal', 583.

will have them or not; we have them! And we bring them to cross-cultural understanding. Thus, the absolutely decisive issue is the values we bring to the task. If commitments are inevitable, the critical question is: to what are we committed when we approach cross-cultural understanding? Are we really committed to cross-cultural understanding? If we are, what commitments are likely to be conducive to, and enhance, it? If there is an issue over which a cultural group on the margins and a powerful dominant group disagree, where will our allegiances lie? Where will we start?

It may appear that these questions are those of a political tract or treatise rather than a book which some would think should be balanced and even-handed. But Harding has demonstrated how something as apparently balanced as science is not. According to Harding, even when science claims to be objective and neutral it systematically distorts social reality in a way that minimises objectivity and defends powerful groups and structures. In this chapter we have found that the social function of impartiality, neutrality and relativism is that of a smokescreen behind which oppressive and repressive social and political forces reign supreme.

Thus, whether the question of allegiances seems as if they come from a political tract is somewhat irrelevant. I might think I am being objective when I do my social science but it is possible that I may descend into some form of ethnocentrism (E_2, that is, arising from within our cultural filters). Likewise, in the context of neutrality turning into its opposite, and tolerance performing contrary social functions, an uncritical approach to cultural baggage is likely to be counterproductive to cross-cultural understanding at best. More significantly, there is the possibility that the very way I approach the task may not only sabotage cross-cultural understanding but perpetuate the very attitudes, beliefs and cultural practices that render it impossible and exacerbate and prolong the very discrimination, ethnocentrism (E_2), and marginalisation that contribute to it. Thus, our commitments can—one way or another—facilitate or obstruct. And because our best and most trusted commitments can so easily turn into their opposites, a key question becomes: whose side are we on? With whom do we want to identify as we approach cross-cultural understanding?

If those western values which we trust to enhance cross-cultural understanding are in fact hostile to it, then an uncritical approach is unlikely to identify with the cultural groups we are attempting to understand. If the values of western social sciences, such as impartiality, neutrality, relativism and objectivity, have let us down so badly, it would seem necessary in the interests of cross-cultural understanding to start from a perspective more likely to allow the full flowering of values consistent with cross-cultural understanding. This is another reason why I suggest that our research begins with those on the margins.

So, to a second point about commitments. It might seem that, as commitments are inevitable, our cross-cultural understanding will reflect our ideologies. Whatever approach is adopted, whatever method is used, as they reflect our commitments so too will they affect our cross-cultural understanding. Yet, there are examples where the pursuit and enhancement of understanding have not been adversely influenced by commitments. For example, few would dispute the fact that Karl Marx advanced our understanding of nineteenth-century industrial England. His work is contentious, of course, but his commitment to the proletariat did not lead him down some blind alley which distorted the results of his research into the conditions in which the proletariat lived and worked.[37]

---

37. Harding, 'After the Neutrality Ideal', 583–5.

Revisionist historians, of whatever commitment, have challenged dominant historical explanations. Even if their work is regarded as questionable, their findings raise issues of fact which require explanation. I am thinking of the challenge by the revisionist historians of the entry of the United States into the Second World War or the timing of the dropping of the atomic bombs on Hiroshima and Nagasaki, or the origins of the Cold War.

Likewise, feminist historians have shed new light on a whole range of shibboleths, ranging from accounts of the past, details of the extent of adverse discrimination, and explanations of inequality. Their commitment is clear. Yet few would doubt that they have provided more than a valuable corrective to the histories of those few, elite and privileged males who wrote most history prior to the last two or three decades. Thus, our commitments are not necessarily obstacles to the advance of knowledge and understanding but inevitable and indispensable to them.

One reaction to this might be to remind me that even Sandra Harding conceded that 'the dominant ideology restricts what everyone, including marginalised people, are permitted to see and shapes everyone's consciousness'.[38] Do the resultant conflicting positions cancel each other out? If our commitments influence our findings, and different commitments yield different findings, and there is no method of arbitrating between them (either the commitments or the findings), aren't we back in the world of countervailing ideologies again?

However, as popular as such a position might be, it does not necessarily follow that the dominant ideology is immutable. As Harding pointed out,[39] previously women, and men, may have thought of sexual harassment as a matter of 'boys will be boys'. That reflects the

---

38. Harding, 'After the Neutrality Ideal', 582–3.
39. *Ibid.*

dominant ideology. Yet, increasingly, both women and men recognise that sexual harassment is a violation of the civil rights of women. Likewise, marital rape was legal and a conceptual impossibility until recently. Without denying the difficulties women who have been raped encounter in the judicial system, the fact remains that sexual relations without consent in marriage is regarded as rape just as it is in any other circumstance.

Again, without being complacent, the dominant ideology does not render change impossible. Harding also conceded that western feminists, like other westerners, are also beginning to sense the Eurocentric bias in our diagnoses of our own and other's problems. Thus, initially, it may appear that these commitments may be ideologies which distort research findings, between which it is impossible to arbitrate. However, these very commitments have led to better knowledge (U_1) and understanding (U_2).

One implication which follows may surprise. To reach it, a little backtracking is necessary. Much of modern science and social science is based on the thought that neutrality is the way to avoid bias. Thus, neutrality is advocated. But if, as argued, neutrality does not necessarily lead to objectivity, if objectivity-as-neutrality can lead to distorted results, then it might be argued that the quest for objectivity as neutrality should also be abandoned. According to this view, objectivity too should be jettisoned because it merely reinforces the adverse influence of our commitments and cultural filters. We have returned to the influence of the cultural filters which we discussed in the first chapter.

However, Harding's position indicates a way to avoid relativism and overcome the problems associated with objectivity as neutrality. It highlights a way to maximise objectivity and advance our knowledge and understanding. Using Sandra Harding's analysis, it is possible to argue that maximising objectivity is a realisable goal.

But it depends on beginning our attempts at explanation and understanding from the position of those on the margins. This discussion is, in turn, based on our commitments to the values of explanation, of under-standing and of maximising objectivity. If so, then our commitments play a pivotal role and lead us to a surprising conclusion—it would be optimal if our values were demonstrably preferable to their opposites. It would be preferable if we could articulate our commitment to certain values as something which we need neither to recoil from nor be coy over. It would be preferable if we could defend and justify our rejection of inferior alternatives.

Yet, as we have seen repeatedly, such a possibility is largely denied in the West, usually on the grounds that we cannot arbitrate between values. Then when, in moments of methodological weakness, the temptation cannot be resisted and one set of values is deemed preferable to another, the values determined to be superior are allegedly imposed on unwilling opponents. We have returned to the problems of e-value absolutism and e-value relativism (and their political correlates). That is heavy ground which we do not need to plough again. However, raising its formidable head again is the importance of defending our values, of showing that certain values are preferable to others without feeling the need to impose them on other people.

However, before the issue of defending our commitments is explored in the next chapter it is worth returning to the matter of starting with the standpoints of the most marginalised, and exploring just what this might involve. Sandra Harding suggested that it is necessary to begin our research from that perspective in order to achieve a less distorted perspective. But if I am conversing with a person from a marginalised position, how it is possible to understand their outlook? How can anyone understand another person's experiences, particularly when I have not had them myself? Are there any further safeguards to ensure that the effect of my cultural filters is minimised? What should count as understanding? What should I regard as understanding? What will convince my cultural interlocutor that I understand?

Laurence Thomas and moral deference

Laurence Thomas addressed these issues by arguing that some people are owed moral deference. As he claimed, 'the attitude of moral deference is, as it were, a prelude to bearing witness to another's pain with that person's authorization—that person's blessing, if you will'.[40] Thus, moral deference comes before understanding. It is a commitment to a value. So it is relevant to our concerns because moral deference is about how it is possible to understand those on the margins and about how we approach understanding. Even if the person's rendition of their experience(s) is inaccurate, which Thomas conceded is possible, their understanding of their situation is what must be explained.[41] Without a full appreciation of their experience(s), we can't know what a full account is, nor can we know what is to be explained. Another reason moral deference is relevant to cross-cultural under-standing is that it often involves westerners attempting to understand non-westerners which, in turn, often means that a member of a dominant group is attempting to understand a member of a non-dominant group.

Moral deference is necessary because of the inadequacy of imagination and reason when we attempt to under-stand another person's pain.[42] There is no vantage,

---

40. Laurence M Thomas, 'Moral Deference', in *Theorising Multiculturalism: A Guide to the Current Debate*, edited by Cynthia Willet (Massachusetts: Blackwell, 1998), 359.
41. Thomas, 'Moral Deference', 374.
42. Thomas, 'Moral Deference', 359, 361, 368, 371.

according to Thomas, from which it is possible by imagination or reasoning to grasp someone else's pain. One explanation for this is that people belong to different social groupings, for example, gender, ethnicity or race. The likelihood of experiencing socially induced pain is likely to be greater amongst those in 'well-defined diminished social categories'[43] than amongst members of privileged social categories.[44] The critical question is: 'How is it possible to be morally responsive in an appropriate way to those belonging to a diminished social category group if one does not belong to that category?'[45] Translated into the scenario of cross-cultural understanding, the question is: how is it possible to be morally responsive to people from a diminished social culture when I do not belong to it? It is at this point that Thomas suggested moral deference.

Thomas pointed out that we understand ourselves, at least in part, as others conceive us. In a just world, all members of a society would be regarded equally and valued equally. 'By contrast', according to Thomas,

> in an oppressive society, the victims of oppression - diminished social category persons I mean - are constituted, in both masterfully subtle ways and in ever so explicit ways, so as not to see themselves as full and equal members of society. I shall refer to this as downward social constitution.[46]

One of the most powerful dilemmas posed by this downward social constitution is that the members of diminished social categories contend with the 'problem of

---

43. Thomas, 'Moral Deference', 363.
44. *Ibid.*
45. Thomas, 'Moral Deference', 365.
46. *Ibid.*

social category ambiguity'.[47] This ambiguity may arise, for example, when a person in a diminished social category is unsure whether a comment reflects their downward social constitution or something else, or both. They are uncertain about the meaning of the comment. It may be innocuous. Indeed, the ambiguity may not have been a result of their diminished social category 'but the very nature of the context of one's social reality as a diminished social category does not allow one to rule out the possibility with confidence'.[48]

Thomas poignantly described the profound sense of vulnerability that members of a diminished social category experience because of gender, ethnicity or race, for example, and the haunting memories of such experiences which can be activated by any number of things, including witnessing similar experiences of other members of their social group or having another experience of their own. Thus, being constituted as a member of a diminished social category involves the constant experience of the social 'claim that they lack the wherewithal to measure up in an important social dimension'.[49] According to Thomas, there is a sense of exhaustion at feeling the need to refute the social claim, vulnerability because there is very little a member of a diminished social category can do to demonstrate the claim is false, and the 'vulnerability of exhaustion stemming from the feeling that one must speak up because no-one else will, although continually speaking up might diminish one's effectiveness'.[50]

Thomas argued that there is a correlation between the way we are constituted socially and the resultant emotional consequences. In other words, emotions are

---

47. Thomas, 'Moral Deference', 366.
48. Thomas, 'Moral Deference', 366–7.
49. Thomas, 'Moral Deference', 367.
50. *Ibid.*

configured by social category. There are different emotional category configurations commensurate with social categorisation.[51] Thus a man who 'abhors violence against females, and understands very well why a victim of rape would rather be comforted by a female rather than a male, nonetheless does not have the emotional configuration of a female'.[52] One reason for this is that the fear of sexual violence is not usually such a problem for a man walking alone at night as it is for a woman. Consequently, they have different emotional category configurations.

Likewise a black and a white man brutally attacked at night have a different emotional configuration to their experience of violation. Thomas, himself African-American,[53] neither condoned the experience of either, nor belittled the pain of the man who is white. However, he maintained that their experiences differ in some respects. It is worth quoting Thomas at length:

> the white's fear may very well be a reminder of the random brutality of some blacks and the moral squalor in which some wallow. The experience may seal his conviction that blacks lack the wherewithal to live morally decent lives. But for all of that, the experience will not be a reminder that he is a second class citizen. It will not make him vulnerable to that pain. He will not have the pain of being scarred by those who in fact have power over so very much of his life. By and large, the white will not really have to concern himself with having to trust blacks who have power over him, as with a little effort and creativity the white can avoid situations of that kind;

51. Thomas, 'Moral Deference', 369.
52. *Ibid.*
53. Thomas, 'Moral Deference', 370–1.

whereas for the black, having to trust whites who have power over him is a real possibility. So whereas some physical distance from blacks, coupled with time, might serve to heal the wounds of the white, this healing route is not a genuine possibility for a black. This is yet another dimension along which the black will live with his pain in quite a different manner to the white.[54]

Thomas emphasised that neither man should have experienced the brutality and pain: 'the wrong may be equal in either case'.[55] However, his point is:

that because the black and the white man have different emotional category configurations, each will experience their respective pain in a radically different manner. While economic differences could be factored in here, I did not develop the point with such differences in mind. The force of the point is not diminished in the least if both white and black are upper-middle-class people enjoying equally high salaries.[56]

In this and similar situations, Thomas claimed, moral deference is the appropriate response. His argument is that if I want to behave in a morally responsible way then I owe moral deference to people whose experiences are shaped by their diminished social category. When they tell me of their experiences from 'the standpoint of an emotional category configuration' to which I have not had access, 'there should be a presumption in favour of the person's account' of their experiences. 'This presumption

---

54. Thomas, 'Moral Deference', 369.
55. Thomas, 'Moral Deference', 370.
56. *Ibid.*

is warranted because the individual is speaking from a vantage' to which I do not have access.[57]

There are three points which are noteworthy about moral deference. Firstly, moral deference allows access to the standpoint of people from different social categories and with a different emotional category configuration. For cross-cultural understanding this is significant. According to Thomas, moral deference enables us to empathise with another person's pain and suffering even if we are unable to completely understand it. It renders possible insights previously denied us. Further, as this is a book about how westerners may optimally approach cross-cultural understanding, moral deference is relevant because many, if not most, of the other cultures which we are attempting to understand will be from a diminished social category, or were from one at some time.

Secondly, to act in ways consistent with moral deference is to 'bear witness to another's moral pain with that person's authorization'.[58] Thomas used the story of a hypothetical woman named Leslie to make the point. A conesquence of successful moral deference is that to bear witness to Leslie's pain with her authorisation is 'to have won her confidence that one can speak informedly and with conviction on her behalf to another about the pain she has endured'.[59] Put differently, it means that if we were to speak with Leslie's authorisation, our own way of thinking, our priorities, our expectations, our imaginings about such pain would be displaced. We would see it as far as possible from Leslie's point of view, such that Leslie trusts and authorises us. We all know that we cannot experience her pain and suffering as she experienced it. However, Leslie feels confident that, as much as anybody

---

57. Thomas, 'Moral Deference', 373–4.
58. Thomas, 'Moral Deference', 375–6.
59. Thomas, 'Moral Deference', 376.

can and more than most, we have seen and can articulate it from her point of view. Indeed, Leslie may be more confident of our ability than we are. Nonetheless, a test of the insights gained from moral deference is that we are authorised by Leslie.

In the cross-cultural understanding context this is significant. In Chapter 1 and 2 the question of what would constitute a test for knowing (U_1) and understanding (U_2) was raised. Can I be confident that I really understand when I think I understand? Or is the test that the person whom I am attempting to understand authorises or sanctions my understanding? To clarify his point, Thomas used the analogy of a person who is near-sighted putting on corrective glasses for the first time. They see details they'd never seen before. As such, moral deference 'is a matter of rendering oneself open to another's concern, and letting another's pain reconstitute one so much that one comes to have a new set of sensibilities—a new set of moral lenses if you will'.[60] We now have a test for understanding, a criterion for measuring it. This does not mean that the person could not be mistaken about the nature of their experiences.[61] It does mean that the presumption will be in their favour because I am not a member of the same social category and, as such, my emotional responses are configured differently. Without moral deference I am not in a position to understand the reality of their experience at all.

Thirdly, moral deference is also relevant to cross-cultural understanding because it offers a much more robust notion of the standpoint of the marginalised. Moral deference both amplifies and reinforces Harding's standpoint while being consistent with it. The standpoint of the marginalised, when bolstered by the idea of moral deference, entails more than merely listening or taking

60. Thomas, 'Moral Deference', 377.
61. Thomas, 'Moral Deference', 374.

another's account as we understand it. It means listening with the presumption in favour of the person's account of their experiences. It involves a prior commitment to their account and explanation of their experiences and, like Harding, uses their standpoint to link the causes of their experience to social injustice.[62]

Concluding comments

In this chapter I began by posing some questions about the social function performed by neutrality and e-value relativism. I ended it with an examination of moral deference. It might seem that the links between the two are rather tenuous. But, in one sense, the seeming distance between them highlights the significance of this chapter to approaching and facilitating cross-cultural under-standing. It also shows how far the discussion has come.

It has been argued that neutrality does not serve cross-cultural understanding—at least not neutrality in the sense associated with western science and the social sciences. Both Marcuse and Harding made the point differently but powerfully: neutrality gives the impression of impartiality while aligning with the most powerful. E-relativism (generally, not exclusively apropos values) is an accomplice in the same process. The clamour to objectivity-as-neutrality in western science and the social sciences has a history which distorts the object of the research. But, as Harding argued, it is one thing to employ objectivity too weakly through a bogus and inept concept of it, and quite another thing to jettison it altogether. It is unnecessary and feckless to displace objectivity by relativism. The latter is socially influenced and serves a similar social function to objectivity weakly used. The corrective to both objectivity-as-neutrality and

---

62. Thomas, 'Moral Deference', 378.

e-relativism is objectivity maximised, particularly when reinforced by beginning our standpoint from the standpoint of those on the margins.

Furthermore, Thomas's notion of moral deference proffers an insightful path for putting Harding's standpoint epistemology into operation. Moral deference is a way of listening to those who have experienced pain and suffering that is used by those who do not usually have such experiences and subsequent feelings. This might be because our paths do not cross, but Thomas also pointed to the differences in social categorisation and the way in which downward social categorisation configures emotional experiences differently.

Thus the chapter has demonstrated what is antagonistic to cross-cultural understanding (neutrality, impartiality, e-value relativism), and has thrown into sharpest relief what is conducive to it. Because this book is about how westerners might approach cross-cultural understanding in order to facilitate it, Harding's standpoint epistemology and Thomas's notion of moral deference are relevant. In all probability the cultures with which we engage will be on the margins, or from a downward social category.

One response to this chapter might be to regard it as a retreat to the sanctimonious. Some may suggest that I am wearing my heart on my sleeve, that all of a sudden what has been a rather demanding intellectual book has sunk into affective depths with talk of moral deference and emotional configurations. More disturbing is the suggestion that as we bring our culturally influenced commitments to the task of understanding other cultures we had better ensure that our commitments maximise understanding rather than minimise it.

There are at least two responses to such comments. Firstly, it is possible, surely, to reason about our emotional responses as about anything else. After all, they influence our thinking. Secondly, discrediting the importance of emotions is symptomatic of western, patriarchal, scientific forms of thought that deny and belittle the emotional. As the dominant, scientific culture does not have the resources to facilitate cross-cultural understanding or, more accurately, has (largely) contributed to cross-cultural misunderstanding, it is not surprising to find that it is being challenged and displaced when we seek to understand other cultures.

Indeed, criticism of the emotional aspect epitomises the very problem with such scientific attempts at cross-cultural understanding. The discounting of the emotional exemplifies part of the hierarchy of knowledge in which reason rules emotion. But, as Thomas pointed out, this effectively denies us access to a precondition of cross-cultural understanding, namely, the capacity to learn, so far as we are able, the depth, the profundity, of what has been experienced by others and what is in need of explanation. If we do not have the fullest possible appreciation of what is to be explained, then our social realm, including its social attitudes and discriminatory practices is incorrigible. Further, if we do not have access to U_1, even a modest understanding of the experiences of others (U_2) is unavailable. In this case, the status quo is preserved and the causes of downward social categorisation proceed unfettered. Now that we have discovered where and how we should begin cross-cultural understanding, the next challenge is to defend those values which facilitate it.

8

Why should we understand and how can we justify it?

Introduction

We have reached a crucial stage in the task we set ourselves and have identified the obstacles to cross-cultural understanding and found that approaching the task is far deeper, more profound and intractable than indicated by the introductory questions in Chapter 1. We have seen how important values are to the task. Thus, justifying values, such as empathy, deference and tolerance (U$_3$), is a precondition for cross-cultural understanding. They are almost a first step to cross-cultural understanding; they inspire and motivate it. Without these values there is neither a rationale for genuinely understanding other cultures and their members, nor for undertaking the task in a particular way. About them we need not be coy; from them we should not recoil. Yet the difficulty remains: how do we justify them? How do we defend them?

One response to what might seem a clarion call is to suggest that defending our values is unnecessary. However, in liberal democracies, the debate between members of ethnocentric or racist groups and multi-culturalists, for example, pivots around what is socially cherished, treasured and valued. The value of national space or of diversity, to name two of many, is debated in the public arena. Nonetheless, defending values is largely discredited in the West. They are regarded as ideological, relative and subjective. According to Marcuse, at least, this inferior, ideological status ascribed to values performs a special social function, namely, to create the power vacuum that gives powerbrokers the opportunity to dictate dominant social values, to camouflage as relativist and pluralist what is politically oppressive and totalising.

This leads to an important conclusion: cross-cultural understanding presupposes that I am able to justify the values on which it is based in a way that are not only good for those who agree with me but in a way that is persuasive to others who do not. This position we previously called e-value absolutism in order to distinguish it from political absolutism or authoritarianism.

This chapter begins by analysing one of the reasons e-value absolutism (or value objectivism) is rejected. The position is rejected because there are no foundations on which value positions can be built and from which they can be defended. Furthermore, such foundations are metanarratives, and those who build from them are (allegedly) insecure. This position is usually called non-foundationalism. Also associated with non-foundationalism and e-relativism is the rejection of truth. I will examine this rejection next, after which I will explore one way to defend our values.

My argument is that, despite some reluctance to concede the point, all positions have the equivalent of a foundation albeit, to continue the metaphor, some not as deep as others. I also argue that the search for truth is not only essential in cross-cultural understanding but is imperative if we are ever to hear and respond to injustice. In addition, I propose that it is possible to defend the view that some values are preferable to others. In any case, most people behave as if they uphold e-value absolutism.

Justifying values: a brief restatement of the problem

In Chapter 5 I distinguished between a theory of knowledge (e-value absolutism), on the one hand, and a political position which was anti-democratic and anti-liberal and involved the imposition of one view on dissenters, on the other (political absolutism). I argued that it was imperative to make this distinction because political absolutism of the imposing-my-view-on-others variety does not necessarily follow from a theory of knowledge which claims that it is possible to arbitrate between conflicting values (no matter how difficult it is and how modest one should be in making the claim). Political absolutism does not follow ineluctably from e-value absolutism any more than a defence of the values associated with democracy and tolerance follows from e-value relativism.

A principle reason why many people reject e-value absolutism is the politically absolutist implications that are seen to follow. In other words, the argument that it is possible to defend the proposition that one value is preferable to another is jettisoned because such a view is confused with, and seen to lead inexorably to, authoritarianism. In the light of the fact of tyranny, past and present, this would be a major concern and an understandable conclusion to reach—if e-value absolutism was in some way inexorably linked with totalitarianism. I have shown that it is not.

Non-foundationalism (sometimes anti-foundationalism)

However, there is another related reason for abandoning e-value absolutism which is also popular, particularly amongst some postmodernists and their supporters. This involves a metaphor, the metaphor of foundations. The argument is that, because it is impossible to arbitrate between values, we simply do not have the underlying premises, the solid bedrock of values, the solid foundations, on which to construct our value edifices.[1] Without a secure foundation on which to build our ultimate values, they fall into relativism. The value edifice is dismantled; the value constructs are deconstructed.

This deconstruction involves more than merely demanding the removal of the scaffolding and the supports around which our values positions are constructed. The foundations are not only laid bare as a relic of modernity in the postmodernist, archaeological dig. If the foundations exist they cannot support the e-value absolutism of modernism. In fact, it is unlikely that there are foundations and, if in fact there are, the post-modernist archaeologist not only bids them goodbye and good riddance, but regards them as unnecessary. This is a significant point.

According to the metaphor, and the associated language, it is not only that the foundations are laid bare, but that they cannot support the construction. Increasingly, in the past two or three decades, a movement has developed that not only regards foundations as unnecessary but as almost hostile to the postmodern project. So foundations become not only an obsolete relic of modernism but one which attracts opposition. Thus, non-foundationalism becomes the name of the game.

For our purposes it is unnecessary to explore this metaphor and its consequences in detail. Several points will suffice. Firstly, if the metaphor of the foundation refers to a base, a starting point on which our value

---

1.   The argument may be more complex although the conclusion is similar. Another way to express the position described is that because we do not have the wherewithal to arbitrate between values we do not have the ability to decide between ultimate values. Without reliable ultimate values as a basis, a foundation, it is impossible to build our value positions.

positions are erected, then all positions have a foundation; if the metaphor refers to a starting point then all positions have one despite protests to the contrary. All positions rest somewhere; they repose on something that can be likened to a foundation (even if their protagonists oppose the idea).

The second point concerns non-foundationalism. What distinguishes, say, a modernist from a postmodernist is not whether they use foundations. Both use them as the first point above notes (despite some non-foundationalists claiming the contrary). A difference between the modernist who claims a foundation for beliefs, practices and values, and the person who eschews foundations, is the depth of the foundations. The former is more likely to search for, and claim, foundations that are deeper, more certain, secure and trustworthy than the latter.

So a religious justification for political values such as freedom, liberty, equality, respect for diversity, and tolerance is more likely to be founded on some notion of the divine or transcendent. It may pass through other attempts which, while effective in some respects, are ultimately unsatisfactory for the religious believer until they reach rock bottom in a theistic notion of some kind (which to others may be quicksand). For example, natural law theorists, who sometimes use religious foundations, claim that there is a universal law binding on all human beings, while conventionalists claim that political values are merely derived from customs and traditions.[2] The

---

2. For example, see Jacques Maritain, *The Rights of Man and Natural Law* (London: Bless, 1958); Leo Strauss, *Natural Right and History* (Chicago: University of Chicago Press, 1953). For more recent analyses see Martha Nussbaum, *Women and Human Development: The Capabilities Approach* (Cambridge: Cambridge University Press, 2001) and Anthony J Langlois, *The Politics of Justice and Human Rights: Southeast Asia and*

natural law theorist and the conventionalist may agree about certain political values (for example, freedom and equality) and their defence at certain levels may coincide. For example, both may agree, whether by natural law or convention, that freedom is based on the dignity of all human beings. But the conventionalist will always rest the case on a social and political convention whereas the natural law theorist will invoke a deeper foundation perhaps based on some notion of the divine or the transcendent.

Thus, the difference between the religious natural law theorist and the social conventionalist or constructivist is the base (rock bottom) or source of the justification for their position. For the natural law theorist the ultimate source or base of their position is a god, or a divine or transcendent being, who is the author of such political values. For the conventionalist or the constructivist the source of the justification is the culture, society or group which enshrined the principles in law or norms of some kind (written or verbal). However, while the foundations might differ, they remain.

In the last few decades pragmatism has emerged as an anti-foundationalist political justification for certain political values. There are many varieties of pragmatism, but it is usually associated with reflecting on experience. Pragmatists are more likely to begin their task by considering what is experienced in order to draw conclusions about what should be normative. For pragmatists the critical issues for reflection are what is happening in practice. They begin with practical issues

---

Universalist Theory (Cambridge: Cambridge University Press, 2001). I would include Richard Rorty in the conventionalist category. See Richard Rorty, 'Human Rights, Rationality, and Sentimentality', in *On Human Rights: The Oxford Amnesty Lectures 1993*, edited by S Shute and S Hurley (London: Basic Books, 1993), 111–34.

and concerns. As crude as this statement of pragmatism is, it does reveal the foundation. What occurs is the foundation; what works is the foundation—and it is regarded as just as objective as anything the natural law theorists might claim (although they may reject the similarity I am forging). But the foundation, the objectivity, originates from within a culture, society or group. Thus, pragmatism has a base, a foundation, something on which other values are built.

Thus we can see that, strictly speaking, non-foundationalists are nothing of the sort. They may reject traditional, religious, modernist foundations (such as those of natural law) but their positions also have a starting point on which the remainder is constructed. The foundations may not be as deep, they may not attempt to plumb the depths of the divine or the transcendent but, nonetheless, the foundation metaphor (with the degree of slippage all metaphors possess) is apt for varieties of conventionalism, constructionism and pragmatism. This is significant for our purposes because, non-foundationalists notwithstanding, whenever values are justified they will be based on some sort of foundation, that is, they will have premises, and reasons on which they depend and rest.

Before we move on, there is just one more point I'd like to make about non-foundationalism. It should be clear that the reasons for rejecting foundations are also linked to the reasons for rejecting e-value absolutism and embracing e-value relativism. If there are no foundations, then all claims to e-value absolutism are spurious and e-value relativism seems to be confirmed. According to anti-foundationalists, if there are no foundations then external building blocks to defend values do not exist; if there are no external reference points then e-value relativism seems to be justified. We have already seen how the latter subverts our attempts at cross-cultural understanding because it cannot defend the values that are required for understanding, such as deference, empathy and tolerance (U_2, U_3 and V_1). Nonetheless, to repeat the point of the paragraph, embracing e-relativism seems to be a response to the rejection of e-absolutism[3] because there are no foundations to support knowledge about values.

An example of non-foundationalism

There have been other attempts to diagnose the problem of defending values and the political implications which allegedly follow. Linda Nicholson, for example, claimed that relativism is parasitic on objectivism. This seems to mean that once e-absolutism has been rejected, then e-relativism seems to be the only alternative. In this way, e-absolutism or objectivity is based on the need for fundamental proof and e-relativism is tied to it because it arises as a consequence of the impossibility of such proof. Hence, e-absolutism as the need for a final grounding of an argument (a foundation) and its impossibility (e-relativism) 'are symbiotic and share a common ideal: fundamental proof'.[4]

It is at this point that Nicholson attempted to overcome the problems with both positions by claiming that (what I would call) e-relativism and e-absolutism are only symbiotic while 'fundamental proof' is required.[5] According to Nicholson, if it is possible to circumvent the ideal of fundamental proof then both e-absolutism and e-

3. I have deleted 'value' from e-value absolutism because epistemological relativism is not confined to values in this discussion.
4. Linda Nicholson, 'On the Postmodern Barricades: Feminism, Politics, and Theory' in *Postmodernism and Social Theory: The Debate Over General Theory*, edited by Steven Seidman and David G Wagner (Oxford: Blackwell, 1992), 85.
5. Nicholson, 'On the Postmodern Barricades', 85.

relativism are rendered unnecessary. Without the need for fundamental proof neither e-absolutism nor e-relativism is required—or so Nicholson claimed.

Nicholson then proceeded to make two very important points. The first is that abandoning the search for fundamental proof does not mean that there are no criteria for truth at all. This may come as something of a surprise, but after suggesting overcoming e-absolutism and e-relativism by forfeiting the requirement for fundamental proof, Nicholson wrote: abandoning the search for fundamental proof 'does *not* entail the abandonment of criteria of truth immanent to the practices which generate them, a position supported by both Lyotard and Rorty'.[6]

This means that abandoning the need for fundamental proof does not necessitate abandoning the search for criteria of truth within the cultures or societies that generated them. This is an important point, although whether it is sufficient is another matter. Nicholson's point is that in a particular culture or society there are conventions and constructions about beliefs, practices and values. The conventions and constructions play the role of aims and objectives which have their own criteria of truth. Provided the criteria come from within the society and culture which generated them, then there are criteria for truth. Like Kuhn's paradigms, the criteria are internally justifying.

Now Nicholson was certainly correct to point to Lyotard and Rorty as exemplifying this position. Rorty is a staunch defender of American liberalism and democracy,[7] which to all intents and purposes works, and that satisfies Rorty. He does not need more argument than

---

6. *Ibid*, (emphasis added).

7. See, for example, the relevant chapters in Richard Rorty, *Objectivism, Relativism, and Truth: Philosophical Papers Volume 1* (Cambridge: Cambridge University Press, 1991).

that. He accepts the American political system as normative for himself and Americans and he consistently calls for what he regards as the principles of American democracy to be more fully invoked. When the principles that apply are implemented all is well and good. When experience does not measure up to these internally generated principles, they should be addressed. The principles of American liberalism and democracy, which are internally spawned, become the truth criteria.

Some who are not American may regard this as a rather insular, smug, perhaps even an overweening approach. But there is another concern. Rorty's view of what is normative is justified by his own standards while he remains in the United States. But as soon as he confronts another culture his view is problematic. Why? Because, by definition, his internal criteria no longer apply; if he proceeds beyond the society which generated the truth criteria they may be no longer relevant, the other person or group may not uphold them.[8]

Rorty would seem to have at least two options. Either he can attempt to persuade others of the normative value of his values, or he can say nothing. If he attempts to persuade others he is undertaking a different project. He is no longer working strictly from 'criteria . . . [which are] immanent to the practices which generate them'. As soon as he begins to confront other cultures the internal application of criteria, norms and values are used externally. The nexus between criteria emanating from within the cultural practices that generate them no longer applies.

---

8.   Of course, I am referring to the consistency of Rorty's case. It may well be—and I would argue it is the case—that values emanating from the United States have clout due to their sheer domination of the world capitalist and political systems. But my argument here is logical rather than descriptive.

Put differently, as soon as Rorty (or anyone else who holds a similar position) attempts to persuade members of another culture with different cultural practices which are perhaps un-American, a wedge is driven between the connection linking truth criteria and the cultural practices that generate them. This poses considerable obstacles to cross-cultural understanding. The two sets of criteria may be at odds; they probably will be. In such an instance we return to the situation of e-value relativism in which it is impossible to arbitrate between the conflicting values, or we are locked within conceptual and cultural relativism in which it is impossible—so the argument goes—to translate and communicate.

But Linda Nicholson is not limited by such considerations. She rejected the argument that bypassing both e-absolutism and e-relativism, by abandoning the fundamental proof ideal, limits the use of criteria to those inherent in the cultural practices that generate them. In fact Nicholson went further. She suggested that abandoning the burden of fundamental proof does not 'even entail the denial of the possibility of cross-cultural tools of adjudication, such as a commitment to dialogue or the law of non-contradiction'.[9] In other words, Nicholson agreed that there are criteria (she called them tools) that enable the arbitration of cultural differences. There may not be universal standards but there are certainly criteria which are external to at least two cultures and which can be applied to both, hence the description 'cross-cultural'. According to Nicholson, such cross-cultural criteria exist when the parties agree to enter dialogue or when they agree that they will not use contradictions.[10]

---

9.   Nicholson, 'On the Postmodern Barricades', 85.
10. But even these two conditions seem to beg some questions. What happens if one side does not agree to enter dialogue? In such circumstances at least one party would be frustrated. Regarding

What, then, are the consequences of the abandonment of the fundamental proof ideal? Nicholson claimed: 'It only brings with it the admission that it is unlikely we will ever be able to identify one value, one category, one theory, or tool of adjudication both big enough and specific enough to resolve all possible conflicts'.[11] If we take seriously her statement that we are unlikely to find only one value, one category, one theory, or one tool of adjudication to resolve all possible conflicts, she is probably correct.

Nicholson then made the point that the criteria of truth immanent in the practices which generate them concern what is admissible as truth in the shared tradition. To her this 'suggests an alternative mode for interpreting relativism; relativism becomes the situation which results when communication breaks down'.[12] Nicholson continued:

> Thus relativism becomes a life possibility rather than a theoretical position. And viewing it as a life possibility, we can begin to speculate about the conditions which lead to difficulties in maintaining communication: when participants lack common beliefs able to mediate conflicting ones; when they possess terms which cannot be translated into the vocabulary of the other; when conflicting interests motivate the construction of conflicting beliefs and vocabularies.[13]

---

not using contradictions, what happens if the party disagrees on this point or on what constitutes a contradiction. My point is that the criteria Nicholson invoked seem to highlight the need for, or presuppose, other deeper criteria which Nicholson left unexamined.

11. Nicholson, 'On the Postmodern Barricades', 85–6.
12. Nicholson, 'On the Postmodern Barricades', 86.
13. *Ibid,*

At first glance this seems quite a useful statement. Relativism arises from the lack of communication and the reasons for it. Certainly those problems arising from the differences mentioned in the quotation above are real; they are sound explanations for the breakdown in communication. But in diagnosing relativism as a life possibility rather than a theoretical position, and identifying some of the causes of the lack of communication, Nicholson was really only describing what we all know. There is a variety of beliefs, practices and values, and for some of the reasons Nicholson pointed out. This is the descriptive or sociological relativism mentioned in Chapter 2. It simply describes and identifies yet does not really grasp the nettle of how to overcome the very problems which characterise a lack of communication.

In so doing, Nicholson's analysis begs the questions: do human beings from different cultures share nothing such that there exist no common beliefs able to mediate conflict? Are concepts and terms really untranslatable? Do conflicting interests outweigh common interests? Before delving into such questions and attempting to show how it might be possible to have a foundation for values and the implications which follow, it is worth summarising Linda Nicholson's suggestion.

Linda Nicholson's position is one of the most carefully articulated attempts to overcome non-foundationalism or e-value relativism and e-value absolutism that I have seen. It will be recalled that, for Nicholson, both positions depend on the idea of a fundamental proof. Nicholson claimed that e-value absolutism certainly depends on fundamental proof; it claims such proof is an achievable goal. When foundations are dismantled and regarded as unrealisable, e-value relativism is adopted. Thus, both positions turn around fundamental proof. As indicated in the previous chapter, Sandra Harding made a similar diagnosis.

In order to overcome the dilemma, however, Nicholson suggested abandoning the search for fundamental proof. This, she insisted does not forfeit the possibility of criteria for validity because all cultures and societies have them. It is then possible to use social conventional or internal criteria to evaluate or judge, defend or justify. This approach may not be problematic (no matter how complacent and smug it is) until, of course, contact is made with another culture and judgements are made. Then the criteria are not merely internally valid; they are being used in a way that transcends the cultural boundaries and internal validity criteria.

Nicholson was undaunted by this—although it exposes a tension in her position. Initially in her statement, criteria of validity and truth were confined to those internal to a particular culture. Later, she recognised that there are criteria for validity that are not merely internal. These include a commitment to dialogue or the law of non-contradiction.[14] Thus, according to Nicholson, there are tools which enable cross-cultural understanding (agreeing to dialogue and to the law of non-contradiction) even if there is not one final, ultimate value which can be used to resolve all conflicts. Commitment to dialogue and to the law of non-contradiction are values which Nicholson claimed have the potential to be used when different cultures meet. In this case, despite her previous statement, it appears that there are some values that are not confined to the culture that generated them.

We also noted that, for Nicholson, relativism can be interpreted as a way of life rather than merely an abstract position. This may jar a little, especially given that one of the themes encountered in our discussion of cross-cultural

---

14. The argument that when e-value relativism is used to deduce and justify tolerance it flouts this law, was developed in Chapter 5.

understanding has been the practical and political implications that have been drawn from it. In that sense, relativism (or e-relativism) is not merely theoretical or abstract (as the alleged link between e-value relativism and tolerance demonstrates). But that is entirely different from Nicholson's suggestion. The connection examined in Chapter 5 between relativism and tolerance is distinct from Nicholson's speculation about the origins of relativism, which she related to certain impediments to communication. The latter indicates an inability to mediate between conflicting beliefs, an inability to translate from one language or vocabulary into another and the existence of conflicting interests that intrude to construct different beliefs.

Although the difficulty with this suggestion is not the description of e-relativism; it certainly itemises some of the salient issues. The problem is that it does not overcome barriers to communication, it merely describes them. As becomes clear, the modernist might insist that there are criteria external to cultures and history to which we might appeal in order to resolve some of the dilemmas mentioned in the description of relativism above. However, this is impermissible in Nicholson's brand of postmodernism which retreats to the internal validity of cultural views. The possibility remains that the modernist and postmodernist may appeal to the same notions of equality and freedom because they are members of the same culture. Even here, of course, disagreement is possible, but the real problem arises when there are no externally recognised criteria for validity as occurs when cultures, nations or societies disagree. The possibilities, tensions and consequences of Nicholson's position are exemplified in the following.

> . . . it must also be stressed that common
> beliefs, values, etc. can be appealed to only as

possible resources. When these are not available as means of mediation, the only resources left might be human ingenuity or luck, and these by their very nature offer no guarantees of success. Thus, a postmodern stance must admit of the possibility of breakdowns in communication. But to admit this is not to deny the many means by which humans do maintain communication, even in the context of differences.[15]

According to Nicholson, there may be no guarantees of success in reaching agreement and understanding; communications may breakdown, reach an impasse or a stalemate. But, as Nicholson conceded, human beings do maintain communication even across cultural, national and social divides. It is approaching this communication in ways which facilitate and foster cross-cultural under-standing that is the topic of this book. Yet there are many views which hinder this understanding. Nicholson's position is that of a 'careful postmodernist',[16] alert to the difficulties and using every possible means to continue the communication. Yet ultimately, as we have seen, as candid as her position is, it really only highlights the issues; it throws them into sharper relief. Clearly, she tried to avoid foundations and anything that smacks of external criteria, of absolutes. Yet she identified some of them (although she would not call them absolute values), including the commitment to dialogue and the law of non-contradiction. Human beings do communicate despite their differences. Our examination continues with this reality.

---

15. Nicholson, 'On the Postmodern Barricades', 88-89.
16. Nicholson, 'On the Postmodern Barricades', 89.

Defending values: a suggestion

The fact that humans do communicate despite their differences is highly significant. Consider two cultural groups. What happens if both believe they would rather live in harmony rather than conflict? What happens if they also believe that peace at any price is appeasement and is not that to which they aspire. The peace for which they yearn is peace with justice, and justice demands that their cultural forms and expressions are not respected begrudgingly and parsimoniously, but celebrated. Justice also demands equality of access to goods and services (such as education, employment, health and housing) and deference offered to members of diminished social categories. Thus, justice demands a tolerance which is not repressive and indiscriminate, but which is intolerant of repression.

I don't think it is naïve to say that if there are people and cultures and societies who agree with something like the above, then they have decided that it is possible that one value, or a cluster of values, is better than another. They are not shy about their position. They adopt e-value absolutism. Inter alia, they have decided that a discriminating and liberating tolerance is preferable to intolerance and repressive tolerance, that justice is preferable to injustice, that freedom is preferable to authoritarianism and that understanding is preferable to misunder-standing. Furthermore, they have decided that it is easy to misunderstand, and particularly to misunderstand those who are in diminished social categories and experience aggravated social assault. They have also decided that these are criteria by which at least some disputes can be resolved. They also realise that their view of these ultimate values is not the only one and that some-times they will disagree with members of other cultures. But they are also committed to getting along, and not necessarily in a way that pampers or acquiesces to their neighbour's cultural proclivities. Such a sycophantic appeasement does not do justice to their right to persuade and challenge even as their neighbours challenge them.

Further, they have good reasons for deciding in favour of deference, equality, freedom, justice and a discriminating tolerance. They mount good reasons in the best of the e-value absolutist or objectivist tradition. They want to live in peace. They know they have different views so they have decided that it is better to attempt to understand than to misunderstand, that it is preferable to live with their differences rather than minimise them by denying the right of others to be different. They are realists in the sense that they know that their differences are real. They intuit them even before they understand them better. It is a tacit knowledge that their interactions demonstrate convincingly, even if inchoately.

And just as they have decided that e-value absolutism is preferable to e-value relativism and act accordingly, so they have addressed (at least to their practical satisfaction) the dilemma of epistemology and ontology, of which comes first, our theories of knowledge on the one hand, or the diverse, heterogeneous real world in which they find themselves on the other. This is a major dilemma. Much of popular modern thought has pivoted on a prior requirement to determine how we know about the real world. We ascertain how we know first, then we work out what it is that we know; we determine how we can acquire reliable knowledge first and then we set out to find it.[17] In the West, for socially validated knowledge such as science, epistemology comes first.

---

17. For a diagnosis and critique see Charles Taylor, 'Overcoming Epistemology', in Charles Taylor, *Philosophical Arguments* (Cambridge, Massachusetts: Harvard University Press, 1995), 1–19.

In the West the questions and answers about this issue tend to be as follows. What faculties do we use to obtain valid knowledge? Reason! What method should we use? Modern science and positivism! What theory of knowledge, what epistemology, should we use? Empiricism, scientific objectivity, neutrality! This has characterised much philosophical thought since the seventeenth-century. In this way, theories of knowledge were decided before investigating the real world. Indeed, according to this view, the only way to know the real world with certainty is to decide beforehand which reliable theory of knowledge to adopt and then investigate using that method. The real world, ontology, could (and can) only be known via an acceptable theory of knowledge, an epistemology, which was chosen first. As noted in Chapter 3, the results of the socially credentialed know-ledge for cross-cultural understanding were disastrous, with scientific objectivity and neutrality resulting in cultural conceit and epistemic and colonising domination of other cultures.

But the starting point for these individuals and cultures in the illustration about the groups who craved peace is different. They accept their intuitive and tacit knowledge about cultural diversity, the multiplicities of human and cultural expression and the heterogeneity of institutional form and organisation. The ontology they experience is different and pluralism and the epistemology they pursue will be commensurate with their overall objective: to live in peace and harmony.

One way to highlight this approach is to compare it with the argument in what we called the 'tolerance school fallacy' in Chapter 5. You will recall that one popular argument for tolerance proceeded from e-value relativism: it is precisely because we cannot arbitrate between values that we should be tolerant. In this position, the theory of knowledge, the epistemology, is identifiable first. It is precisely because we cannot arbitrate between values that we should be tolerant.

But the interactions of those groups from different cultures I am describing begin from their real world, their ontology. They argue that it is precisely because of the diversity that we want to respect, encourage and foster, that we say that some values are preferable to others. If we have these goals then certain values are essential, they are preferable to their opposites. It is possible to arbitrate between them; it is imperative that we do!

Those committed to living in peace and harmony have come to understand that even their theory of knowledge is a cultural by-product, it is a function of their own culture. As far as the West is concerned, that has been part of the problem. In particular, as a culturally approved theory of knowledge, science claimed to be able to find the truth. Yet it has peddled distortions in the name of veracity, espoused objectivity but operationalised it minimally or too weakly (to use Harding's terminology), claimed a neutrality when the theory of knowledge and the ensuing results were partisan, and claimed a tolerance when it was repressive.

A commitment to truth

But this does not mean that the two groups I discussed above are afraid of truth. Unlike Nicholson, who eschewed fundamental proof, those in the example are committed to living in peace, harmony and under-standing are committed to getting to the truth. By truth they are referring to something quite specific. Their commitment to all the values mentioned above means that they want to know how others understand their world, how they experience other cultures, the conesquence of being a member of a diminished social category (even though they may not be a member of it), and what happens when they experience aggravated social assault.

They want to know in detail, and as accurately as possible, whether a person has experienced structural racism, what happened, who were the perpetrators, what charge was alleged, what real treatment was received —and so on. Understanding demands it. Justice demands that what has been closed be disclosed; that what has been hidden be exposed.

Without this commitment to the truth, to what really happened, the cultural groups I am discussing feel that justice cannot be done, understanding cannot be achieved, freedoms cannot be restored and violations of justice cannot be addressed. It is not so much that they believe they have some privileged access to The Truth, but they do not allow difficulties with the alleged compulsive nature of truth to obstruct their commitment to discover what actually happened, or the closest representation of it possible. Approximating as closely as possible the circumstances of structural racism, discrimination, false accusation, wrongful arrest and imprisonment, for example, presupposes the deepest commitment to truth for the most emancipatory reasons.

Further exploration of the issues: constructionism

In this chapter I began by noting the importance of justifying our values. If it is inevitable that cross-cultural encounters are influenced by our values, then the salient issue is not the presence and influence of our values (these are inevitable) but the values to which we are committed. Ethnocentrism of the E_2 variety is such an obstacle to cross-cultural understanding that it is imperative that we, at least, ask the question: with what values do we, should we, approach understanding across cultural divides? Further, are they the values which facilitate and foster cross-cultural understanding, or are they the values which obstruct or stymie it? In summary, just as our commitments are inevitable and the pertinent issue is to what we are committed, so our values are just as inevitable, and the issue concerns the values we uphold to justify and approach our cross-cultural exchanges.

However, as we have seen all along, this is a major problem; defending our values is sabotaged in the West by e-value relativism and the criticism of e-value absolutism. The latter has the potential to be helpful if it were not accused of, and confused with, political absolutism. But this chapter has also highlighted another reason why defending values is treated with suspicion, namely, that according to the non-foundationalists, the foundations on which previous prevailing values were constructed have been deconstructed to such an extent that they are merely social constructs which perform repressive social functions. In other words, the foundations are based on quicksand and soon collapse. The grand theories, the metanarratives, the edifice which is built on the foundations, sink into oblivion.

The notion of social construction is a very useful analytical tool. It poses an immediate challenge to cultural and social practices, particularly when they are regarded as natural, neutral and unchallengeable, when they are seen as absolute or originating from some source other than the culture or society in which they arose (as in religious explanations). For example, expectations based on sex differences are sometimes regarded as emanating from a source that is supposedly transcultural, such that they possess a moral status which justifies moral coercion. Western views about gendered labour stereotypes and roles are an example. Similarly, the inequitable distribution of wealth in most western countries is often explained as being a result of inadequate individuals. Likewise, failure in school is often explained as the fault of poor students and dysfunctional families. The dominant history of a culture or society is usually taken for granted.

Deconstructing such beliefs, exposing their cultural and social origins and the social functions they perform, is an extremely useful analytical tool. Deconstructing sex roles not only reveals their social origins but highlights the way they have been used to systematically repress women. If they are set in concrete it is cultural and social concrete; as they do not transcend culture and society, they have no more validity (despite their social power) than the culture and society that generated and grants them. Likewise, deconstructing the explanations for educational failure and for poverty exposes the institutions which are involved and suggests structural rather than individual causes. Potentially, at least, this is emancipatory. Deconstructing the history which was written by the victors, which excludes as much as it includes, is very challenging, but it is a corrective to those histories which masquerade as being correct by the powerful.

Thus, the idea of the social construction of beliefs, explanations, expectations, practices and values, and the equivalent deconstruction, is a very useful analytical device. Construction helps to explain the present; deconstruction offers the potential to reconstruct the future for the better. Thus, if tolerance has been socially constructed as protecting social structures, it can be deconstructed, that is, exposed for what it is and the social functions it performs. It can also be reconstructed in ways that are consistent with its original objectives prior to the distortion of social constructionism. It is also very useful for cross-cultural understanding because it is a constant reminder that our most cherished beliefs, expectations, practices and values are socially constructed, a realisation which, in turn, has the potential to challenge the immutable way our socialisation has taught them to us. In this way, it is a very useful concept as we approach cross-cultural understanding.

However, as analytical and probing as constructionism and deconstructionism might be, they cannot be exempted from scrutiny. For example, if cultures and societies have been constructed, then so have the forms of social inquiry that attempt to examine and explain them. Hence, if what counts as valid knowledge has been socially constructed, then on what grounds are the social sciences which purport to examine and explain them exempt from the diagnosis of social construction and the prescriptive deconstruction? This is also significant as we approach cross-cultural understanding. In addition, if everything has been socially constructed then everything can be socially deconstructed, including what counts as valid knowledge, the privileging of our own culture even if unintentional, what comprises understanding, and what characterises other cultures and their members.

So, while acknowledging the potential of social construction, deconstruction and reconstruction, the salient issue here is the problem of self-reference and reflexivity. This refers to the potential for a critical concept to rebound on its proposers. Consider social determinism. If sociologists say that everything is socially determined then it would seem that sociology is also socially determined. A similar problem was found with metanarratives. If postmodernists reject modernist explanations as metanarratives, then one wonders why their postmodernist explanations do not fall into the same category. Thus, social constructionism, social determinism and critiques of metanarratives are all potentially reflexive, rebounding on the concepts and nullifying their influence. The devices used to criticise are constructions too; as such, they can be deconstructed!

This conclusion can be explored a little further. If the very foundations of our culture are constructed then the way we approach cross-cultural understanding will be similarly conditioned. If my own culture has created barriers to the task, then I carry those very barriers into it.

If it is argued that deconstruction is possible, at least in the sense of challenging the constructions and exposing their social function then, in the absence of external criteria by which to judge, it is difficult to imagine on what basis the new, reconstructed order could be defended.

Concluding comments

The conclusion reached in this chapter is that every position is based on something, every position has a foundation. Operating value positions are based on something. The difference between, say, the foundationalist and non-foundationalist, is that the former is prepared to say the foundations run deeper and the positions on which they are built are more secure. Yet despite protests to the contrary, pragmatism, post-modernism and relativism have foundations. They might be covert, unrecognised, tacit, by default and not as deep, but the positions are built on foundations nonetheless.

Ask a pragmatist why pragmatism is worth upholding and the answer will probably be because it works. But works for what? For whom? Why is it good that it works for such groups? The answer might be that it is better than the alternative. But on what grounds is it better? Why is it preferable? If there is an answer to such questions, then the answer exposes the foundations.

Ask an e-relativist why pluralism is better than totalising political absolutism and the answer will probably be that people should be treated with dignity and that cultures should be respected. I agree. But why does the relativist maintain this stance? Aside from the inconsistency we have already found, the answer will probably have something to so with respecting diversity, tolerance and, if pressed, the relativist may even invoke values such as freedom and justice.

This shows that we need not be chary about having foundations. Non-foundationalism is a ruse. All positions have them. Sure, some run deeper. Certainly, some invoke grand metaphysical systems. But the mere fact that there are foundations is uninformative. It tells us very little. It gives us no reason to end our search for a defence of the values that will justify our commitment to approach cross-cultural understanding sympathetically (U_2 and U_3). In fact, the conclusion is that we will have foundations; there will be a base from which our defence of the values required for cross-cultural understanding will spring.

Another approach used by those who are wary of foundations and totalising metanarratives is to use internal criteria for their values. However, as we discovered, this renders cross-cultural understanding impossible at worst, or begs all the questions at best. Just because one culture may say that it is worthwhile to embark on cross-cultural understanding rather than misunderstanding does not mean that other cultural interlocutors are committed to the same value. Further, it is impossible for the representatives of one culture to persuade the representatives of another if they are only working from criteria which are immanent to the practices which generate them, which may be inherently reasonable and integral to one culture but not to another. That strategy does not work either—it is akin to being locked in by cultural frameworks.

At first blush the suggestion that relativism is a life possibility may seem an attractive way out of the dilemmas created by e-value relativism. However, very little is gained by seeing e-value relativism as a breakdown in communication or a life possibility. The reason is that such a view begs questions such as: why is there a breakdown in communication? What has caused the breakdown? Nicholson suggested breakdowns are caused by the lack of common beliefs, the inability to translate across cultural boundaries and conflicting beliefs motivated by conflicting interests. But this is merely to describe the situation which we already know. What is required is an explanation for this situation—and one way or another the most adequate explanations are those which have recurred throughout our analysis, namely, the issues of conceptual and cultural relativism and, specifically, that there are apparently no methods by which we can arbitrate between values. These are the obstacles which require explanation and no amount of 'making a virtue out of necessity' (that is, relativism out of the life situation, as Nicholson suggested) is going to change the need to defend values which motivate, and are part of, cross-cultural understanding.

After addressing these matters in turn, I turned to defending these value positions. I chose a premise and used a foundation. The particular value position I chose concerned two cultures who wanted to live in peace and harmony. Now some e-value relativists might claim that this cannot be demonstrated in the way I have claimed. They might argue, for example, that I have fudged the issues. I might have thought I could circumvent the e-value relativist insistence that the burden of proof was on me to demonstrate that peace and harmony were preferable to their opposites, but I cannot. Further, they may insist, I have not actually demonstrated that peace and harmony are preferable to their opposites. I have only stated the positions of two groups who happen to want to live that way.

But for the two cultural groups I am discussing there is absolutely no doubt about the mutual value position and that they could provide reasons for them. They agree that there are times when it might be impossible to live in peace and harmony, when issues of justice are more important than peace at any price, where appeasement is not a satisfactory way forward and where varying degrees of disagreement and disharmony are inevitable in order for a resolution to take place. However, as far as they are concerned, that peace and harmony are preferable to war and disharmony can be defended with reasons.

In fact, this is the way most people in the West operate—as e-value absolutists, that is, as being able to decide that at least one value position is preferable to another and which then is used to arbitrate between conflicting values. For example, protagonists in an abortion debate have already decided that it is possible to arbitrate between values before they begin their debate, even if neither side has studied epistemology or issues akin to those in this book. It is impossible to argue genuinely about abortion being right or wrong if the protagonists think that it is impossible to arbitrate between conflicting values.

Put the other way, if it is impossible to arbitrate between conflicting values it is impossible to argue about abortion with the intention of resolving the debate. Why? Because a prior position has been invoked which precludes the very possibility of resolution. If it is impossible to arbitrate between competing values it is impossible for the protagonists to argue about their position on abortion with a view to convincing each other. That has been ruled out; after all, if a position insists that it is impossible to arbitrate between conflicting ethical, moral and value positions how can a specific issue (such as abortion) be decided? Thus, even before most debates, the e-absolutist conclusion has already been reached that, for example, it is possible to demonstrate that tolerance is preferable to intolerance or that abortion is morally right or wrong.

The net result of this is that, despite the popular e-value relativism, most people are e-value absolutists. Certainly, politicians, advocates of abortion law reform, and civil liberties groups opposed to capital punishment, to name just a few, act as if they are e-value absolutists.

Further, as soon as they try to persuade other cultures and societies of the worthiness of their choice they have gone beyond supporting their values from within the practices that generate them. They are saying, in effect, what I am arguing is not only good for me and my partisans, it is worthy of your acceptance too. In so doing they are adopting e-value absolutism; their recommendations reveal the general epistemology they have adopted.[18]

Some of you may remain unconvinced. You may still be inclined to think that I have not really demonstrated that it is possible to show that one value is preferable to another, that I have not really argued the case for e-value absolutism One reaction might be that all I have done is stated the obvious, namely, that we do have values, some of which are foundational, that we have decided that one set of values is preferable to another and we act accordingly (or, at least, make the attempt). In this way, we act as if we are e-value absolutists. That is what we do—and describing what we do is a different project from justifying a theory of knowledge.

I did start with what we do, with actual experience and practice. However, in this way we avoid the difficulties of e-value relativism which confuses e-value absolutism with political absolutism, which confuses an epistemology with its alleged political implications, and rushes to e-value relativism and tolerance and confuses the two. In fact, the e-value relativists not only confuse both e-value absolutism and e-value relativism and their political implications, but they argue that we cannot arbitrate between values and then paradoxically, use that position to defend tolerance. The contradiction noted in Chapter 5 seems to elude them. Further there are other

---

18. See the discussion of this in Chapter 5; James Flynn, *Humanism and Ideology: An Aristotelian View* (London: Routledge and Kegan Paul, 1973).

deleterious consequences. We have previously seen the social function performed by neutrality and impartiality. One result is the potential for repressive tolerance. Another consequence is that we cannot defend intolerance when warranted.

Such difficulties are avoided by e-value absolutism. If it is possible to say that one value is preferable to another then we can at least promote values which further cross-cultural understanding. E-value absolutism makes cross-cultural understanding possible. Neither political absolutism nor e-value relativism allow this, the former because it imposes views, and the latter because it cannot with any consistency defend the values required.

Starting with practice, however, has another strength. Beginning with practice allows us to explore the foundations of our beliefs. It does not necessarily rest with them. The example I used invites the exploration of values that are more specifically about justice, equality, the value of human beings, the conditions under which they should live if they are to flourish, the standards by which this could be measured and the values associated with them. In particular, the groups to whom I referred wanted to live in peace and harmony. But this invites questions about their reasons and purposes, all of which point to the values from which peace and harmony were themselves derived. As the foundations are being explored it is discovered that they are deeper than imagined.

Thus, the argument advanced is that e-value absolutism is not only imperative for cross-cultural understanding, but it also has profound advantages over e-value relativism and its variants. But I do concede a problem. It is not about the possibility of e-value absolutism but it does concern the possibility that the values I have chosen and attempt to defend are inadequate. There is also the possibility that there is so much dirt on my cultural lenses that my vision is distorted in ways which disadvantage my cross-cultural interlocutor and I benefit myself. It may be unintentional, but in this way I display my ethnocentrism (E_2), and we know how quickly E_2 can be twisted into an intolerant E_1.

This is a variation on the theme that one way or another we bring our values to cross-cultural understanding. So the question is: which values will we bring? To what are we committed? To what will we align ourselves? The importance of this cannot be over-emphasised. One way to counter this danger is to embark on the cross-cultural understanding enterprise from the standpoint of those who are marginalised, who have relatively less power than I do, to align myself with them —which is an application of Sandra Harding's argument in the previous chapter. Another corrective, which constantly requires my vigilance, is to use the notion of deference outlined by Lawrence.

It is now possible to summarise the analysis thus far. We have noted the importance of defending our values, of avoiding ethnocentrism (E_2) and the cultural imperialism of the powerful and popular view of western science, and the spurious objectivity that can result. We have also seen how it is possible to defend our values, to say that one is preferable to another, without the political absolutising, totalising metanarratives which concern some critics. We have also seen how it is necessary to be critical of our version of values. Tolerance is preferable to intolerance, but how do we avoid the tolerance we espouse becoming repressive? How do we recognise it when it is repressive?

However, does our conclusion mean that we should avoid scientific imperialism and extreme conceptual and cultural relativism, or does it warrant complete acquiescence to the beliefs, practices and values of other cultures and their members? Is there a method of social inquiry which avoids the twin dilemmas of scientific ethnocentrism and attempting to understanding another culture only on their own stated terms? It is to this important issue that the next chapter is devoted.

9

Is there a method of social inquiry suitable for cross-cultural understanding?

Introduction

Among other things, the previous chapter examined some of the values underpinning cross-cultural understanding and how we might defend them. This chapter addresses another important issue, namely, finding a method of social inquiry which will facilitate cross-cultural understanding, while hopefully avoiding the pitfalls which we have found thus far. One set of obstacles comes from the social sciences which seeks to emulate the methods of the natural and physical sciences, particularly those akin to the epistemology as propounded by the Vienna Circle and their protagonists in the social sciences. The other problem results from the conclusion that we should not negatively judge members of the culture that we are attempting to understand, that we should accept their understanding on their own terms.

Consider, firstly, the problem which comes from a social science based on the model of the natural and physical sciences. As I outlined in Chapter 3, there are problems with this approach, including using a scientific theory of knowledge to analyse cultures which, by definition, do not adopt the same standard of rationality. This is an inevitable outcome of the use of such methods, and one that does not show the sympathy and tolerance, let alone the deference and empathy, required for genuine cross-cultural understanding.

Another pitfall is the almost opposite problem. We have not paid it much attention until now, although it is one implication sometimes drawn from conceptual and cultural relativism and ethnocentrism (E_2). Here the point is: if we are unable to move beyond our own concepts and cultural beliefs and practices, if we are locked into our own perspectives and worldviews, if our standards of rationality are so different from the culture we are attempting to understand, if our standards are necessarily alien to another culture, does that mean we should make no judgments at all so that their cultural beliefs and practices are immune from criticism (positive or negative)?

Does conceptual and cultural relativism entail accepting another cultural belief, practice or value by default (because we are locked into our own conceptual and cultural worlds)? Does our attempt to overcome the problems associated with ethnocentrism (E_2) and its political absolutism (no matter how unintended) lead us to be so tolerant that we cannot be intolerant of those things which might arouse our disapproval. In other words, must we take the culture we are attempting to understand exclusively on its own terms so that its beliefs, practices and values are accepted as uncontentious?

For example, imagine that I am desperately trying to avoid the problems of E_2 by accepting as my understanding the stated position of those cultures in which animal fighting (bullfighting, cockfighting) is part of their belief system and cultural practice. Suppose that I am also an activist opposed to animal fighting for human entertainment. There is a dilemma here. On the one hand, I could accept the other culture's perspective on such beliefs and practices without judgement. On the other hand, my activism over animal fighting for human entertainment, and my attempt to persuade others, would seem to adversely influence my attempt to approach understanding without pre-judging.

A variation on the position that understanding necessitates suspending judgement comes from the insistence that we should be tolerant of the other culture and this too, necessitates understanding their culture on their own terms. In other words, we desist from making any evaluations at all. If our standards of science mean that another cultural belief or practice is irrational, then we avoid using our beliefs and values by which the other cultural belief or practice falls foul. If our standards of rationality inevitably mean that another cultural belief or practice is irrational, then we resist the temptation to use our standard. If, by our standards of technology, the beliefs and cultural practice of another culture are regarded as pre-technological, then we abstain from using our standards. When this applies to practices (such as animal fighting for human entertainment or betting) it involves the suspension of judgement, the net result of which is that the cultural beliefs and practices in question are unchallenged.

My suggestion so far in this book has been that we approach the task of cross-cultural understanding with deference and empathy until we have the degree of understanding which a representative member of another culture would attest as authoritative for that culture or a part of it. But what happens if they agree that we have understood the importance of animal fighting in their culture, and we still loathe the practice? Should we suspend judgement? Should we be uncritical? Should we avoid challenging their culture? Should we desist from challenging their culture even if they challenge our practice of culling kangaroos or cockatoos or the battery farming of chickens, eating beef, or dog racing (to name several practices which are not necessarily identical, but for the sake of argument, may meet with disapproval by members of another culture)? Does understanding preclude such judgements? If so, their culture is regarded as immutable and not subject to challenge. If so, we accept their understanding such that their culture is incorrigible, to use Charles Taylor's term.[1] In other words, the other culture is immune to challenge, and members cannot correct their ways because they are unchallenged.

Considerable care is required at this juncture else we fall into the traps we have been at pains to avoid. We may have thought we were on the final leg of conceptualising understanding. But it seems that, whenever we advance, another obstacle is encountered which, in turn, seems to involve one of the many culs-de-sac into which we have stumbled. This time it threatens our entire project.

In a nutshell, the dilemma puts us between the devil and the deep blue sea. The devil is that ethnocentric western science judges other cultures as unreasonable or irrational or pre-technological—or worse. The deep blue sea is that in our attempt to be understanding there is the danger that we must accept a particular culture's way of seeing their world even if we disagree with it.

My task in this chapter is to find an alternative to the devil of western scientific ethnocentrism and the deep blue sea of accepting the beliefs, practices and values of another culture without questioning them. Attempting to find a method of social inquiry which is equal to the task is a tall order but Charles Taylor, I think, provided the most promising approach. In his article entitled 'Understanding and Ethnocentricity'[2] Taylor attempted to overcome what he regarded as two unacceptable methods

1.   Charles Taylor, 'Understanding and Ethnocentricity', in Charles Taylor, *Philosophy and the Human Sciences: Philosophical Papers 2* (Cambridge: Cambridge University Press, 1985), 123–5.
2.   Taylor, 'Understanding and Ethnocentricity', 116–33.

of social inquiry and proposed one which overcomes both.

Taylor's statement of the problem

The first approach which Taylor opposed is the scientific approach in which the social sciences adopt the methods of the predicative natural and physical sciences. According to Taylor, this approach offers a 'bogus objectivity'.[3] Accordingly, 'The confused model of value-free, culture-transcendent science hides from its practitioners both their ethnocentrism and their norm-setting'.[4] Or again: 'allegedly scientific languages, by claiming to avoid understanding, always end up being unwittingly ethnocentric'.[5] How unwitting is a moot point, particularly if and when the social scientists in question know the ethnocentric consequences of their theories of knowledge and methods. That notwithstanding, an example of Taylor's focus here is the claim of western anthropology that the magic of other cultures is 'a kind of proto-science/technology, an attempt by primitive people to master their environment, to do what we do better by modern science and technology'.[6]

The second approach which Taylor wished to avoid is that which, in its attempt to steer clear of ethnocentrism, claims that social inquiry necessitates adopting the point of view of those we are attempting to understand. Taylor called this the 'incorrigibility thesis' by which he meant that the attempt to avoid ethnocentrism 'rules out an account which shows them up as wrong, confused or

---

3.   Taylor, 'Understanding and Ethnocentricity', 131.
4.   Taylor, 'Understanding and Ethnocentricity', 132.
5.   Taylor, 'Understanding and Ethnocentricity', 126.
6.   Taylor, 'Understanding and Ethnocentricity', 127.

deluded. Each culture on this view is incorrigible'.[7] In other words, in avoiding ethnocentrism (E_2) the other culture becomes to us unchallengeable, incapable of modification or improvement. This approach of the person attempting to understand is uncritical. Those who adopt this approach acquiesce to the other culture in the sense of raising no objection to it.[8]

Incorrigibility refers to a tacit agreement which largely follows from the view that understanding another person (particular from another culture) necessitates adopting that person's point of view, or describing and accounting what the person does in their own terms or those of their culture and time.[9] It is largely agreement by default rather than an earnest commitment to understand. It follows as much from an objection to ethnocentric social science, which uses the model of the so-called neutral and objective natural and physical sciences, as it does from attempting to avoid the rampant ethnocentrism of past anthropology. It is like jumping to relativism because the objections to absolutism and objectivism appear over-whelming, because there seems to be no other choice. Similarly, incorrigibility is adopted because of the fear of ethnocentrism. So to avoid ethnocentrism some social scientists switch to an approach to social inquiry which exclusively explains by using the accounts of members of the other culture.

Taylor's alternative

Taylor rejected both possibilities. According to Taylor, the problem is that both are based on the belief 'that the language of cross-cultural theory has to be either theirs or

---

7. Taylor, 'Understanding and Ethnocentricity', 123.
8. Here acquiescence does not mean deference (lest it be confused with the discussion in the previous chapter).
9. Taylor, 'Understanding and Ethnocentricity', 117.

ours'. He continued: 'If this were so, then any attempt at understanding across cultures would be faced with an impossible dilemma: either accept incorrigibility, or be arrogantly ethnocentric'.[10] According to the view Taylor rejected, incorrigibility is intended as an antidote to the previous ethnocentrism epitomised in describing magic as a primitive and inferior form of western technology.[11] Taylor offered an alternative which he called 'the interpretation thesis',[12] or 'the interpretive view, or the *verstehen* view'.[13]

There are several characteristics of Taylor's interpretive social inquiry which are worth noting because they assist in overcoming the ethnocentricity of science or social science, on the one hand, and the incorrigibility thesis in which we surrender our right to account for social reality in exchange for someone's else account, on the other. Firstly, Taylor claimed that empathy is an essential ingredient of social science, but that it is neither the main aim of social science nor a characteristic or quality of the interpretive social science notion of understanding. That is, according to Taylor's interpretive thesis, empathy is a precondition for understanding, but it is not all that is involved in social scientific understanding as explanation.[14] This is similar to what has been argued in previous chapters. U_2, empathy, is a prerequisite for U_1, knowledge about other cultures. If Taylor's interpretive thesis can be sustained we will have a fuller idea of the ingredients of U_1 as social science (hereafter U_{ss}).

The second aspect of the interpretive thesis is that it does not rest with the account of the world offered by a

10. Taylor, 'Understanding and Ethnocentricity', 125.
11. *Ibid.*
12. Taylor, 'Understanding and Ethnocentricity', 121.
13. Taylor, 'Understanding and Ethnocentricity', 123.
14. Taylor, 'Understanding and Ethnocentricity', 117.

person from another culture (hereafter an agent). In fact, Taylor's suggestion is that avoiding ethnocentrism and incorrigibility, and developing an adequate social science, entails clarifying the actions of agents so that they may be clearer to the social scientist than they are to the agents. There may appear to be a tinge of conceit or paternalism here.

But perhaps if we backtrack a little we can see, as Taylor claimed, that humans can be mistaken, deluded or confused. If we accept their version of reality unquestioningly, then we will never know if agents are mistaken and, if so, to what extent. Before I read King's analysis of tolerance I was not really aware that to advocate tolerance as generally understood in the West was to advocate a change of attitude in individuals while leaving the intolerant institutions intact. Before I read Ghassan Hage I had only the faintest idea of the social function which tolerance performed against minority cultures in Australia. Before I read Marcuse (over two decades ago) I did not appreciate how tolerance could be repressive and that, in the West at least, repression was tolerated and opposition voices were not tolerated.

Now, I would not suggest that everyone is necessarily as gullible as I am! However, human experience attests to mistakes, to having the wool pulled over our eyes, to degrees of myopia and having blind spots which serve to protect self-interests. This does not mean I have a negative view of human beings. On the contrary. Agents often come to a similar awareness of their frailty. But there are people who defend female genital circumcision on the grounds that it is allegedly for the betterment of women, while camouflaging their own self-interest. There are people who justify ethnic cleansing on grounds which many people find abhorrent. And so on. Agents are immersed in their own cultural worlds so that analysis exposes inconsistencies and mistakes in cultural and social worlds.

Hence I am not too troubled by Taylor's claim that a social science of the interpretive variety he advocated (U_{ss}) attempts to explain actions in ways that are clearer than the agent's account. I would be very troubled if that meant that I should be neutral as in the natural and physical scientific approach, and ignore the agent's self-understanding altogether. That could result in judging other cultures by my cultural standards (E_2 at least).

But, felicitously, Taylor denounced and circumvented such a move; he rejected the possibility that social science should be neutral. Further, he did so by taking the agent's self-understanding seriously. In effect, he seems to have argued that both self-understanding and a sympathetic approach are required for an adequate account of an agent's actions. There is a sound reason for this. We do not even know what has to be explained if we ignore the agent's account, the agent's self-understanding, or we have only our own perspective of what is in need of explanation. If we ignore or reject the agent's account, the agent's self-description, there is nothing to explain, or, to use Taylor's term, we have no 'explananda' (that which needs to be explained). If, Taylor argued, we want to penetrate to the depths of what must be explained, it is imperative to approach the agent sympathetically and to sense their own understanding as they express it. But taking the agent's account seriously does not mean we must formulate our account in the agent's language and terms. It does not necessitate using the same account, the same explanations, or explanatia.[15]

There is obviously a danger here, namely that we will impose our account on the agent, perhaps even to the extent that the explananda and the explanatia will be skewed (E_2). But even here Taylor's suggestions are helpful. Even though he argued that 'our language of

---

15. Taylor, 'Understanding and Ethnocentricity', 118.

understanding' is unlikely to yield an understanding of another culture, this does not mean that understanding is impossible. In fact, in their proper place, in the context of a sympathetic, interpretative approach, as Taylor advocated, our experiences and understandings are indispensable. As he claimed: 'it will almost always be the case that the adequate language in which we can understand another society is not our language of understanding, or theirs, but rather what one could call a language of perspicuous contrast'.[16]

By this, Taylor seems to mean that it is possible to represent features of two contrasting cultures in ways that members of both believe are accurate. This can occur when cultural beliefs, practices and values are compared and, particularly, when they are contrasted, juxtaposed, in relation to what he called 'human constants' such as birth, death, marriage, and times of scarcity and plenty.[17] The sociologist in me hastily questions whether there are constants that are not socially constructed and understood. But Taylor's position does not necessarily deny that rites of passage, for example, are socially constructed. Of course they are. But that is the point; it is the different social constructions and understandings that we find hard to communicate that require understanding. Taylor's suggestion is that by contrasting them we can increasingly understand.

For example, consider what appears to the western mind to be the magical beliefs and practices of certain traditional cultures. There seem to be two western responses to this. The first is that, for example, rainmaking practices are unscientific, and do not work; if it rains it is not because of a rainmaking ritual. The second approach is that of the incorrigibility thesis, namely, that the practice must be understood in terms expressed by the

---

16. Taylor, 'Understanding and Ethnocentricity', 125.
17. Taylor, 'Understanding and Ethnocentricity', 125, 127.

member of another culture as symbolic of something else, in terms of the cultural beliefs, practices and values which generated it. The two approaches seem worlds apart and we have no reference point that might render understanding possible.

However, Taylor argued that both conclusions are ethnocentric; one suggests that the rainmaking ritual represents an inferior explanation and technology, the other suggests that it is merely symbolic, only representing the search for meaning and significance when for members of that culture it is much more than that.[18] In the West one or other will be accepted; it is either/or but, according to Taylor, both are ethnocentric. Why? Because in western cultures science and the search for meaning are two different things. Thus, even making the distinction is characteristically western. One concerns the scientific enterprise and the resultant technology; the other is more like what we might find in religions or describe as religious. The dominant secular culture of the West not only makes the distinction between science and symbols, but privileges the former over the latter.

The point Taylor was making is that either approach is ethnocentric because it presumes the very western distinction made between science and the symbols which are part of the culture which practises what we call rainmaking magic. Even the distinction exposes our cultural assumptions; the division depicts western values. What in our culture is separated is combined in theirs. Yet, presented in this way, in the form of easy to understand and clear contrasts—perspicuous contrast as Taylor designated it—we not only begin to understand their culture but we understand something of ours. That we could previously only see either a proto or primitive technology, or merely myths and symbols engaged in meaning in the

---

18. Taylor, 'Understanding and Ethnocentricity', 128.

practices we dub magical, exposes our cultural biases and the values we used in our attempt to explain and understand another culture.

Previously, according to Taylor, understanding another culture was limited or foredoomed until the alternatives were identified, the hierarchy of knowledge exposed and the contrast made. Then, it became possible to find periods in the history of the West before the distinction between science and myth or symbol was made, before the scientific and technological outlook of the West assumed control. When the contrast was made it was possible to perceive alternatives hitherto unknown by many westerners, even in their own culture. Just think how different our views about the environment, forests, waterways, poverty and personal relations might be if our ontology, if our understanding of the natural and physical order or realm, of science and technology, the separation of science from religion, and the privileging of the former over the latter, was different.

Further, Taylor's analysis is not necessarily one-sidedly anti-western. He is not opposed to challenging the agent's self-descriptions. It may be suggested to them that they use some of the scientific explanations and particularly the resultant technologies to enable them to improve the health of their members, to save lives or whatever. If we are in genuine dialogue, those alternatives may be outlined and explored. The encounter of the two cultures may open up new opportunities, new self-descriptions, alternative means and ends, aims and objectives. Taylor claimed that the example of magic and the western reaction to it is:

> meant to show how the interpretive approach, far from leading to ethnocentrism, ought properly [be] understood to bring about the exact opposite, because it will frequently be the case that we cannot understand another society until we have understood ourselves

better as well. This will be so wherever the
language of perspicuous contrast which is
adequate to the case also forces us to redes-
cribe what we are doing.[19]

Thus, what the West calls magic:

forces us to see the separation of knowledge
of and attunement with the cosmos as something we have brought about, one possibility
among others, and not as the inescapable
framework of all thought. We are always in
danger of seeing our ways of acting and
thinking as the only conceivable ones. That is
exactly what ethnocentrism consists in.
Understanding other societies ought to
wrench us out of this: it ought to alter our
self-understanding. It is the merit of the interpretive view that it explains how this comes
about, when it does.[20]

Exploring Taylor's position: a fabricated example

Consider an example.[21] Suppose a colleague and I are
examining the political structures and institutions of

---

19. Taylor, 'Understanding and Ethnocentricity', 129.
20. *Ibid.*
21. This example is based on a teasing out of Taylor, 'Understanding
and Ethnocentricity'. However, while the example is mine some
readers may sense some similarities between it and the method
and argument in aspects of Charles Taylor, 'Interpretation and the
Sciences of Man', in *The Review of Metaphysics*, 25/1 (1971):
3–51; Charles Taylor, 'Neutrality in Political Science, in *The
Philosophy of Social Explanation*, edited by Alan Ryan (Oxford:
Oxford University Press, 1973), 139–70; and Charles Taylor,
'Understanding and Explanation in the *Geisteswissenschaften*' in

another culture. I acknowledge that the West has a pre-conceived idea of the political but I assume that most, if not all, cultures have methods of governance, of decision making, of stating their beliefs, expectations, practices and values, methods of ensuring compliance, and of rein-forcing, legitimating and rendering plausible the existing institutions, structures, beliefs, practices and values.

My scientific approach and conclusions

I set out to discuss the political with my cross-cultural interlocutor. However, I soon run into problems of understanding. Assume first that I am a political scientist who believes that my discipline should emulate the natural and physical sciences (as popularly conceived in the West). I am not really trying to understand my cultural interlocutors, the cultural representatives with whom I speak, because self-understanding, under-standing the culture as its members understand it, is not my objective. My cultural interlocutors' self-under-standing is far too subjective. Let's assume that neutrality is my aim so my findings can live up to all the objective claims I make about them, and can stand up to the tests of scientific rigour my colleagues will demand of it.

So I write my paper and argue that my cultural interlocutor's culture does not have political institutions as in western democracies. While I can detect the general political mechanisms I conclude that there is no political mechanism whereby the interests and views of in-dividuals are heard. Elections are not held. The idea of a representative, someone who re-presents the views of smaller groups at a larger assembly, is unknown. The idea

Wittgenstein: to Follow a Rule, edited by Steven H Holtzman and Christopher M Leich (London Routledge and Kegan Paul, 1981), 191–210.

of bottom-up politics is unknown; in fact their approach seems top-down, top-heavy.

The incorrigible approach of a colleague

Imagine a colleague from the same political science department at my university is also interested in the political institutions of the culture I have been studying in my strictly scientific way. However, my colleague accuses me of rampant ethnocentrism. Initially, he accuses me of the unavoidable ethnocentrism (E_2). However, as we continue our exchange about our different approaches he makes an outrageous claim—at least to my ears in this imaginary story.

He has the temerity to suggest that even though I may not want to impose my views on others there is something imperious about my brand of political science. I am offended because I insist my political science is neutral as an investigative device. It does not take sides. I maintain that my political science is like a test. As popularly conceived in the West, a test or exam is not designed to fit one particular student; the student is supposed to fit the test and is measured against it. The test or exam is impartial just like the science I use. In recording the results I am acting according to scientific principles which are based on neutrality and objectivity. How dare a colleague suggest I am being ethnocentric! If I found no democratic institutions, then that is the way it is!

My colleague decides to test my conclusions but uses an entirely different approach. The cultural interlocutors' self-descriptions are taken very seriously. The political institutions are articulated and explained thoroughly and the conclusions drawn are totally different. My colleague's conclusion is that the way of politics in the culture we are exploring is different. The central theme is a belief system which connects that culture with its environment. Further, there are some members in that culture who are ascribed the responsibility of ensuring that the political system (as westerners might describe it) is part of a much broader belief system. They believe there is an order in the universe, that they are part of it, and that it is the role of governance to ensure that the culture is connected to that order and their daily routine is in harmony with it.

In fact, my colleague suggests I misunderstood almost every aspect of the political system we both investigated. Thus, I did not detect the political systems in place. He agrees that western-style elections are not part of the system of governance but claims that there are mechanisms for ensuring that members of the culture have a say and feel part of the process. He also discovered that other institutions are linked to the system of governance through the family and clan which are represented at the highest levels of decision making. In this way, decision making is not top-down as I had supposed and, in any case, the members of the culture do not feel repressed.

My colleague suggests that I cannot see the broader picture because I live in a western culture that has the individual as its fundamental unit. Whereas I see my western culture as comprising individuals, he insists that my cultural interlocutors are more wholistic in their approach, more concerned with members flourishing according to their cultural beliefs, practices and values.

I respond by saying that he was being hoodwinked. I accuse him of being gullible, of accepting an account of their culture on their terms, of being acritical. I suggest that his account is merely subjective compared to my more objective account.

Criticisms of our conclusions based on Charles Taylor's 'Understanding and Ethnocentricity'

Imagine that an academic who has read almost everything Charles Taylor has written (which is a lot), and adopts his approach to political science, joins the political science faculty of which my colleague and I are members. Both my colleague and I submit our research findings to the newcomer and eagerly await her comments and adjudication. However, when we receive her feedback, we are both bitterly disappointed and stunned by her adverse response.

My new colleague suggests that my findings are riddled with ethnocentric bias. I find this very difficult to comprehend. When I reply that I was using a neutral and objective method, she replies that both my method and my findings are ethnocentric (E_2). Evidently, I used a research methodology (with its associated theory of knowledge) which was entirely different from that adopted by my cultural interlocutors. Consequently, I missed those aspects of the culture which were beyond the reach of my research epistemology and methodology and so my findings were adversely affected. I did not take the cultural spokespersons' self-understanding seriously —in fact, I was deliberately trying to avoid it because I regarded it as merely subjective. Moreover, according to our new colleague, I also missed some important clues. Notably, I failed to see how members of that culture perceived the whole and the parts to be linked, how different positions were represented, and how decision-making occurred.

I may have thought I was being objective but, according to my new colleague, my results apparently reveal my western bias. I may have thought I was applying external yet independent, transcultural criteria but, according to her, I was being ethnocentric (E_2), and

my results confirm her conclusion. When I protest that my position is distinguishable from the Ku Klux Klan or other supremacist groups (E_1), she reminds me how in the nineteenth century many indigenous nations were regarded as inferior on the basis of so-called scientific research. I am reminded that in the twentieth century so-called objective intelligence testing was used to propose restricted migration policies. I am shattered by her reaction to my research.

To my surprise, however, my other colleague, who arrived at conclusions at variance with mine, fares no better. Our new colleague notes that his approach took the self-understanding of our cultural interlocutors very seriously. In fact, he took it so seriously that he accepted the cultural spokespeople's account fully—as if their account should be the social scientific account. He is accused of mere acquiescence, of attempting to see the world as the representatives of the other culture saw it. Even to imagine a member of another culture could do that successfully, is regarded as smacking of ethnocentrism by our new colleague.

Some of my adversary's conclusions are confirmed, but overall he is accused of seeing the world through the representative's eyes, which is not consistent with a social science which attempts to explain in ways which are at least more universal, which transcend any particular culture. The newcomer summarises this by saying that my adversary has fallen for the incorrigibility thesis so that the cultural interlocutors' position was immune from proper social scientific scrutiny and criticism.

Our new colleague certainly surprises us—but she is not finished with us yet! In other comments made when we are together she repeats her conclusion that we are both ethnocentric although in different ways. My approach is ethnocentric because I regard the scientific approach I use as the only means to obtain reliable knowledge, and because I assessed my cultural interlocutors'

political institutions only from my perspective. As the other culture does not have the same political structures which perform the same political functions as in western democracies, a negative judgement about their system was inevitable. Moreover, I smuggled into my science implicit assumptions about the primacy of the individual in western democracies, about a position Taylor called 'atomism' and the notion of the political system as a means to an end, which he called 'instrumentalist'.[22]

The newcomer also suggests that my adversary is ethnocentric because his analysis assumes the political is symbolic rather than real. From the agent's self-description it seemed to him that the political is merely a means to a more religious or transcendent end that connected and explained the past, present and future. Identifying something as symbolic invoked a distinction from the West, between the real and its symbol, which did not do justice to the complexity of the notion in our inter-locutors' culture.

Our new colleague's alternative approach based on Charles Taylor

To our mutual chagrin, our new colleague then proposes an alternative approach. My original colleague, whose research yielded different conclusions, is challenged about the western distinction between the objective and the mythical, the real and its symbol, which seems to be implicit in the way the position of the cultural inter-locutors is presented. He is also challenged to listen to dissenting voices in the culture, to hear the murmurs about the way certain powerbrokers closed ranks against the urging to adopt some of the apparent health and technological benefits of the West, and to hear the

---

22. Taylor, 'Understanding and Ethnocentricity', 131–2.

multiplicity of voices and not only those of the representatives with whom the consultations occurred.

Then our new colleague begins to challenge me again. This time she begins with a quotation from Taylor:

> We are always in danger of seeing our ways of acting as the only conceivable ones. That is exactly what ethnocentrism consists in. Understanding other societies ought to wrench us out of this; it ought to alter our self-understanding.[23]

She suggests that the perspicuous contrast facilitates that challenge to our self-understanding. In my case, a potential contrast could be between my atomistic, instrumentalist and means–ends orientated politics, and a view of politics as an end in itself, the good, the good life, and harmony with other people and the natural, physical and social world. This reminds me of reading the classic political philosophers and their legacy in the work of Leo Strauss, Eric Voegelin and even the Frankfurt School of which Herbert Marcuse was a member. Politics is not 'the art of the possible'; it has a telos, an end—the creation of the good society. It is driven by the goal and not just the reduction of all the really important ethical, moral, political and religious questions to mechanical and technical solutions.[24]

According to our new colleague, my emphasis had been so atomistic and individualistic that I had forgotten an underlying, now subterranean, trend in liberal

---

23. Taylor, 'Understanding and Ethnocentricity', 129.
24. See Herbert Marcuse, 'Repressive Tolerance', in *A Critique of Pure Tolerance*, in Robert P. Wolff and Barrington Moore Jnr, and Herbert Marcuse, *A Critique of Pure Tolerance* (London: Jonathon Cape, 1968), 95–137; Leo Strauss, *Natural Right and History* (Chicago: University of Chicago Press, 1953); Eric Voegelin, *The New Science of Politics: An Introduction* (Chicago: University of Chicago Press, 1952).

democracies which concerns the role of the state to provide for its citizens, and that the idea of the welfare state has its origins (or at least some of them) in liberalism. I had ignored a significant element in the formation of liberal democracies, namely, the existence of the glue which keeps societies together, about what it means to be a community where the community is more than merely the sum of its parts. For example, many people regard taxation as an attack on their freedom to spend the money they earn as they see fit. Alert to this, or in order to attract support, politicians and political parties invoke the 'the taxpayers' money' when it suits, when they want to expose spending from a slush fund, or the waste of taxpayers' money by opposition politicians.

Ignored, however is the idea that taxation is a community resource to assist communities to meet needs that are difficult for individuals to meet alone. The idea that we depend on others for a whole range of goods and services is denigrated. Yet even surgeons cannot take their own tonsils out! The way people are linked together in providing for their mutual needs, the way they are interdependent, is lost when the emphasis is atomistic and individualistic. My narrow, complacent ethno-centrism was being challenged and I was beginning to question my own culture and its political beliefs, practices and values—which is just what Taylor recommended as part of understanding another culture.

Concluding comments

The chapter began with a discussion of what appeared to be two intractable obstacles to cross-cultural under-standing. There was the problem of western science, including social science, applying its own standards even while regarding itself as objective, neutral and above the ethnocentric position (E_1) which it denounced. As the chapter proceeded, we saw that this problem doesn't only apply to standards of what constitutes valid knowledge; it also applies to other values. As a student of political science I also smuggled in, however unwittingly, western liberal-democratic and allied values which completely sabotaged any claim to neutrality and objectivity. In Chapter 3 we explored the possibility that science could be a neutral ground on which to adjudicate the competing claims of cultures and to facilitate cross-cultural understanding. We found the dominant view of western science wanting.

Yet, now we have discovered ethnocentrism in a second, although less obvious form (at least to westerners). The charge of ethnocentrism (E_2) is not only levelled at the western social scientist who follows the natural and physical sciences. It can also be levelled at the western social scientist who, rejecting the claims of the social science which emulates the predictive, natural and physical sciences, claims we should accept the self-description of other cultures without question, that all we can do is accept their explanations, in their terms. Both views have their defenders; both have their problems.

However, an interesting issue arose in the light of the discussion of deference in the previous chapter. At first glance it might be thought that Thomas' and Taylor's positions on deference and incorrigibility are at odds with each other. After all, Thomas argued that we should defer, which means to accept or submit to someone else's perception of their experiences. This sounds like the incorrigibility that Taylor rejected.

In fact, I would argue that deference is an essential aspect of cross-cultural understanding just as much as incorrigibility undermines it and that, by and large, Thomas' and Taylor's positions are compatible. Several comments are noteworthy. Firstly, deference includes the possibility that those to whom we are to defer could be wrong about the nature of their experiences.[25] Likewise, the potential to be misguided or wrong is one of the reasons Taylor rejected the incorrigibility thesis. In this, Taylor and Thomas concur—as does Harding.

Secondly, moral deference and Taylor's critique of the incorrigibility thesis share another attribute, namely, they begin with the standpoint of another person (to adopt Harding's term). Taylor emphasised the importance of what he called the 'agent's self-descriptions'[26] as an integral part of interpretative social science. Even the demand that our account should 'make the agent's doings clearer than they [are] to him'[27] does not annul the obligation to understand the agent. Indeed, this is one of the reasons why Taylor is critical of a social science which emulates the natural and physical sciences: it cannot make sympathy and other values a precondition of its account (because it is allegedly value-free and neutral), and self-understanding is excluded as an aim (because it is subjective and evaluative).[28]

There is a third point worth emphasising and which supports the conclusions reached on Thomas's moral deference and Taylor's critique of incorrigibility, namely, that deference may be regarded as referring to what must be explained (our explananda) but the agent's explanation is not necessarily our full account or explanation (our explanatia). Taylor was insistent about the need to couch that which must be explained in terms of the agent's self-understanding. Otherwise, how could we know what we were attempting to explain? How would we know the

---

25. Laurence M. Thomas, 'Moral Deference', in *Theorising Multiculturalism: A Guide to the Current Debate*, edited by Cynthia Willet (Massachusetts: Blackwell, 1998), 374.
26. Taylor, 'Understanding and Ethnocentricity', 118.
27. Taylor, 'Understanding and Ethnocentricity', 118.
28. Taylor, Understanding and Ethnocentricity, 119–121.

object of the social scientific exercise? However, he was equally insistent that we must not allow the agent's self-understanding to completely dominate our explanations. Again, deference and Taylor's critique of incorrigibility have related aims and implications.

A fourth point concerns the link between the individual, the agent, and the structural causes of their pain and suffering. They approached this issue differently (Thomas from moral deference; Taylor from social science) but their objectives are similar. Both want to understand the consequences of social structures. For Thomas this is an important issue. He claimed that:

> to engage in moral deference is to allow oneself to become affected in a direct inter-personal way by the injustices of the world. While it is not the only way to do this, it is a very important way. Thus, it is a fundamentally important mode of moral learning. It is a mode of moral learning which those who have been oppressed are owed in the name of eliminating the very state of their oppression. In the absence of such learning, oppression cannot but continue to be a part of the fabric of the moral life. Indeed, the absence of such learning, the studied refusal to engage in such learning, is one of the very ways in which oppression manifests itself. Worse, the studied refusal to do so adds insult to injury.[29]

Thus, moral deference tutors on social injustice with the aim of eliminating oppression. Taylor (and Harding) also attempted to account for the structural explanations of the pain people experience. Both emphasised that explanation at the social level is the prime concern. They

---

29.   Thomas, 'Moral Deference', 378.

are attempting to account for, to explain, social phenomena. They both maintained that understanding the social forces at work must start from the standpoint of those who are marginalised (Harding) or from the self-understanding of agents (Taylor). However, both claimed that explanation in social science is more than starting from the standpoints of the marginalised or the self-descriptions of agents per se (as important as they are). It is about the institutional or structural explanations of social problems people experience. Again, in this sense, Thomas's and Taylor's positions are complementary.

Having highlighted how deference and Taylor's critique are at least complementary I would now like to ask a question of Taylor's position: is his conception of understanding as articulated sufficient to understand another human being? Is Taylor's conception of under-standing commensurate with the task of social science? Will we really know what is to be explained if we derive it, as Taylor suggested, via the self-understanding of the agent? What might self-understanding involve? Could we interpret inaccurately or understand minimally rather than maximally?

If I only use Taylor's method I think there is a possibility that my understanding will not be maximised. And this is important because if my understanding is limited, then my explanation will be too. This is obviously not good social science. It also explains why deference is an important complementary concept in cross-cultural understanding. It is not merely a theoretical question; the practical implications are enormous. The extent of the pain we detect may well influence where we search for answers to account for the pain others experience. Failure to recognise the depths of pain will influence the explananda and the explanatia. An account which fails in this way would neither expose the cause of the pain nor explain the extent of the pain. It could even legitimate existing practices and priorities rather than challenge them. The research could be a whitewash and the agents the scapegoats.

Hence I would argue that, in the interests of maximising cross-cultural understanding, it is helpful to bolster Taylor's position with that of moral deference. I acknowledge that Taylor believes that understanding the agent is a prerequisite for social science accounts. He certainly made a strong case that 'the presumption of equal worth' of cultures is a precondition of under-standing.[30] In that, his position is extremely helpful for advancing cross-cultural understanding. The argument I am putting forward suggests that the very nature of understanding will affect social science. In fact, there is a relation between the two. An unreflective understanding will yield different accounts of what needs to be explained than an understanding that begins with a pre-sumption in favour of the experiences of those in diminished social categories. Understanding which minimises what must be explained will lead to a commensurately inadequate account. As tautologous, or obvious, as the point is, it is significant. And it is so because moral deference contributes to the extent or level of the agent's self-understanding that it is integral to cross-cultural understanding.

In other words, in Taylor's terminology, I agree that the incorrigibility thesis impedes our research scope and findings. In alerting us to this Taylor has made a significant contribution to our approach to cross-cultural understanding. But it could also be that the under-standing Taylor recommended to ascertain the explananda reduces the agent's self-understanding so that

---

30. Charles Taylor, 'The Politics of Recognition', in Charles Taylor, *Multiculturalism: Examining the Politics of Recognition*, edited by Amy Gutman (Princeton, New Jersey: Princeton University Press, 1994), 72, 66.

the resulting misunderstanding unnecessarily constrains the explanatia. Thus, it is not only the incorrigibility thesis that limits the social science account; it is our conception of the explananda. If what is to be explained is misconceived or minimises the agent's understanding of the extent of the pain or other experiences, then the explanation may be too simple or even distorted; a limited explananda may, by definition, limit the explanatia, to use Taylor's terms.

This is *not* to retreat to the incorrigibility thesis. On that score Taylor's analysis remains entirely valid. Furthermore, his critique of a value-free, objective social science which replicates the methods of the natural and physical sciences is also cogent and bears some resemblance to Harding's suggestion that we maximise objectivity by beginning our research from the standpoint of the marginalised. Against the value-free social scientist, Taylor certainly values the agent's self-understanding and believes it is integral to how we ascertain our explananda. However, my argument is that, while emphasising the agent's self-understanding as the basis for our explananda, it may be possible to go further than Taylor's method when attempting to acquire such understanding.

My point is that our understanding of the problem per se requires the reinforcement provided by moral deference. This is imperative in order to ensure that as far as possible, and further than can be guaranteed by Taylor's analysis, we have maximised our understanding that is so essential for our explananda and explanatia. Again, this is not to deny Taylor's contribution to my overall argument. Clearly, his attempt to overcome the problems associated with a value-free social science and the incorrigibility thesis are significant advances on both options. However, a commitment to moral deference augments the significant contribution Taylor has made.

Taylor's notion of perspicuous contrast is another helpful concept because it encourages a critical appreciation of our own culture. This is an essential and indispensable aspect of cross-cultural understanding because the values to which we might be committed are so easily distorted, as exemplified by the examination of tolerance in Chapter 6. One of the most useful aspects of Taylor's position is the possibility that cross-cultural understanding has the potential to wrench us out of the ethnocentricity that perceives our cultural beliefs, practices and values as the only ones. It is then that we can both alter our own understanding and begin to understand others.

This ability to challenge our own beliefs and begin to understand both our culture and our cultural inter-locutors emanates from Taylor's suggestion about perspicuous contrast. This, in turn, arises as alternative beliefs, practices and values are compared. There is a consequence of this that has important implications for extreme cultural and conceptual relativism. Unlike the latter, which holds that we are locked into our own worlds, Taylor obviously thinks it is possible to identify another culture in a manner which does not render cross-cultural understanding impossible. It is possible to translate concepts.

This is nicely stated in a book on Gadamer, whom Taylor acknowledged as an important influence on the development of his own position. Georgia Warnke discussed Jurgen Habermas' reaction to Gadamer. She wrote:

> For Habermas's purposes, Gadamer's most valuable insight here is the recognition that translation involves neither resocializing oneself nor finding a set of rules through which to reduce one language to another. It

involves, rather learning to say in one's own language what is said in another.[31]

Learning to say in our own language what is said in another; this would seem to be an accurate restatement of Taylor's position. The options are not incorrigibility and resocialisation, the latter being learning to be part of another culture as members learn to be through all the stages of life. Rather, translating and the ensuing understanding, requires a new method, a new approach. Warnke continued:

> Translation does not require producing a correlate in one's own language for each word that is expressed in the other but being able to say in one's own words what one finds in the words of someone else. To this extent translation is not in principle different from the achievement of understanding through dialogue. On the one hand, one has to make sense of someone else's position and can only do so through the lens of one's own understanding in terms that make sense to oneself. On the other hand, making sense of someone else's position leads to an expansion and refinement of one's own.[32]

What is required for adopting optimal cross cultural understanding is adapting our words to concepts from the other culture and then testing ours by the ensuing contrast which, hopefully, extricates us from the potential for ethnocentricity. The reality is that people do translate. The critical question is not whether we can, but the accuracy of the translation.

---

31. Georgia Warnke, *Gadamer, Hermeneutics, Tradition and Reason* (Cambridge: Polity Press, 1987), 110.
32. Warnke, *Gadamer, Hermeneutics*, 110–11.

What Taylor offered is an invitation to social inquiry which seeks to avoid the two main horns of the ethno-centricity-incorrigibility dilemma. Explanations are part of that science. In the inter-cultural context, 'what is demanded of a theoretical account is that it make[s] the agent's doings clearer than they were to him'.[33] This might invite a challenge to his self-descriptions. The anti-ethnocentric corrective to this is that 'we cannot under-stand another society until we have understood

---

33. Taylor, 'Understanding and Ethnocentricity', 118.

10

What are some of the features of optimal cross-cultural understanding?

Introduction

Our introduction to approaching cross-cultural understanding is nearing its end. We have looked at many issues, most of which have involved negotiating some thorny paths. It has not been an easy task, although by highlighting some of the problems, some real, some alleged, I have tried to show that it is possible to secure some of what is required as we approach cross-cultural understanding. In fact, I have tried to demonstrate that there are a number of issues that are behind the scenes, that are often smuggled into cross-cultural understanding, largely unreflected, taken-for-granted. There are more obstacles to cross-cultural understanding than meet the eye. Yet by identifying and examining these, teasing out their implications, it is possible to obviate some of them.

The following conclusion is organised around themes which cut across those of the previous chapters and synthesise the preconditions of cross-cultural understanding. This book aimed to enhance some aspects of our approach to cross-cultural understanding and to identify the optimal features or qualities of understanding cultures other than our own. It is now possible to glean those features.

Cross-cultural understanding is facilitated by the awareness that culture is a construct

The development of the idea that social reality is constructed has been a powerful analytical tool in the social sciences, particularly sociology. What characterises a society and culture is not given but made; it does not come from above for all time, but has been forged in the past and adapted and adopted here and now. To realise the constructed nature of social and cultural reality is to be able to determine its origins and motivation, to trace its emergence, to determine how it has been adapted to meet changing cultural and social functions, to discern how current social arrangements serve and preserve certain interests and detect how the burdens and benefits are inequitably distributed.

Exposing such constructions as social, as time and culture-bound, has resulted in our seeing how, for example, gender, deviance, and religion are culturally and socially constructed. Whether this means that everything is socially constructed is a different matter. If it is, reflexivity demands that we also conclude that sociology is socially constructed too. This may come as a shock to those who maintain, simultaneously, that everything is socially constructed—with the exception of their diagnosis. If all perspectives are socially constructed, then what grounds are there for exemptions? However, the point here is a caution about how far social construc-tionism should be taken; that if all cultural and social reality is constructed in the way described, then academic disciplines that espouse the view, and use the technique, are not exempt from the same conclusion.

Particularly germane to cross-cultural understanding is that members of cultures are socialised into their culture, as we are into ours. We learn and act as if our cultures are not socially constructed, as if they are as natural as the trees, neutral and immutable. This time-bound charac-teristic of cultures is not something that is normally introduced in the socialisation process. With very few exceptions, we grow up in, and into, a monoculture which is usually monolingual, and has quite specific expectations about how things should work, and has explanations if they do not.

An obstacle to cross-cultural understanding is that our cultural interlocutors have also been socialised to similar degrees. It is not only citizens of the West who have been socialised in this way. The problem is that the power of the monoculture into which we are socialised—and that it actually is an excluding monoculture—is camouflaged, even though it is crystal clear to others, including our cultural interlocutors. Again, this is not because we are gullible, but because of the social structure into which we have been absorbed, the social mechanisms which reduce the many dimensions of human activity and diversity to the dominant one, and the power of the socialisation process.

Integral to this absorption of the monocultural is that our culture has a perspective on other cultures; it perceives them through monocultural spectacles, it has constructed them as other than us, as 'the other' or 'the others'. Thus, they, the 'others', are identified in a certain way—and often resent and reject the identity imposed on them. It is what the other sees as the caricature imposed on them that is one of the main obstacles to cross-cultural understanding. The peremptory nature of this imposition may be offset to some extent by the fact that our cultural interlocutors may suffer the same obstacle too, only this time we are the other. But that only accentuates the problem: that both sides come from their respective monocultures and have expectations and perceptions of the other, and impose an identity on each. The problem is further exacerbated if members of one party are unaware of power imbalances in previous encounters, and how the members of the other culture associate their interlocutors with a more powerful cultural group.

For example, we know the frustration and sense of being excluded when other cultures do not understand our position, when our cultural interlocutors misunderstand our position, our expectations, the reason why we act, feel and think in certain ways. We know it from a western perspective. But, does this mean that we know it from the point of view of our cultural interlocutors who experience the legacy of the colonialists, the imperialists, the invaders, the dominant white group?

At this point my western reader may feel betrayed; you may think I am a quisling. It might seem that I am advocating the very incorrigibility thesis that I previously tried to avoid. You may want to remind me that you have distanced yourself from western colonialism and imperialism, that you denounce it, and do not want to be associated with. So do I!

However, my point is that whatever we may think and feel about this, the critical issue is how do our cultural interlocutors feel about our western culture? Consider cross-cultural understanding with indigenous people and nations in say, Australia, Canada, New Zealand, South Africa, or the United States. Our white colonial culture has a constructed perspective on their culture that was mainly negative (and largely remains so). We are not the only ones who do that; they too, have constructed their culture. It may even be the case that they have a monocultural perspective on our culture. But in the context of the colonialism, imperialism, invasion and White domination of the past, whose construct has the most power? Whose construction prevails? What are the implications of the inequalities in the strength of the constructs, particularly as we engage in dialogue aimed at mutual understanding?

It might be argued that our cultural interlocutors have constructed their own culture, and their perspective on our culture—and we have constructed our own culture and have a perspective on their culture. In this way, then we are both in the same boat. We might be. But that does not warrant the conclusion that as we approach cross-cultural understanding our respective and mutual constructions of ourselves and our cultural interlocutors cancel each other out, or that there is some balance in ignorance and misperception.

Both participants in the dialogue may be expressing their construction of their own culture, and their constructions of their cultural interlocutors. But what if there is a difference in the strength of the construction that comes from the West, the one we have of ourselves, and that which emanates from our cultural interlocutors, the perception they have of us? Both groups may have constructed the other, but what are the implications if one construction is vastly more powerful, or is associated with dominating nations or groups of people (largely white and western)?

I am white. I can neither help nor change my skin colour. It should be irrelevant in cross-cultural communication. I wish it was. But to my cultural interlocutors my skin colour may be powerfully relevant. The culture into which I was born and socialised may be of negligible importance to me as I approach the task of understanding another culture, but it may the critical issue for those whom I am attempting to understand. I may denounce and repudiate the actions of some of my ancestors. But what for me might be sufficient distance from my white ancestors may be insufficient for my cultural interlocutors.

White invaders may have played a determining and definitive part in their lives, culture, history or stories. I am the same colour as the colonisers. The issue of what that represents, or my native culture, or my mother tongue, may by totally irrelevant to me when I come to cross-cultural understanding—but may evoke the most painful memories of the blackest pages of history to members of another culture.

This does not mean that I was involved personally; I was not. It means that through the accident of birth, colour, language, sex, I may re-present to those cultures with which I want to engage, and understand the powerful colonising power that subjugated and decimated their nation. My skin colour is a powerful symbol; it evokes painful memories. To be serious about cross-cultural understanding demands that I allow the possibility that I may be associated with the construction (which may amount to the destruction) of another culture.

I may feel very deeply about this. I may be involved in deconstructing the social myths of the superior white –inferior non-white other. But that does not change the possibility that for my cultural interlocutors, who I am may be a barrier to cross-cultural understanding. Why? Because I represent a group that has constructed the other, I am engaging with people of a culture that my own culture has constructed, and then with the might of its weapons (both intellectual and technological) de-cimated. Even if I can extricate myself from what I have been taught about the constructed other, a commitment to cross-cultural understanding invites me to consider the possibility that my cultural interlocutors will not perceive it that way—as I think, Sandra Harding and Laurence Thomas have pointed out.

One point should be made clear: I am not suggesting that indigenous people are totally defined by the constructed other, by the distortion the West has construc-ted. They have resisted such a construction just as they have resisted in a variety of ways all manner of the things done to them. My point is that there is a construction of other cultures which the dominant culture has created and legitimated. A similar point could be made about my cultural interlocutors who come from an Islamic background. They might associate my culture with (their experience of what they regard as) Christianity even though most Australians may be secular.

Cross-cultural understanding is facilitated when I do *not* preclude the possibility that there are issues of power and perception when I embark on understanding other cultures—even if I denounce what my forebears have done. It recognises that the dominant culture of which I am a member has constructed this perception of 'the other' to usurp and retain its power over them. Ignoring such possibilities, refusing to face up to the possibility, may impede cross-cultural understanding. I say 'may' impede because I do not want to presume how the person with whom I am engaged will respond. But, optimally, an awareness of such possibilities will facilitate the approach to cross-cultural understanding.

The dangers of cultural filters

Undoubtedly, our cultural background influences how we conceptualise and understand. If I live in a culture where water is plentiful, I may value water differently from those who live in a culture where water is scarce. If I live in an environment where snowfalls are an annual occurrence, then I may have more concepts for snow than if I live in an environment where it rarely snows. These quite simple examples make it clear that cultures can have different concepts and values.

This influence is common, and it is camouflaged by the process that we call socialisation. In fact, social processes hide the source of our cultural and social beliefs, practices and values. This neither denies that, as individuals, we mediate and process what we learn, nor that we are necessarily resigned to it. As individuals we process information and, at times, challenge what we learn. This is why the notion of social construction is potentially liberating: if we are aware that social claims are socially constructed then we can attempt to deconstruct them.

However, there are manifold bits and pieces of learnt information which are invoked at times. We rarely think about them but they are there ready to be used. We have learnt about our past; we have learnt that institutions are there to protect us or help us in some way. Yet on these two relatively straightforward issues alone we can detect the imprimatur of our society and culture. We have learnt about our past, but it is usually the socially approved version of the past. History is usually written from the perspective of the victors, not the vanquished. We have learnt that institutions are there for our sake, yet quite clearly the dominant groups benefit more than others. Institutions which we extol, because they exist to protect all citizens from violence, may protect us (relatively speaking), but perpetrate violence against other groups. These structures are usually exempt from criticism, or the criticism is finessed or modified in some ways in which individuals are targeted as the prime explanation for the violence used.

There are many other ways in which cultural factors have an impact. They are not denied here; they are axiomatic. The critical issue, however, is not whether cultural factors influence any sort of understanding—they do! The critical issue is how they influence, and the extent to which they influence. My argument in this book is that cross-cultural understanding neither entails a socially approved ethnocentrism nor the conceptual and cultural relativism popular in some academic circles. Cross-cultural understanding need not be stymied by them. The next section amplifies the point.

The different forms of knowledge

Early in the book I argued that more than factual knowledge or scientific knowledge is required for cross-cultural understanding; a sympathetic approach to cross-cultural understanding is essential. If we approached another culture with anything less it is likely to jaundice our attempt at understanding. However, more than a culturally neutral approach is required, because we come with prior knowledge, judgements and values. Literally, being understanding is essential.

However, this raised a problem, since to be understanding is a value. It presupposes that we value understanding (U_1) and being understanding (U_2), namely, a sympathetic approach to our cultural interlocutor is necessary. The problem arises because in the West, at least, e-value relativism makes it difficult to justify our value commitments. They become merely our own ideologies between which it is impossible to arbitrate. Nonetheless, if there are value preconditions for understanding then it is essential to be able to defend our commitments.

If this is impossible, as the e-value relativists claims, then the commitment, the determination, to be understanding is no more valid than to be misunderstanding—as absurd as the latter sounds! In Chapter 2, defending the value of understanding was designated U_3. Cross-cultural understanding involves all knowledge of beliefs, practices and values (U_1), empathy as a precondition (U_2) and the ability to defend the value of cross-cultural understanding (U_3) and, hence, the ability to defend our cultural values generally (V_1).

The dangers of ethnocentrism

Cross-cultural understanding rejects ethnocentrism. You will recall that this was defined in two ways (E_1 and E_2). Those who advocate or adopt E_1 see their cultural world as the centre and act as if all others are on the periphery; they see their culture as being the standard against which all others should be judged. When other cultures are judged against such standards they are found to be inadequate or deficient in some way. E_1 purports to understand (U_1), but ethnocentrism neither knows nor is understanding (U_2). It is malign, usually, racist, bigoted and supremacist. Unrecognised prejudgements lead to twisted attitudes and perceptions (not necessarily in that order). This form of ethnocentrism renders genuine and optimal cross-cultural understanding impossible.

However, before this is interpreted as rather sanctimonious, complacent platitudes of the 'they-are-ethnocentric, we-are-not' variety there is an important caution to observe. We may abhor E_1, but it is relatively easy to slide into E_2, for we are immersed in our own culture that, with few exceptions, is a monoculture. We are not to be blamed for that; it is the way it is. Unless parents of different cultures practise their respective cultures, or a child lives close to different cultures, we are socialised into one culture. It is not surprising that we internalise it absolutely, entirely, because there are very few, if any, alternatives. From birth—perhaps before—we are absorbing this culture. It is not surprising that our culture becomes our window to the outside world.

So, is the more benign ethnocentrism of E_2 unavoidable? Is it benign? You will recall that it is possible, and, probably inevitable, to be ethnocentric (E_2) even if we are committed to tolerance and human rights, and appreciate diversity and celebrate difference. Why? Because in seeing and judging with these concepts we are seeing other cultures from our elevated, superior centre. These values (including respect for diversity, celebrating difference) might be conducive, even essential to cross-cultural understanding, but if the extreme conceptual and cultural relativist is correct, then we are locked into our own concepts and cultures and cannot do anything else but judge by our own cultural standards.

Some like Rorty almost regard this form of ethnocentrism as a virtue. But our discussion has shown how E_2 can so easily slide into E_1, and even if we do not see it that way, it is possible that our cultural interlocutors will. We may not be members of the Ku Klux Klan or a neo-Nazi, but if it is inevitable that we see and judge other cultures from the perspective of our culture, how is our position different from such groups? Now, it may differ on political grounds; we might repudiate the diagnosis and prescription of the racial supremacists, and their violence. But we have seen how something we value, such as tolerance, can be distorted, oppressive and repressive. It may not involve direct violence from our point of view but, all the same, repression is violating the rights of others. I am not saying than E_1 *is* E_2, that there is a one-to-one correspondence. My argument is that E_2 can easily become closer to E_1 and that such a danger looms large, particularly with extreme conceptual and cultural relativism (although I hasten to add, devoid of the rabid bigotry and violence associated with E_1).

However, there is an even more important reason for urging caution about E_2. That is, we may not regard the slippage from E_1 to E_2 as significant or likely. We may do everything to prevent it. But our cultural interlocutors may see it differently. For example, they may see our calls for more democracy in their cultures as political interference. They may see it as imposing our political values and institutions on them. For this reason, optimal cross-cultural understanding repudiates ethnocentrism (E_1), attempts to overcome what some regard as inevitable ethnocentrism (E_2), yet is vigilant about the possibility of slippage from E_2 to E_1.

The problems of incorrigibility

The concern about the ease of falling into ethnocentrism, and for some its inevitability, may tempt us to revert to what is considered the opposite position, namely, what Taylor called incorrigibility (the other culture cannot be corrected, mistaken or improved). According to this view, the dangers of ethnocentrism are so great that the most dependable and viable option is to suspend our judgment about other cultures and take their self-under-standing as the criterion, the standard, for cross-cultural under-standing. To understand in their terms, to use their self-descriptions, does appear to decrease the chance of ethno-centrism (E_2) sneaking into our attempt to understand.

However, as Harding, Thomas and Taylor pointed out, albeit for different reasons, it is possible even in good faith to be misguided and misinformed—and simply wrong. There is a difference between submitting to another culture's viewpoint, accepting their self-descrip-tions, acquiescing to their worldview, their beliefs, practices and values, on the one hand, and understanding them in the social science sense, on the other. The latter requires testing their worldview against their own stated objectives, the study of which may find unintended or unforeseen consequences. In a nutshell, cross-cultural understanding does not ultimately rest with agreeing with our cultural interlocutor's claim.[1]

Further, understanding does not require us to jettison our own culture and become as they are; it does not require re-socialisation into another culture. Even the possibility of re-socialisation could be viewed as ethno-centrism, particularly if it was argued that we are capable

---

1. This is particularly important for those who are chary about multiculturalism because it appears to attenuate their own cultural beliefs. Questioning our cultural beliefs is part of understanding another culture, but not because we must of necessity agree with them or adopt their perspective.

of jettisoning our culture while claiming simul-taneously that it is impossible for our cultural inter-locutors! We can be tolerant even if they can't—a position which is inimical to the cross-cultural understanding and which may be regarded as conceit!

Further, accepting incorrigibility as the antidote to ethnocentrism is unnecessary. Incorrigibility presupposes a certain form of understanding. It may even smuggle in the pretence of understanding when there is little or none. It may lead to a complacency or presumption of under-standing. It may lead to the conceit of understanding when there is little or none (in which case, it is closer to ethnocentrism E_1, just as Taylor suggested). Thus, ul-timately, a social scientific understanding does not require total submission, but it does presuppose and require a sympathetic approach and the challenge to one's own cultural perspective and ways—issues to which we now turn.

The challenge to our own culture

As we have seen, cross-cultural understanding is facilitated by steering away from both incorrigibility and ethnocentrism, that is, by neither adopting the stated view of another culture, nor by imposing our views on others (in the form of either E_1 or E_2). It is also advanced by a wil-lingness to challenge our own cultural beliefs and systems. In some respects, this should be clear from the content in the previous chapters. Most have included a critical component, whether it be of western science (Chapter 3), postmodernism (Chapter 4), the alleged justification for tolerance and its repressive tendencies (Chapters 5 and 6), or the social function of e-value relativism and neutrality (Chapter 7). Perhaps the issue was most explicitly addressed in Chapter 9 in which Taylor's position was examined.

Taylor emphasised the necessity of comparing our own social beliefs and customs, expectations and institutions with the other culture's in order to better understand their culture and our own. This comparison, which evaluates those things which we regard as socially normative in our culture, not only corrects or mitigates any tendency towards ethnocentrism (E_1 and E_2) but augments the possibility of cross-cultural understanding. It will be recalled that Taylor emphasised that there is an inclination to approach cross-cultural understanding through our own eyes, believing that our cultural ways are the only conceivable ones. The approach he suggested is intended to 'wrench us out' of that inclination and to alter our self-understanding.

Thus, approaching cross-cultural understanding entails a commitment to increasing our understanding of another culture but the very process involves enhancing our understanding of our own. This has a significant consequence, namely, that approaching cross-cultural understanding is not, to use the vernacular, 'a one way street'. It is not only my attempt to understand another person or their culture, it also involves a commitment to understand my own culture in more critical and profound ways.

Now, I do not know what influence this may have on my cultural interlocutors. They may sense (with some relief) that my self-evaluation is the result of the comparisons I have made between their description of their culture and my reflection on mine. Or they may begin to ask questions of their own culture on the basis of my observations and reactions. It is difficult to predict what the reaction might be. By using Taylor's approach, however, I have suggested that cross-cultural understanding is not optimally approached with a smug complacency about my own culture. A better understanding of another culture necessitates being willing to put my own culture under the microscope, to analyse it, to learn about it, and to do so in ways which may challenge my understanding.

Willingness to explore the structural problems of our own society

It is important to note that the challenge to my own culture involves questioning the structural explanations for those things that are distinctive or, perhaps, regarded as social problems in it. This self-referential aspect of cross-cultural understanding was first exemplified in the discussion of imperious western science and in the postmodern diagnosis from which the other is excluded. It was also alluded to in the examination of tolerance. Indeed, we noted Preston King's point that to ask someone to consider being more tolerant was a minimalist request that they could ignore. It merely involved attitudinal or psychological change in individuals rather than structural change in our institutions. Likewise, Ghassan Hage regarded tolerance as camouflaging deeply-seated white notions of power and control over national space, while Herbert Marcuse noted that in powerful institutions tolerance became repressive.

The challenge to contemporary culture was also seen in the examination of the social function of neutrality, and also in Harding's critique of the way objectivity-as-neutrality is used to buttress the socially dominant assumptions. Likewise, Thomas' notion of deference is a response to inequality epitomised in his notion of downward social constitution and diminished social category which, in turn, result in corresponding and different emotional configurations. A further challenge from Harding is that research should begin from the standpoint of the marginalised. Likewise, Thomas' suggestion that deference is due to the experience of those people from diminished social categories.

At first glance the questioning involved in the above may seem to be mitigated by the fact that they are just that—largely ideas. It is the case that the focus of this book has not been mounting a critique of the systems of education, justice or welfare. But a significant part of it has involved parring back the layers of often preconceived working assumptions and operational definitions which are brought to cross-cultural understanding. They are no less powerful because they are not obviously connected to institutions or social systems.

I would argue that ideas are linked to such institutions and that is why they are important and powerful. It is also one reason why it is necessary to challenge them, because the obstacles to cross-cultural understanding are not necessarily personal or private, even though the intention may be understood in such terms. At least some of the barriers to cross-cultural understanding are more systemic in the sense of being linked to institutions which legitimate past and present socially dominant attitudes, beliefs and practices. This is another reason challenging cultural beliefs is a pre-requisite to cross-cultural understanding.

Defending the values on which cross-cultural understanding is based

With some qualifications, I have argued that approaching cross-cultural understanding requires both a sympathetic approach to our cultural interlocutors, and a willingness to challenge our cultural and social institutions and the beliefs and values on which they are based and made to seem legitimate. Yet both involve using values which, in turn, creates real problems in western societies. As indicated in Chapter 1, values are regarded as merely personal or private and above all, subjective; they do not possess objective status as facts are alleged to do.

In the previous chapters I took considerable care to be very clear, and to unscramble the issues as far as possible. We noted that some social scientists, and particularly sociologists, are wary of the role of values in their disciplines. Postmodernists also are chary about values because they believe they have or can become oppressive metanarratives. It should be clear that I am opposed to political absolutism and any values which are used to defend it or camouflage it. That is one of the reasons why I distinguish between e-value absolutism and political absolutism, the former being a position about the epistemological status of values from which the ineluctable drawing of authoritarian political conclusions is unjustified, the later being an oppressive political position.

I have argued that values are indispensable when approaching cross-cultural understanding. They motivate it in the sense of approaching the task (U_1) and are used when there is a commitment to undertake cross-cultural understanding with sensitivity and sympathy (U_2). It is also necessary to defend such values (U_3) and furthermore, values are used when we compare the contrasting perspectives of various cultures and defend our respective cultural values more generally (V_1).

Undertaking this task requires that it be possible to defend the proposition that one value or cluster of values is preferable to another. Against the non-foundationalists and e-value relativists, it has been argued that defending prefered values is possible. It is sometimes very difficult; it requires a humility and modesty about those values; they may be even conditional in the sense that they are examined and re-examined to ensure that they have not turned into their opposite, or become distorted in some way, or that they are not merely representing taken-for-granted western values.

Nonetheless, e-value absolutism allows the defence of values with some consistency, a consistency which is denied by e-value relativism. The latter insists that it is impossible to arbitrate between values; it is impossible to argue that one is preferable to another. If this is the case, then any argument advancing the superiority of tolerance or understanding contradicts the tenets of the position. It is inconsistent to argue that it is impossible to demonstrate that one value is preferable to another, and then say that tolerance is preferable to intolerance or understanding is preferable to misunderstanding.

It is akin to saying 'no' and meaning 'yes', or disallowing something and then allowing it. Such things might happen in everyday life although not without some degree of frustration. It depicts a world in which some have the power to be whimsical and capricious. Usually, however, even when the English words 'yes' and 'no' are used differently they are used consistently; if they were not, a hearer would detect a contradiction or inconsistency.

For example, there are cultural variations in an affirmative answer to the question, 'Haven't you finished reading this book yet?' I would answer 'No' (meaning 'No, I haven't finished this book yet') but the answer 'Yes' (meaning 'Yes, I haven't finished reading it') is just as acceptable and understandable, albeit confusing if we are not accustomed to such usage. The point is that even when 'yes' and 'no' are used differently there is no contradiction in the answer because the precise meaning can be determined. The answer to the question is never equivalent to saying that 'no' could mean 'yes'. Yet when e-value relativism is used to defend cross-cultural understanding, multicultural or tolerance, that is what appears to happen; the law of non-contradiction is not applied.

So, optimally, what does approaching cross-cultural understanding mean and involve?

It might appear as if approaching cross-cultural under-standing requires negotiating some thorny issues. It does —but the success of the understanding is likely to be considerably advanced by some consideration of the issues presented in the previous chapters. Throughout, the focus has been on approaching as 'coming toward' or 'preparing for' cross-cultural understanding. However, it has become clear to me that an approach could easily be derived from the arguments advanced in this book. It is an approach which will have the some of the following features.

Ideally cross-cultural understanding involves the following.

Recognising the pitfalls of cultural relativism and ethno-centrism.
Cultural relativism is attractive to those who emphasise the plethora of cultures and their practices and values. Yet we are neither entirely locked into our cultural prisons, nor do we only see things from them. The capacity of human beings to translate languages and come to degrees of understanding that are authorised by individuals and groups of various cultures attests to this. The other danger is imposing our own cultural perspective onto others even when this is not our intention.

Approaching cross-cultural understanding ideally challenges western scientism and the incorrigibility thesis.
The twin dangers here have been examined at length and, ideally, cross-cultural understanding will avoid them. Although at opposite ends of the continuum, they both concern the way we approach understanding across cultural divides. Western scientism uses the scientific

method and theory of knowledge to assess other cultures whose beliefs and practices are often regarded as irrational. The incorrigibility thesis claims to take on the cultural analysis and description of a culture as it is expressed by members of that culture. In accepting their version the net result is that their culture is incorrigible. If western scientism has made imperious judgements, accepting another culture as requiring no modification is not necessarily conducive to cross-cultural understanding. This does not deny the imperative to be understanding (U_2) or approach the task with sympathy.

A commitment to e-value absolutism without political abso-lutism, to tolerance without e-value relativism.
The distinction between theories of knowledge and the political values that we adopt has been a major theme of this book. E-value absolutism is essential if we are to be understanding (U_2), to defend a sympathetic approach (U_3) and to defend the values by which we assess our own and other cultures (V_1). E-value-absolutism does not refer to political absolutism that is authoritarian, but without e-value absolutism it is unlikely that we can defend values. Likewise, as open and appreciative of diversity as e-value relativism may seem, it cannot defend the very values required for cross-cultural understanding.

A recognition that issues of the past, and power may influence how others see my involvement in cross-cultural under-standing.
Cross-cultural dialogues that lead to understanding acknowledge the history of our cultural interlocutor's relations with my culture and any power imbalances that have resulted. They may not affect my involvement, but a genuine and effective attempt at cross-cultural under-standing is likely to be stalled (at least) or sabotaged (at worst) if I do not recognise that the person with whom I am engaged configures the past and present differently

from the way I do—and that I may re-present or symbolise that to them.

An acknowledgement that the popular understanding of past inter-cultural relations is that of the victors rather than the vanquished and that, optimally, approaching cross-cultural understanding begins from, and defers to, the perspective of the most marginalised or the downwardly constituted.

This does not involve the incorrigibility thesis. It does recognise that where inequalities are prevalent, experiences vary. In approaching cross-cultural understanding, an awareness of the way these experiences affect those who engage in dialogue is critical. The salient issue is not whether we bring our cultural values to the task but how we regard them and which perspective is privileged. Thomas's notion of deference provides a basis for the way we may approach understanding another person (contrary to those who claim we are locked into our cultural prison) and allows for such understanding that the other person authorises us to speak on their behalf.

This does not mean that we would actually speak on their behalf, or that we would relish the thought, that we have to agree with each other, or there would be an opportunity for us to so speak. The very idea of speaking on behalf of someone else may be judged as anathema to everything that is optimal for cross-cultural understanding. Certainly, there is no sense in which condescension, patronage or paternalism is being advocated here. Such fears should be allayed by my emphasis that it is not we who decide the degree of understanding but someone else.

Perhaps this last point is controversial because it seems that cross-cultural understanding is not just a cognitive or intellectual activity and a matter of defending our values—as difficult as that is in the West. It is also an ethical and moral activity involving a decision on whom we will stand with, with whom we will start our research, and by whom we will be found sufficiently trustworthy to share the experience of others as they would want to state it. This does not mean that we submerge ourselves in someone else's experience or become their mouthpiece. It does suggest that the other person senses that, to some extent, we are committed to aligning ourselves with the way they configure their experiences. Perhaps the 'understanding' (U_1, U_2) in cross cross-cultural understanding involves a deliberate attempt 'to stand under' the experience of our cultural interlocutor. This is not intended to sound mawkish or unctuous for it also requires the courage to evaluate and challenge our own cultural positions and social institutions.

Conclusion

Introduction

Rather than summarise the book, in this conclusion I will briefly apply my argument to what seems to be an intractable sticking point in cross-cultural understanding, namely, religion. You will recall that in the Introduction I argued that culture and religion have coalesced in the past two or three decades and that both are so intertwined that to speak of one is to refer to the other. This, of course, may be an exaggeration and controverted by those who would identify with atheism or agnosticism or with secularism.[1] But a moment's reflection will highlight the reality that atheism, agnosticism and secularism, while rejecting a religious position, are approaches, attitudes or dispositions towards religion. By definition, the secular West may not be religious, and may even abjure or disavow religion, but even allowing their differences, western nations are characterised by an approach to or worldview of religion. Yet there is a real sense that, as events have unfolded since the end of the Cold War, and

---

1.   By secularism I refer to those nations in the West in which, largely, religion is a private and personal matter, Church and state are separate and the idea of a country adopting religious laws in a theocracy is anathema. Furthermore, I am *not* suggesting that in other nations religion is more cultural than personal, Church and state are inseparable and the nations are theocracies. There are many degrees and permutations in the meaning and implementation of the three variables as there are of equivalent issues in the secular West.

reported with lightning speed in the media, religion is often the contemporary face of culture.

Thus, using the conclusions of the previous chapter, I will briefly attempt to apply the argument put forward in this book to understanding religious differences. This is a vexed issue and, in order to delimit its scope, this conclusion will largely concentrate on differences between cultures that state they are religious and those that are not. In recent times, this is most keenly reflected in relations between nations and peoples of the Islamic faith and those of the secular West. Such differences (and even antagonisms) are also felt by minority groups and individuals in the nations to which the former have migrated.

Cross-cultural understanding is facilitated by the awareness that culture is a construct

Immediately when religion comes into consideration, the footprints of the West can be detected. What is not necessarily contentious when analysing culture per se becomes an identifier or signpost exposing western values of knowledge when examining religion. The reason is as follows. If, in keeping with my attempt here, religion is substituted for culture, the heading above becomes 'religion is a construct'. Now, in one sense that could be interpreted benignly as 'religion was created by God'. While possibly flinching at the wording, and pressing the need to qualify the phrase in a multitude of ways, mono-theists may be able to accept such a claim.

But this interpretation would be foreign to many westerners, particularly extreme social constructionists. According to this view, culture is not merely constructed; it is *socially* constructed—and exclusively socially con-structed. Feuerbach resoundingly echoes in our ears; God didn't make human beings; humans beings made God. Religion is an outpouring of human creativity, a giant human projection.[2] By itself, this claim would be a challenge to many theists. Yet, the very phrasing, seemingly axiomatic and innocuous in the secular West, is likely to be seen by theists as reflecting the chasm between people of faith and secularism.

Nonetheless, a dominant view in the West has been that religion is constructed by cultures and societies to serve certain social functions, to protect and legitimate certain vested interests. Religion makes adverse circumstances seem plausible, excuses hardship and poverty, censors behaviour, invokes standards, regulates relationships.[3] Thus religion is a social construction, the very invoking of which is a marker of the western predisposition to atheism.

However, Peter Berger, who was a major contributor to the social constructionist literature,[4] made at least two important points about social constructionism. He pointed out, firstly, that if every social thing is socially constructed then so is the analytical tool and heuristic device called social constructionism.[5] If religion can be discredited because it is merely a social construction, then so can the extreme social constructionist position itself. If the sport was fencing, and after repeatedly being struck by the social constructionist the religious opponent finally parried successfully with a quick riposte, the latter might counter 'touché'.

---

2. Peter Berger, *A Rumour of Angels: Modern Society and the Rediscovery of the Supernatural* (Harmondsworth: Penguin Press, 1970), 62–3.
3. For example, Peter Berger, *Social Reality of Religion* (Harmondsworth: Penguin Press, 1973).
4. Peter Berger and Thomas Luckmann, *The Social Construction Of Reality: A Treatise in the Sociology of Knowledge* (Harmondsworth: Penguin University Books, 1971).
5. Berger, *A Rumour of Angels*, 58–9.

But the second point Berger made is more significant; not all social constructions point to the social. He noted that mathematics has all the hallmarks of a human projection yet 'Put crudely, the mathematics that man projects out of his own consciousness somehow corresponds to a mathematical reality that is external to him, and which his consciousness appears to reflect'.[6] This is 'possible . . . because man himself is part of the same overall reality, so that there is a fundamental affinity between the structures of his consciousness and the structures of the empirical world'.[7]

The concept of social construction has made an enormous contribution to how we understand and explain the social and political realities in which we live. It has also enabled us to explain the way such realities have been organised in favour of the rich against the poor, men against women, the colonisers against the colonised, majority against minority. Thus, social constructionism is a two-edged sword. In its extreme form it exposes Western secularism. Yet, when used to emphasise that representations of other cultures and religions are socially constructed for certain purposes, the subsequent cross-cultural understanding will be heightened, and we will be sufficiently alert to critically examine such constructions.

People of religious faith are constructed by others in certain ways. In the West, for example, the proportion of citizens and residents of the Islamic faith in the population is exaggerated, the views of the majority of that faith who are opposed to terrorism are rarely published or aired, and comments made by the small proportion that offends the dominant population are propagated by the free press, which rarely provides the

---

6. Berger, *A Rumour of Angels*, 64.
7. *Ibid.* Similar issues are examined in Paul Davies, *The Mind of God: The Scientific Basis for a Rational World* (New York: Simon and Schuster, 1992), chapter 6, 140–60.

equal or greater space or time which would more accurately represent the view of the members of that faith. In other words, religious beliefs are homogenised to create certain impressions, and being alert to the reality that religious groups are being so constructed in adverse, often demeaning, and pejorative ways, will advance the cause of cross-cultural understanding. However, as probing as this heuristic device can be, when social construction claims that religion is socially constructed it can be a marker exposing western assumptions which are counterproductive to understanding people of another religious faith.

The dangers of cultural filters

The argument in the previous section is an example of the point being made under this heading. In the previous section the secular presuppositions of the West were exposed in the position that religion is a social construction. Such a position is a filter through which the secular West is predisposed to interpret religious belief. But what may be constructive in the secular West has now been identified as a constraint which the western mindset has imposed on our religious neighbours.

There are other examples of our cultural filters apropos religion to which I will refer as we proceed. But there is something else that the previous discussion elicits that is also relevant to this section. The example of social construction being a secular western concept is certainly one of our deeply entrenched cultural filters. But that it was exposed suggests that it is possible to be aware of their dangers and yet not be rendered impotent by them. Thus, the dangers of culture filters are like orange traffic lights—caution required! But just as we are cautious when we spot an orange light we are not completely stymied by it, so it is with our cultural filters. That they can be exposed suggests that we are not locked into our own cultural barricades.

The different forms of knowledge

In the previous chapter, I argued that more than a neutral approach was optimal for a cross-cultural dialogue that led to understanding. I argued that a precondition for factual knowledge (U_1) was U_2, a sympathetic predisposition to our cultural interlocutor's culture. But, if religious belief is so antithetical to the secular West, how is it possible for its citizens to enter dialogue with people whose religious faith is not only central to, but motivates and prompts their cultural practices, beliefs and values?

However, you will recall that, in addition to U_1 and U_2, understanding is also optimised by the ability to defend the values associated with cross-cultural understanding (U_3) and to defend our values more generally (V_1). Here there may be some common ground that can be used to foster and promote cross-cultural understanding. For example, in addition to agreeing on the basic requirements for human health and wellbeing, the religious and non-religious may have some common ground when invoking notions of peace, justice, and rights. Both groups might have different understandings of such political principles but, for all practical purposes, they can work together and find some common ground and may foster cross-cultural understanding. Perhaps that is all we can hope for. However, it does not deal with the underlying differences about knowledge as indicated in the western distinctions between reason and faith, church and state.

The dangers of ethnocentrism

The reason–faith and science–religion binaries are paradigmatic ways in which the West examines religion and religious belief. Such investigations may not always be of the E_1 variety that is intractable and supremacist.

However, the point has been made that if we are perceiving and interpreting from the inside of our cultural filters it is relatively easy to slide from E_2 to E_1, that is, from a position which acknowledges that it is difficult to see the world as others do because of our cultural filters, to a view which positions others on the margins and regards their culture as inferior. Perhaps more likely is the possibility that others who are on the margins will judge what we believe is a candid E_2 to be a censorious, judgmental and overweening E_1.

They may judge in this way because they perceive the West to be materialistic and obsessively individualistic. They may also judge what we regard as E_2 to be E_1, and perhaps because of what Charles Taylor labelled western 'closed world structures'.[8] By this phrase Taylor was referring to the western preoccupation 'which leave[s] no place for the "vertical" or the "transcendent", but which in one way or another close[s] these off, render[s] them inaccessible, or even unthinkable'.[9] Such a vertically closed world may seem to be an example of E_1 to people of different religious faiths.

The problems of incorrigibility

It will be recalled that sensitivity to incorrigibility arises from an awareness of the dilemmas associated with ethnocentrism (E_1 and E_2) and that the temptation is to proceed to the opposite position. For, in one sense, if religious ethnocentrism is regarding one's religion as the centre and marginalising all others, then incorrigibility is giving credence to the other person's religion as the centre

---

8. See Charles Taylor, 'Closed Word Structures', in *Religion After Metaphysics*, edited by Mark A Wrathall (Cambridge: Cambridge University Press, 2003), 47–68.
9. Taylor 'Closed Word Structures', 47.

as if we are on the margins (or at least not in the centre). Of course, in reality this description is a charade that is one of the reasons an attitude of incorrigibility can descend to ethnocentrism (E_2).

You may be hard pressed to think of examples where a perspective of another religion is characterised by incorrigibility. Who accepts religious adherence and belief as expressed in a member of another religion's terms? In the secular West, religious belief is regarded as controvertible, and those who are religious in some way simply compare and distance their own beliefs with those of the religious interlocutors from another faith.

However, there are instances when it would be appropriate to not take as incorrigible the beliefs of others. For example, why should we regard as incorrigible, Christians who believe they can handle snakes with impunity, or believe that human affairs are divided into a Manichean 'axis of evil', or that God is on the side of one army to the exclusion of another? Why should we regard as incorrigible the claims of some (who regard themselves as) Islamists and who defend (what they regard) as their acts of war on the basis of their religion? Such incorrigibility is not only unnecessary, it does not demonstrate understanding, particularly of the diversity of religious belief in both Christianity and Islam. Seeking the diversity of religious belief is one corrective to incorrigibility.

The challenge to our own culture (in this case, our own cultural response to religion)

My analysis in the preceding chapters emphasised that a precondition of understanding another culture or religion is to be responsive to the suggestion of reflexivity and challenge our own cultural and religious beliefs, practices and values. If this was done for religion, the secular West would inquire about the deeply entrenched binaries which a perspicuous contrast would invite. We could begin to ask questions like the following. Was there a time when the distinctions between science and religion, reason and faith, were much more blurred that they are today? This is not to deny the subtleties of religious belief in the West, including a renewing of interest in religion and spirituality.[10] Yet such changes have not had any great influence on the implications of the privileging of science over religion, epistemology over ontology, reason over faith, the supposedly objective over the subjective. If anything, the new interests in individualistic notions of religion and spirituality seem to reinforce them.

We could also ask if the dominant and popular view of science and rationality has become so imperious and aggrandising that it has infiltrated to where it has no right to be? For in the West the prevailing secular theory of knowledge is not confined or restricted to science as practised by scientists in their everyday work. It has tentacles which reach much further so that some who promote this secular world view have no inhibitions, feel no unease, have no compunction, about entering other debates about, for example, ethics, morality, and education and health policy. While some critiques are caricatures and parodies, secular views are taken seriously and are seen to have implications for all areas of life.

This is why the privileging of one popular theory of scientific knowledge is so significant. It has colonised the way, and determined the extent, that we in the West examine all problems. If a conclusion is not scientifically grounded, it is not objective. If it is not objective it is relegated to the subjective, to ideology, to personal

---

10. See Gary Bouma, *Australian Soul: Religion and Spirituality in the Twenty-First Century* (Cambridge: Cambridge University Press, 2007).

opinion. Moreover, it cannot have any higher status. Thus, in areas of morality and ethics, in discussion about the best political regime, and in religion, there can be no higher status for knowledge than the subjective, the ideological, or the private opinion.

And, because of this encompassing scientific world view, the staggering thing is that this conclusion is drawn even before such areas of human activity and experience have been examined. For it is not only the privileging of the scientific world view vis-à-vis religion that is relevant here. It is also the privileging of the scientific world view as the manner in which we should come to understand all areas of human activity and thought. This is the privileging of one epistemology over ontology, the privileging of one epistemology that should be used to analyse all other domains of human activity. And it is staggering because this judgement about what theory of knowledge should be used occurs even before the matter has been studied. It could be called the apriori exclusion of some forms of human activity (ethics, morality, politics, and values) from the very possibility of yielding knowledge regarded as socially valid.[11] In the middle of the twentieth century the political philosopher, Eric Voegelin, called this the 'scientistic creed', the 'positivistic conceit'.[12]

This analysis is not a call to have more religion in politics; it is not to advocate the infusion of the Church into the state or the withering of the secular state. It is prompted by the conclusion reached in previous chapters

---

11. See Rodney Fopp, 'Gnostic Messianism and Catastrophe of the Twentieth Century in Eric Voegelin's Political Thought', in *Messianism, Apocalypse and Redemption in 20th Century German Thought*, edited by Wayne Cristaudo and Wendy Baker (Adelaide: ATF Press, 2006), 302.
12. Fopp, 'Gnostic Messianism and Catastrophe of the Twentieth Century', 300–2.

that a condition of optimal cross-cultural understanding is that it challenges our culture; by perspicuous contrast there is the potential to be wrenched from our cultural filters and shibboleths.

For the increasing number in the West with religious sensibilities, a challenge from other religions reverberates onto the individualised understanding of popular Christianity in the West. As has been recently highlighted by sociologist and Anglican priest, Gary Bouma,[13] it is well known that the mainstream Christian churches are 'greying', and that the churches which are experiencing growing congregatons are large, regional, non-liturgical, informal and less traditional. In this largely, but not exclusively, Protestant phenomenon, religion is like a smorgasbord, which means that those religiously inclined pick and choose according to their individual proclivities. The questions which could be asked on the basis of perspicuous contrast concerning religion include the following: are such populist churches more reflective of the dominant individualism of our time? Are they more attuned to broader culture priorities (such as materialism and individualism) and culture which, compared with many other parts of the world, is healthy and wealthy?

Willingness to explore structural problems in our own society

The issues raised here follow on from the previous analysis. One matter is the extent to which the dominant religion, Christianity, adopts the same explanations, uses the same discourse, as the dominant groups who determine who is defined as abnormal or who is excluded. Now there are some exceptions here as attested by the

---

13. Gary Bouma, *Australian Soul*, 1–30.

criticisms of some politicians that the Church should stay out of politics and concentrate on spiritual matters.

But in the growing and popular churches—and in mainstream churches—is the understanding of tolerance a private or public affair? Is tolerance ever seen as a repressive or fulfilling social function to manage conflict and dissent? Is tolerance ever seen as being withdrawn from dissident or minority groups but expected of government policy? Do the churches with thriving congregations, for all their national and international welfare programs, accept the popular discourse of the causes of social problems? Are they ever seen as socially constructed? Against the popular view which is residual in its explanations, is the possibly ever explored that our social structures contribute to social problems? Whether they be religious or otherwise, optimal cross-cultural understanding would invite an examination of such structural explanations.

Defending the values on which cross-cultural understanding is based

Here, religions have the opportunity to use their beliefs about the creation of diversity, respect for human life, and peace and concord to enhance the possibilities for cross-cultural and religious understanding. Unfortunately, religion is often seen as the cause of conflict rather a solution to it. In some instances religious symptoms are confused with other broader causes. But that should not stop people of goodwill and peace, both religious and non-religious, from giving due consideration to their cherished value positions and how to defend them.

Finally

In this conclusion I have briefly applied my analysis to religion. Undoubtedly religion is at the cutting edge of cultural difference. And so without retracing our steps it is perhaps pertinent to refer to a religious saga as I conclude. In the Jewish scriptures, the *Tanakh*, there is a story about the Gileadites defeating the Ephraimites. The account continues:

> The Gileadites held the fords of the Jordan against the Ephraimites. And when any fugitive from Ephraim said 'Let me cross [the river],' the men of Gilead would ask him: 'Are you an Ephraimite?'; if he said: 'No'; they would say to him: 'Then say "Shibboleth"'; but he would say 'Sibboleth'; not being able to pronounce it correctly.[14]

The foe, the defeated Ephraimites, attempted to escape by crossing the river Jordon by disguising themselves as friends. But their accent gave them away. They had trouble pronouncing the 'sh' in 'shibboleth'. Instead, when ordered to say the word to distinguish between friend and foe, they said 'sibboleth'.

From this story we derive our English word 'shibboleth' which I have used occasionally. It refers to a principle, the deep things we live by, or to which we adhere and which reveals something about one. There are shibboleths which are part of our approach to cross-cultural understanding. Just as the accent of the Ephraimites exposed their identity, in this book I have attempted to disclose and analyse an approach to some aspects of understanding other cultures. The underlying assumptions, methods and premises which we bring to dialogue are like accents—so much part of us that they are difficult for us to detect and disguise, yet obvious to

---

14. Jewish Publication Society, *The Jewish Study Bible, Tanakh Translation* (Oxford: Oxford University Press, 1985), Judges 12: 5–6a, 538–539.

people and groups from other cultures with whom we engage. Accentuating cross-cultural understanding necessitates reflecting on and challenging such assumptions, methods and premises.